• *Rosie* •

· *Rosie* ·

ROSIE O'DONNELL'S BIOGRAPHY

by James Robert Parish

Carroll & Graf Publishers, Inc.
New York

First Carroll & Graf edition 1997
First paperback edition 1998

Carroll & Graf Publishers, Inc.
19 West 21st Street
New York, NY 10010

Library of Congress Cataloging-in-Publication Data is available.
ISBN: 0-7867-0542-6

Manufactured in the United States of America

• Acknowledgments •

I wish to thank the following individuals, researching centers and institutions for their outstanding assistance and support: Academy of Motion Picture Arts & Sciences: Margaret Herrick Library; Acme Rosie O'Donnell (Internet Web) Page (Patrick Spreng), Jim Albrecht, Kathy Bartels, Joe Becker, Larry Billman, Billy Rose Theater Collection of the New York Public Library at Lincoln Center, Rick Ceifer, Paul R. Clemente, John Cocchi, Ernest Cunningham, Annette D'Agostino, Audrey De Lise, Dickinson College (Sue Baldwin-Way), Joyce Drzal, Steve Eberly, George Fergus, Film Favorites (Linda Rauh), Bill Fishman, Sharon R. Fox, Charlene George, Bruce Gold, Ken Hanke, Amy Harper, David Hofstede, Homage to Rosie Internet Web Page (Caryl Byrd), Andrew B. Hurvitz, Igby's Comedy Cabaret (Jan Maxwell Smith), Jani Klain, Steve Klain, Steven Lance, John Lavalie, Retta Lewis, Ray Li, Mitch Lutsky, Bet MacArthur, Vinnie Mark, Lee Mattson, Doug McClelland, Mrs. Earl Meisinger, Merv Griffin's Resorts Casino Hotel, Jim Meyer, Minnesota Film Board (Mary Gilstad), Museum of Television & Radio (Jonathan Rosenthal—Research Services), Dr. Martin Norden, Photofest (Howard Mandelbaum), Sayrl Radwin, Linda Rebecca Rash, Barry Rivadue, Jerry Roberts, Rosie is the Queen of All Things (Internet) Web Page (Jane Dorsey), Rosie's Unofficial (Internet) Web Page (Maryellen O. Smith), Brenda Scott Royce, Andrea Sachs, Mike Sauter, Margie Schultz, Arleen Schwartz, Les Schwartz, Seth Poppel Yearbook Archives, Don Shay, Walter A. Smalling, Les Spindle, Dot Stenning, Kevin Sweeney, Sygma Photo Agency (Kathy Cessario), Vincent Terrace, Tom Walsh, Don Wigal, Robert Young.

Above all, I want to thank my agent, Robert G. Diforio for his support and encouragement.

Editorial Consultant: Allan Taylor

• Contents •

For

Rosie O'Donnell

The *New* Queen of All Things

· 1 ·

I have a marker in my head of March 17, 1973. Everything in my memory is either before or after that date. After that date, my life was changed forever.

Rosie O'Donnell, July 1996

*I*n the early 1970s, life was full of concerns, priorities and interests that seem both passé and irrelevant to life today. For example, globally, in mid-March 1973 representatives of the United States and 13 other key trading nations were meeting in Paris, France to discuss ways to counteract economic reverberations due to excess U.S. dollars abroad. Across the world, in Saigon, the Vietcong were accusing the U.S. of shipping war materials into South Vietnam, skirting the inspection procedures required by the cease-fire agreement. A few weeks later, after a decade of fighting in Vietnam, weary American troops would be withdrawn from the war-devastated area and the North Vietnamese would release the last—according to them—American prisoners of war.

Back in the United States in March 1973, Congress was proposing bans on meat exports to curb rising consumer prices. President Nixon's administration was urging Congress to sanction a $300 million loan guarantee to revive Amtrak, the nation's passenger train service, while the recently negotiated national railroad labor contract would provide a 10.7% wage and benefit increase for over 500,000 workers in 15 unions. Meanwhile, in the escalating Watergate scandal, the White House had just announced that the prior offer, by Acting FBI Director

1

L. Patrick Gray, to permit U.S. Senators to examine privately the crucial Watergate files was no longer an option.

In Connecticut, at this time, two self-proclaimed "unfrocked Byzantine Priests" were being charged in federal court of stealing valuable antique books, manuscripts and atlases from the Yale University Library which, for years, they'd been selling on the black market. In New York, the Big Apple's Mayor John V. Lindsay revealed that the city would fight a proposal that the state take over the city's off-track betting operation.

Saturday, March 17, 1973 was a rainy day on the eastern seaboard, punctuated by thunderstorms and, at times, very heavy winds. Nevertheless, in New York City, 800,000 hearty souls, undaunted by the adverse weather, gathered on the streets for the 311th annual St. Patrick's Day parade. The onlookers were ready to cheer the 120,000 marchers—including members of 197 bands from seven states—who were being led by this year's grand marshal, John W. Duffy. Less adventurous New Yorkers ducked out of the inclement weather to attend Radio City Music Hall's spectacular stage show ("Glory of Easter") and to enjoy the movie (the musical *Tom Sawyer*) on the Hall's giant screen. Other entertainment options included seeing Jack Lemmon onscreen in the drama *Save the Tiger* or the new chiller *The Vault of Horror* with Curt Jurgens. For children, several neighborhood cinemas were offering special matinees of *Son of Lassie*.

For those in the tri-state area who remained home that rainy day, television offered on-the-street coverage of the five-hour Irish parade. On the tube, marchers strode past the reviewing stand on the steps at Manhattan's St. Patrick's Cathedral where Cardinal Cooke, the special honorary grand marshal, stood under a black umbrella. Later that weekend day, TV viewers had a choice of such evening fare as the sitcom *The Partridge Family* and the detective drama *Griff* (with Lorne Greene) on ABC or the hospital show *Emergency* (with Robert Fuller and Julie London) followed by a network movie on NBC. However, most TV watchers tuned to the CBS-TV network with its unbeatable Saturday night programming lineup of *All in the Family*, *M*A*S*H*, *The Mary Tyler Moore Show*, *The Bob Newhart Show* and *The Carol Burnett Show*.

Despite the festivities and holiday distractions offered on this March 17, one middle-class family in Commack, Long Island had no cause to celebrate 1973's Wearing of the Green, even though it was an Irish Catholic household and its head, Edward J. O'Donnell, was Irish-born.

For this St. Patrick's day, 39-year-old O'Donnell, who designed cameras for spy satellites at the nearby Grumman airplane plant, lost his wife, Roseann, age 38. Grief-stricken Edward was inconsolable, as were his five children (Eddie Jr., Danny, Roseann, Maureen, Timmy) and his widowed mother-in-law, Kathryn Murtha, who lived with them.

Mrs. O'Donnell's death was neither sudden nor unexpected. Several months earlier, she had been diagnosed with terminal cancer of the liver and pancreas and, as the deadly disease took its painful final course, she had been repeatedly hospitalized. During this protracted ordeal, the numbed Mr. O'Donnell coped with his wife's fatal sickness mostly by not dealing with it, turning increasingly inward, and becoming emotionally inaccessible to his dazed family.

Taciturn Edward O'Donnell had reacted to his wife's plight by burying himself in work and relying on hard drink to ease his pain. Locked in his emotional shell, he could not bring himself to discuss his wife's negative prognosis with the children, even refusing to label her diagnosis as cancer. Thus, for the five young O'Donnells—ranging in age from twelve (Eddie) to seven (Timmy)—the months preceding their mother's death were bewildering on the surface and full of denial on a subconscious level. All of the kids suspected or inwardly knew their bedridden mother was seriously ill. However, they never fully comprehended or consciously accepted that the sickness which increasingly caused her to withdraw from everyday family life was linked to dreaded cancer.

For ten-year-old Roseann, the middle of the five O'Donnell children, her mother's vague ailment was exceedingly painful. Far more than her three brothers or 15-month-younger sister, Maureen, young Roseann was extremely close to her mom. They shared so many similar interests: the theater and movies, pop music and an adoration of Barbra Streisand. Most of all, this tomboyish girl had inherited her mother's sense of humor and a love of making people laugh.

As Mrs. O'Donnell grew increasingly immobilized, little Roseann did everything possible to take over her mom's household chores. When not attending fifth grade classes or helping out at home, this child tried her best to keep her ailing parent (and herself) diverted. Years later, she'd recall, "I refused to believe my mom was dying, I wanted to keep her laughing."

Even when Mrs. O'Donnell was hospitalized for her final, full-time period at Huntington Hospital in Huntington Station, the young Roseann and her siblings refused to acknowledge openly their mother's critical condition. Instead, they insisted to one another and to others that, of course, she would get better . . . she just had to! Meanwhile, their daily routine now included visiting their failing mother at the medical facility some twenty miles away. The future star has remembered, "At the time, you weren't allowed to go in if you were under 12 so the nurses would sneak us up in the emergency-room elevator." This little "game" was one of the many ways in which the O'Donnell youths disguised the seriousness of the situation.

Then came the fateful March 17, 1973, four days before young Roseann's eleventh birthday. Her father broke his increasing silence with the family by announcing to the perplexed children that their mother had just died. Years later, O'Donnell would say, "My father told me, 'Your mother passed away,' and I didn't know what that meant. And that was the end of the discussion." Even at this critical moment, Edward's extensive denial with his loved ones kept him from going into particulars about the funeral arrangements at the Clayton Funeral Home on Meadow Road in Kings Park, let alone acknowledging that his wife was a cancer victim.

Decades later, a still-traumatized O'Donnell would explain, "The family has been brought up to ignore the elephant standing on the kitchen table. For instance, when my mother died, I didn't even know what she died of until I was 16 [and a neighbor blurted out the truth to the unsuspecting teenager at a local bike-a-thon for the American Cancer Society]. They told us she died of hepatitis. Figuring we were little and wouldn't know what that meant. I looked it up. I was in fifth grade, and it said a disease you get through dirty needles. I remember thinking, in a 10-year-old's rationalization and justification, that it was from sewing."

Making the loss even more unreal to the children, the deeply brooding Edward decided that his offspring should *not* attend Mrs. O'Donnell's funeral at Christ the King Roman Catholic Church. Added to this, he immediately got rid of all his late wife's personal possessions. According to O'Donnell in 1996, ". . . there was sort of the removal of everything 'her' from the house in some kind of tragically wrong 1970s version of grieving that my father partook in. There was nothing left. I only have two pictures of her and none of her things. No jewelry, nothing." (At one time O'Donnell proudly wore a ring that had belonged to her mom. However, it was stolen while she was on a ski holiday in 1990.)

Not having any kind of closure to her mom's passing, Roseann refused to accept that her mother was truly gone. "For a long time," as she told *People* magazine in 1992, "I didn't believe it. Patty Hearst had just been kidnapped, so I came up with a fantasy that that was what had happened to my mom too, and nobody was telling us [differently]." On other occasions, highly sensitive Roseann fantasized that her mother, perhaps, tired of bringing up five children, had run off to California, but one day would certainly return. For years thereafter, she found herself imagining that her mom was always there—somewhere . . . somehow—watching over her. If the youngster played basketball, she would tell herself that her mother was in the stands watching.

These fabrications were intertwined with Roseann's idolization of her late mother. As she has explained it, "You know, when someone dies you make them a saint. I think what I remember of my mother is half fantasy. I never really thought of her as a grown-up, but as the Sainted Child Mommy who died." Another time, this bereft daughter would observe, "It's funny: When your mother dies before your adolescence, you have a child's image of your mom. In adolescence, you go through puberty, you rebel against your mom, you separate, and you come back, hopefully, in your late teens, early 20s, as friends. Well, if you never got to do that, you always idolize your mother, you know? The first time I ever thought of my mom as a full human being was when I held my son [in 1995]. And I realized that she felt all these things for me and for my siblings. And that she knew she was going to die and leave us, and what could that have been like for her? And that's when I started seeing her as a woman as opposed to a child's version of mommy."

It was awful enough for Roseann to lose one parent. However, in effect, she and her brothers and sister virtually also "lost" their dad, if not in body, then in spirit. According to the comedian in a 1996 *US* magazine interview: "It's very hard not to have a mom. Especially when you have a father who is incredibly grief-stricken, introverted, not expressive of his feelings and very traditionally Catholic who is struggling to get through in his own way, which meant not necessarily nurturing his children."

In short, Mr. O'Donnell, who was away during the workday, was hardly more visible once he returned to the house each night. To the kids, he seemed perpetually "away" in his own little world, unable or unwilling to exert a healing guidance to his devastated family. As one of the O'Donnells' former neighbors at the time recently told the media: "We heard he often left the kids to fend for themselves."

5

This unremitting, strained situation would have a profound effect on Roseann's—and her siblings'—ongoing relationship with their dad. In fact, its scarring effect on her would still be raw thirty years later. Per O'Donnell, "My father is very distant and emotionally unavailable and I rarely speak to him. After my mother died, the five children fused together and became one functioning parent/children unit. We took turns being those roles for each other. . . . My father was from a different world and different school. He's very Irish and very unwilling to change. . . .That's too bad for him, perhaps. Not for me. . . . Everything I've gone through in my life brought me to where I am, and I don't really have regrets about it or about him. He has his own destiny and his own journey. He'll heal himself when he chooses to. Until then there's nothing I can do about it."

Expectedly, Mrs. O'Donnell's death created a wealth of changes for the early teen. As the future star once analyzed, "I was quite grief-stricken and inaccessible as most children are who suffer that kind of tragedy at that age." One of the O'Donnells' neighbors in Commack, Long Island remembers that back in 1973:

> "Rosie was tiny, but she stepped right up to become the little homemaker. . . . She didn't just care for her older brothers and younger sister, but also her ailing grandmother—'Nanna,' her mother's mother—lived with the family. She had diabetes and went blind. . . .Nanna became Rosie's responsibility, and she took care of her as well as the rest of the family. . . . She grew up fast. Before her mom died, everyone called Rosie by the nickname 'Dolly.' Soon after her mother's death, I called Rosie 'Dolly'—and to my amazement this little girl drew herself up with great dignity and told me, 'I think from now on I'd like to be called Roseann [which a decade later, when she became a professional stand-up comic, she would change to Rosie]. . . . The family invited me to dinner one day. Rosie had organized the meal. And when it came time to clean up, she assigned the chores to her older brothers—and they did what she told them without a murmur."

If 11-year-old Roseann seemed mature at home, the youngster was full of crippling emotional turmoil that churned within her for years. Sometimes her surface "adjustment" to the parental loss would crack and her unresolved trauma at dealing with her mother's death would be visible to the world at large. Decades later, one particularly vivid such illustration remains firmly planted in Roseann's mind: "Well, when I was in elementary school, everyone knew my mother died, because she was the president of the PTA. But then we went to junior high school, and no one knew. And on, like, the third day of school, I hadn't done my homework, and the teacher said, 'Roseann? What's your mother's name? I'm calling your house.' And I didn't say anything. And there's 20 kids in the class, and seven of them knew about my mom because they were from my elementary school. And you hear this buzzing. Then the teacher said, 'What's her name?' and I wouldn't answer. 'What's her name?' And I ran out of school and hid in the woods until it got dark. All the teachers got together and had a meeting and talked about how you can't be this insensitive."

Some of these debilitating emotional reactions within Roseann might have been avoided or corrected *if* only she had had an adult with whom she felt comfortable to share her confusions and profound hurt. But, she did not. As a result, Roseann's weight was affected. "Mom got very thin before she died. I associate getting thin with getting sick and going away." Thus, after her mom's death, Roseann began stuffing herself. "Putting all that food inside me made me feel I was being filled up with love." It was not only Roseann who began to pack on the pounds: ". . . I noticed before my mother died, the pictures of my family, we were all fairly normal sized. And then a year after, there were some pictures, and we were all big. We were all, you know, trying to satiate ourselves, in ways that we were no longer nurtured, through food."

Likewise, Roseann's means of escape and survival became even more important to her. "I lived all my emotional reality through theater, movies and books. I come from an Irish Catholic family that suffered a tragedy where emotions weren't dealt with on any kind of real level."

Roseann's future handling of interpersonal relationships would be strongly affected: "To know the pain of being left makes it nearly impossible to do it to someone else. So with people I get involved with, it's usually forever—I keep them in my life."

And it increased her drive to succeed: "My mother died when she was in her . . . [mid] 30s . . . and I remember thinking as a young child, wow, she hadn't done all that she could have done, even at 10. And I was very driven to succeed in my own level at my own rate early in my life, because of my mother's death." Along the same lines, Roseann reasoned that if her mother had appeared in films and/or TV, she would have left something of herself behind for her loved ones and friends. It cemented Roseann's childhood whim—and now growing desire—to become a film and TV star. It gave her a goal and determination: ". . . I had to succeed before that [her mother's death] age so that if I died, I would have left something tangible."

In tandem with the drive to succeed, her mom's passing created an urgent desire within Roseann to achieve major fame. "When my mother died of cancer, I remember thinking that if Barbra Streisand had gone on *The Tonight Show* and asked everyone to donate ten dollars to find a cure for the disease, there would be one: Everyone loved her so much they'd get millions of dollars. I knew there was power involved in fame."

Finally, some observers have insisted that the virtual "loss" of her father as she was trying so hard to cope with her mother's death, bred in the future show business star an underlying mistrust of men in deeply emotional situations.

In the midst of all this turmoil, the bereaved youngster underwent yet another devastating experience. It occurred when she finally visited her mother's grave site at St. Charles Cemetery in nearby Farmingdale. If she—or others—thought the confrontation of her fantasies with this reality would make her mom's death more real and final for the girl, the visit hardly accomplished its purpose. Instead, it created more angst within the eleven-year-old, for when she reached the cemetery on Conklin Street in Farmingdale and walked up to her mother's grave in section 16 of the memorial park, she had a very strong reaction to the inscribed marker which read "Roseann O'Donnell . . . Forever In Our Hearts." As O'Donnell has mentioned, in true understatement, "To see a tombstone with your name on it is very startling."

Given all that happened, it is little wonder that the Rosie O'Donnell of today admits, "I have a marker in my head of March 17, 1973. Everything in my memory is either before or after that date. After that date my life was changed forever."

For Roseann O'Donnell, the nice girl from Long Island who would make good, the journey from being an emotionally needy eleven-year-old in 1973 to the bright and witty multimedia darling of the late 1990s would be long and tough. It was a case of strong needs feeding a growing determination to make her brash presence felt in the world— especially in the sphere of entertainment.

How this youngster developed into today's major star of TV, films, Broadway and the stand-up comedy circuit is a miracle tale. That she so successfully survived the many pitfalls of years on the road in the highly competitive and then male-dominated world of stand-up comedy is near magical in its unfolding. And how she evolved into the unconventional single mother of today makes Rosie O'Donnell's remarkable life story intriguingly real.

· 2 ·

Most comedians I know have severely dysfunctional families or have survived horrible traumas. I truly believe the comedic spark is lit by sadness and tragedy. Comedy is a lot like a combustion heap: if you throw enough shit on the pile, it eventually sparks.

Rosie O'Donnell, August 1992

*S*tretching 120 miles eastward from New York City into the Atlantic Ocean, Long Island is assumed by many out-of-towners to be mostly a dreary stretch of "endless" tract housing eclipsed by the razzle-dazzle of The Big Apple. Like most generalizations, this is only partially true. As one drives (or rides the Long Island Railroad) across the island—in which no point is more than four hours away, on a good traffic day, from midtown Manhattan—the topography alters gradually from heavily populated urban and industrial centers to farmlands, vineyards and even woodlands. Along the south fork of the island heading toward Montauk and Montauk Point, there are the famous Hamptons, the swank summer resorts with their fine homes, "in" restaurants, lush golf courses and a gilded social life that now operates year-round.

The island is divided into two counties: Nassau to the west and Suffolk to the east. (With populations in the latter 1990s of 1.35 million and 1.4 million respectively, Nassau and Suffolk counties fall within the United States' 25 largest counties according to the U.S. Department of Commerce's Bureau of the Census.) From Orient Point on the far eastern extreme of the island's north fork you can still take a passenger/auto ferry to New London, Connecticut. Along the isle's southern coast, at Bay Shore, Patchogue and Sayville there are seasonal passenger ferries to the many communities situated along the Fire Island National Seashore: Kismet, Ocean Beach, Point of Woods, Cherry Grove, The Pines, etc.

Up and down Long Island the many historical museums attest to the isle's rich past. For example, in Glen Cove there is the Garvies Point Museum and Preserve, boasting dioramas of long-ago Indian settlements as well as archaeological digs. In Oyster Bay sits Sagamore Hill, the famous estate of President Theodore Roosevelt. At both Cold Spring Harbor and Sag Harbor, once major whaling towns, there are whaling museums. Old Bethpage Village Restoration provides a recreated, active working community representing typical village life on the island in the nineteenth century. Out at Montauk, besides the state park with its miles of nature trails, there is the famed Montauk Lighthouse commissioned in 1795 by President George Washington.

While there is evidence that Long Island was inhabited by Indians as far back as 10,000 years ago, the island's present-day history dates back to 1524 when Italian explorer Giovannia Verrazano sailed along its southern shore. In 1614, Dutch trader-explorer Adrian Block actually went ashore at Montauk, leading to Dutch settlers crossing the waters (separating Long Island from Manhattan Island) in 1636 to establish what is now southern Brooklyn. By 1640, British colonists—sailing from Connecticut—crossed Long Island Sound to found Southold and Southampton, both of which claim to be the island's first English settlements. It was in 1699 that the infamous British pirate, Captain William Kidd buried a fabled treasure hoard on Gardiner's Island. In 1744, at Montauk Point, Deep Hollow Ranch was started, making it the United States' oldest cattle ranch. After the American Revolution, Long Island became noted as a farming community, supplying a majority of the food needs for a rapidly expanding New York City.

In 1834, the Long Island Railroad was established and, by the time of World War I, Mitchell Field had become a vital aviation training base for the U.S. Air Force. During World War II, the area's industrial productivity grew enormously, paralleling the expansion of the local Grumman and Republic Corporations, huge major firms supplying the U.S. government with many of its airplanes. After the Armistice, millions of discharged GIs moved to the island with their wives to follow "the American Dream," leading to the isle's baby and residential boom of the 1950s.

Long Island has long been a favored settling ground for Catholics,

11

dating back to 1683 when the Catholic Duke of York appointed Thomas Dongan (a Catholic) to succeed the abusive Edmund Andros as royal governor of New York. Reportedly, the island's first Mass was celebrated by Dongan's chaplain. The Catholic influx really began in the 1750s when French immigrants—Arcadians—from Nova Scotia relocated to Long Island to find religious and political freedom. By the early twentieth century, Long Island, long noted for its cultural and religious diversity, had become a favorite destination for many Catholics emigrating from Ireland.

• • •

In 1962, Edward J. O'Donnell was 34 years old. He was one of the many Irish immigrants who had relocated to the United States and settled on Long Island. He and his parents came from Donegal when Edward was quite young. After completing his schooling and joining the work force, the now-adult Edward married. His 100% Irish, but American-born bride-to-be, Roseann, was the only child of Daniel and Kathryn Murtha. Roseann was one year younger than Edward and also a staunch Catholic. Once married, the couple eventually put down roots in Commack which is in the heart of Long Island, ten miles southeast of Huntington. Commack, then with a population of under 33,000, is a typical middle-class suburban community which can be reached by exiting the Long Island Expressway, (affectionately known as the "Long Island Parking Lot"), or Jericho Turnpike (Route 25). The area of Commack (more a region than a town) in which the O'Donnells lived is actually in the township of Smithtown.

From Commack, it was a short drive on Long Island roads to the Grumman Corporation where Mr. O'Donnell was employed. He was among the many workers involved in designing special cameras custom-made for the U.S. government for use on their spy surveillance satellites. Years later, the stand-up comic would quip about her dad, "I'm still not really sure what he did. But he always used to tell us, 'Right now in Russia, they can read your license plate.' I'm like, 'Well, thanks, Dad. That's a comforting thought for an 8-year-old.' I'm in the bathroom thinking, 'They can probably see this in Russia, you know?'" Another quip she employed in her act in discussing her dad's great— and to Roseann inexplicable—overt enthusiasm for his Cold War spy equipment work at the Grumman Corporation was "he was very depressed when the Berlin Wall came down."

Typical of Irish Catholic couples at the time, the O'Donnells quickly started what would become a large family. Their first-born, Edward Jr., was born in 1960, followed by Daniel in 1961. Then, on March 21, 1962, came the birth of their first daughter, whom they named after Mrs. O'Donnell. Little Roseann (no middle name) was only fifteen months old when her sister, Maureen, was born. The final O'Donnell child, Timothy, was born in 1966. Regarding the latter, O'Donnell has recalled, "When my mom was pregnant, she asked us kids what we wanted to name him and since our favorite book was *Timothy Turtle* [1940], we said Timmy. Thankfully our favorite book wasn't *See Spot Run*, or his name would've been Spot."

The O'Donnells' home at 17 Rhonda Lane, situated a few miles north of the busy Northern State Parkway, was compact and comfortable. It was a two-story brick and cedar-shake home, with a two-car garage, a porch/balcony in the rear of the house, and a basketball hoop in the driveway. There was a big picture window in the front on the right, with the front door between this window and the garage doors. There were four windows facing the street on the second level.

The O'Donnells' home was an average dwelling, modest like the town itself which was more noted for its middle-class restaurants and motels than for historical or cultural landmarks. Many years later, O'Donnell would say, "Well, if you lived in Dix Hills [a Long Island community to the southwest on Route 231], you had money. Everybody in Dix Hills got a Corvette for their 16th birthday. If you lived in Commack, the not-so-rich part of the neighborhood—you didn't. We had one Plymouth Volare that we all had to share." Another time—when her good friend Madonna was interviewing her for the August 1993 issue of *Mademoiselle* magazine—O'Donnell described Commack as, "Well, it's just like New Jersey—it's suburban hell. Tract row houses one after another, the same exact. Different-colored shutters. It's the only way you tell them apart."

O'Donnell depicts her close mouthed father as being "Black Irish" and would refer to her dad—in her act and in interviews—as the "Lucky Charms elf" or "Lucky Charms leprechaun." He was a die-hard Irishman, exemplifying all the stereotypical traits of the "Black Irish" label: Catholic, ultra conservative, hard-drinking, stern, serious and very down-to-earth. He also had, at times, a heavy brogue. According to O'Donnell: "Well, there wasn't really an assimilation problem. I mean, he was pretty much as American as they get. You know, it [i.e., his brogue] gets thicker as he wants it to—sort of like my

New York accent. I don't really realize I have a New York accent. Then I watch myself on TV and . . . all of a sudden . . . I'm talking like this [heavy New York accent]. . . . But I never realized, so I don't think he ever realizes that his is as pronounced as it is. But, you know, we sort of fit right in there, suburban Long Island."

(Some time later, O'Donnell, who relied heavily on her family life and strict Catholic upbringing for her comedy routines in her early years on the road and on TV, would often poke fun at her father's shamrock-tinged accent onstage. Not only was this useful grist for her work, it was a way to repeatedly "get even" with her parent whom she felt had not really "been there" for her or her siblings during their childhood. "So it's nice to be here in California. I like it here. You know, my family—My family is still in New York. My dad is from Ireland. And he's nervous whenever I fly in a plane, 'Darling, be careful over there, you'll—.' Can't even understand him, you know. My friends couldn't understand him, either. When I was a little kid, my friends used to call and make fun of my father on the phone. He had no idea. He had no idea they were making fun of him. They'd call, he'd go, 'Hello, who's calling, please?' And my friends would go, 'Oh, he's after me Lucky Charms, the frosted oat cereal with sweet surprises.'")

In contrast, Roseann had a far stronger attachment to her American-born mother, an individual far more accessible to her children than the reserved, old-fashioned Edward O'Donnell. Mrs. O'Donnell was a dark-haired, blue-eyed beauty who bore a resemblance to the young Elizabeth Taylor. In particular, Roseann was drawn to her mother's sense of humor and, from a very early age, it prompted her to want to be a jokester too. As O'Donnell would later tell talk show host Sally Jessy Raphael: ". . . my mom was very funny. And I remember being a little girl, going to PTA meetings, being 5 or 6, what a great thing that was. Everyone wanted to be her friend. Everyone wanted to talk to her. . . ."

Early onward, it was obvious that Roseann shared her mother's passion for the theater, dance (ballet and tap dancing), movies and especially an admiration for pop singer and budding movie star Barbra Streisand. Some of Roseann's fondest childhood memories are of she and her mother listening repeatedly to Streisand recordings as Mrs. O'Donnell did her daily household chores. (O'Donnell remembers, "I loved Barbra Streisand and I would go into the kitchen and imitate her to make my mother laugh.") O'Donnell also insists, "I knew when I was four years old I wanted to be in show business. There was no choice for me. I used to practice signing my autograph. . . ."

Looking back, if the comic had to pick her most favorite times with her beloved, cheerful mother, it would be those occasions when Mrs. O'Donnell took her by train into bustling Manhattan. There, they'd head for the lavish stage and film show at Radio City Music Hall. Seated in the third balcony of this immense movie palace, mother and daughter would be enraptured by the entertainment, all the while sharing a package of lemon drops. For Roseann, life didn't get much better.

At home, for the pre-schooler, there was the family dog (Happy) with whom Roseann and her siblings played. Her favorite toy as a youngster was the game "Ker-Plunk," later replaced in affection by her record player. However, outside the family house there were exciting adventures waiting to be explored. If the sizable O'Donnell brood wasn't unusual in Commack, neither was their spilling over into the surrounding streets in search of new playmates: "We—every house had, like, five or six kids on the street. There were like all these big kick ball games and kick the can, Ring O'Leary, so it was a great childhood. It really was in that way." Early in her childhood Roseann proved to be an athletic, robust tomboy who wanted to tag along after her older brothers. They, of course, in typical fashion, didn't want their little sister pestering them for inclusion and attention.

By the time Roseann was six she was attending Rolling Hills Elementary School. Already, she was an extrovert who thrived on being the center of attention by entertaining others with jokes and impressions. "In first grade show-and-tell, I would do Bazooka Joe jokes from the comics." According to O'Donnell, "Most of the kids in my class wanted to entertain each other, but my goal was to amuse the adults. I was the teacher's pet because I could make the teachers laugh." However, one bit of notoriety she didn't appreciate was when her classmates (or neighborhood pals) would tease her by using her nickname and chanting "Rosie McDonnell Had a Farm, ee-i, ee-i, oh," or "Rosie O'Donnell Duck" whenever the plumpish youngster came into sight.

When she moved on to the second grade, her mother encouraged her elder daughter to sing "Second-Hand Rose" for the class talent show. This number, along with "Marty the Martian," was among Mrs. O'Donnell's favorites from Barbra Streisand's new LP album, *A Happening in Central Park* (1968). In short order, Roseann memorized all the numbers on the disc. "I used to listen to it every day on my 'close-and-play' record player. It was my mother's record, so I had to sneak it away from her. Then I would do all the songs and, with

Streisand's cadence, do all of the jokes, which I didn't even understand at the time."

Later that year, 1968, Roseann's mother took her show biz-struck offspring to see Streisand's debut movie, the musical, *Funny Girl*. The experience fortified the child's love of this singular entertainer. Additionally, it demonstrated that perhaps it was within the realm of possibility that she too could aspire to being a screen actress. After all, as Streisand had proved in this box-office winner (which earned her an Academy Award), conventional good looks were NOT required to be a screen luminary. Thus, little Roseann reasoned, there was career hope for herself.

From a relatively early age, Roseann had sensed that she was different from her peers. It was not only her very outgoing nature, her love of show business and her strong need to communicate and please by entertaining others that separated her from her classmates. She was, in truth, big-boned and pudgy in face and body. Sometimes she longed to swap her plump appearance for the svelte Ann-Margaret look. However, she inherently understood that such a transformation would never occur.

Generally, Roseann was far too independent to thrive on the strict daily classroom routine of her school. So she would suffer impatiently through the day, anxious to race home after school to share the day's experiences with her mom. While Mrs. O'Donnell would rush in and out of the kitchen as she prepared the family's dinner, Roseann sat glued in front of the TV set. By this point in the ritual, the youngster had already grabbed her favorite snacks: a Ho-Ho and a can of juice. Mother and daughter were joined in their daily television watching by Roseann's maternal grandmother, who had come to live with her only child. Even the acrid smell caused by Mrs. Murtha's constant smoking wasn't enough to spoil the tube-watching ritual for young Roseann.

Clearly the hours planted in front of the family TV were the happiest part of the day for Roseann. Years later she would enthuse, ". . . I used to run home from school and watch Merv Griffin [a popular daytime TV talk/variety show] with [guests like] Captain and Tennille, Zsa Zsa Gabor, and Totie Fields. It was a wonderful program that I watched ever since I was six. . . ." Other similar shows that drew her interest were the afternoon talk shows of Mike Douglas and Dinah Shore, who also boasted a constant procession of show business celebrities. Watching their routines was an excellent training ground for Roseann, the future performer.

Roseann was such an ardent TV watcher, absorbing unconsciously every bit of detail and trivia on any given program, that these television shows soon became the foundation and bellwether of her entire life. One of her favorite TV series at the time was *Bewitched* with Elizabeth Montgomery playing the pert young witch who marries a mere mortal (Dick York). When York the actor left the sitcom in1969 and was replaced—without fanfare—by similar-looking Dick Sargent, it had a profound effect on young Roseann. The unacknowledged substitution of players was as dramatically impressive to her as say the swapping of pod people for humans in the classic science fiction movie, *The Invasion of the Body People*. It caused the unsettled Roseann to constantly study and reexamine the quiet adult in the O'Donnell household who claimed to be her father. Repeatedly, she would check again and again to see if this being was truly her dad.

Another of Roseann's beloved TV programs was *Flipper*, about the cute and helpful dolphin who was the pet of the sons of the chief ranger at Coral Key Park, Florida. Thus, when Roseann joined her classmates for a boat trip to the Statue of Liberty, she has insisted—years later in a satirical tone—that it was she who kept calling "Flipper! Flipper!" from the boat's railing throughout the sightseeing trek. Later, by the time she was eight, Roseann had a new fixation—David Cassidy the pop rock singing star of TV's *The Partridge Family*. Looking back to this impressionable period, the Rosie of today reflects, "I never wanted to be a comedian—I wanted to be a rock star!"

There was something else Roseann wanted to be . . .a baseball player. According to the future star, "I played Little League on Long Island when I was about eight years old. My two older brothers—at the time [they] didn't let girls play Little League, so I would go down with them while they were working out and . . . the coach would let me play because he thought it was so funny that this little eight-year-old girl could catch fly balls in the outfield. So I would play before the game and after the game and put on my brother's uniform when he was at school and pretend like I was in Little League." O'Donnell—with tongue planted somewhat firmly in cheek—also likes to remind people that "I was always the first girl picked for the neighborhood teams. I got picked ahead of my three brothers, which I think still affects them."

Until she was well past eight years old, Roseann's family still called her Dolly. She earned the name because ". . . my older brothers couldn't pronounce my name when they were little, and they also thought that I looked like a dolly." (When Roseann became a professional entertainer she would shorten her first name to Rosie, which had been one of her childhood nicknames.) O'Donnell had another nickname in the neighborhood. One of the youngsters she baby-sat for was little Patty Cossick across the street. Patty called O'Donnell "Dolly Bloomer Bottoms" because Roseann wore bloomers instead of the more typical shorts.

Life was generally good for ten-year-old Roseann who was entering the fifth grade in the fall of 1972. She had occasional bouts of asthma, but there was always Primatyne Mist to stem any attack before it got serious. (In later life as a professional entertainer, one of Rosie's favorite gambits when interviewed on TV would be to rattle off the full Primatyne commercial, much to the amazement of interviewers and viewers alike.) She still went to church each Sunday with the rest of the family and got through the ordeal by daydreaming through the service.

As part of a large working-class family, the fast-growing Roseann was used to the fact that money was sometimes tight in the O'Donnell household. According to the future TV talk show host, "We didn't really have many luxuries when we were children. We didn't have matching socks. Or top sheets for the bed, just the bottom sheet. We didn't have a blow dryer, we used an Electrolux vacuum cleaner with the hose on the turnaround side."

As before, her days were filled with school, then rushing home to the still-hypnotic TV set. By now, the girl was a veteran devotee of the daytime drama, *All My Children*, which had begun in early 1970 on ABC-TV and starred—and still does—Susan Lucci as the fascinating, self-absorbed Erica Kane. This network soap opera provided a complex tapestry of intrigue, romance and surprising turns of events which had immediately drawn the approval of Roseann, her mother, her grandmother and the latter's sister (whom the O'Donnell kids called "Mary Ha Ha") who sometimes came to visit. Over the years, as one of its super-devoted fans, daily doses of *All My Children* would give Roseann the sense of continuity that was often missing in her real life.

Then (as now) Roseann was so totally absorbed by television that she became a human trivia magnet. She admits in retrospect that "I annoyed my family my whole life. They were always trying to get me to shut up." By now, she had informed her family "'I'm going to be a movie star.' So they always knew what I wanted to do. I just don't think they ever thought I would do it." Also, by this point, she'd seen her first Broadway play, a Sherlock Holmes drama.

According to the 1990s Rosie, ". . . when you hit fifth grade your hormones kick in and you try to assess who you are as a person and that includes sexually and who you are attracted to and why, where and how. . . ." As such, she recalls that, at this time, she had a crush on a classmate named Billy. But, he was going steady with a girl named Laurie. However, Roseann still managed to receive her first non-platonic kiss. It was from Craig Blitz, another fifth-grade classmate. It happened one day, after school, when she and Craig were shooting hoops outside his house: "The basketball bounced into the garage, he kissed me, and it bounced out again." End of story? Not quite. Twenty-four years later when Rosie had just begun her daily TV talk show aired from New York City, she received several phone messages at the program's offices from an insistent Craig. For whatever reasons, he wanted to personally remind her of that long-ago kiss. As she told the studio audience and home viewers that day, she remembered. Enough already!

And then, just when everything in her life seemed to be running as predictably as it should or could for a pre-adolescent, everything dramatically changed . . . and nothing would ever be quite right again. Roseann's mother, then only in her late thirties, suddenly got sick and, within a few short months, died.

Deprived of her favorite parent, Roseann's life took a warped direction, depriving her of what should have been normal, safe and happy teen years to come. Years later she would look back and reflect, "I never learned those traditional mother-taught-you things."

• 3 •

My mother died when I was little, so I liked all the [TV] shows with single parents—Nanny and the Professor, Eight Is Enough, The Courtship of Eddie's Father. *They represented what I was living.*

Rosie O'Donnell, August 1993

*S*till reeling from the loss of her mother, stunned, eleven-year-old Roseann found herself operating in near robotic fashion. It did not help or speed up the healing process that, since Mrs. O'Donnell's death, the household was a far different place than before. The loving parent who had been so openly demonstrative in encouraging and paying attention to the children was gone—forever. Equally missed was Mrs. O'Donnell's infectious sense of humor. And worst of all, following the example of her tight-lipped dad, the much-missed mother was never discussed or even referred to in the grieving household. Roseann would blame this bizarre situation on "Being a typically repressed and emotionally detached Irish Catholic family. . . . "

• • •

During the summer of 1973, Edward O'Donnell took his five children on a visit to his homeland. The trip to Ireland, which included a stopover in London, lasted several weeks and allowed Edward to introduce his brood to relatives and friends. Despite the novelty of going abroad, the O'Donnell children were still too upset by their mother's death to enjoy the change of scenery and, of course, their father—although with them—remained distant.

Looking back to that trip, Rosie recalls, "I remember eating salt and vinegar potato chips and having sweets. . . . We used to go to the woods and my cousin would shoot cap guns and we'd hide in the bushes and watch the helicopters come because we were in Belfast for part of it." She further adds, "It's all sort of a fuzzy, hazy memory, but I do remember playing soccer all the time, which we never did in the U.S. and picking up the brogue right away and speaking that way the whole time we were there and all my siblings making fun of me."

One result of the trip to Ireland would be Roseann's growing fascination with bagpipes. Later, when she was fourteen, her uncle, Jim O'Donnell, who was a piper, gave her lessons and she continued learning the instrument at a nearby church on Long Island. To this day, Rosie can still play the pipes ". . . a little bit, but not well."

• • •

Meanwhile, life, of sorts, did go on. Looking back, Rosie can now be more charitable in discussing her dad's frightening plight: "His wife had just died, he had five small children . . . and a mother-in-law in a small house, and he didn't have a clue how to do laundry. I remember one of the first meals he made, he actually mashed the potatoes in the boiled water and then tried to tell us, 'That's how Mommy used to make them.' I said, 'Dad, this is potato soup! This is not mashed potatoes!' He'd go, 'Shut up! This is good!' . . . He was not really ready for what life dealt him and he coped with it the best way he could, which was by checking out."

Before long a whole new set of duties and responsibilities settled upon the single-parent O'Donnell home. For example, Roseann's oldest brother, Eddie, did a majority of the cooking and cleaning. (Months earlier, when Mrs. O'Donnell knew she was dying, she had taught each of her children to prepare at least one actual meal, so now they would occasionally rotate the kitchen chores.) Mostly it fell to little Roseann to assign tasks, referee fights and even get into scrapes at school while protecting her younger siblings—sister (Maureen) and brother (Timmy)—from schoolyard bullies.

The family unit was quickly divided into two opposing, uncommunicative camps: the five children versus the repressed, despondent father (teamed, by default, with the increasingly ailing and unassertive grandmother). Meanwhile, Roseann and her siblings made a useful discovery: "In my family, comedy was the only way you were able to tell the truth without getting into trouble." By being (mock) humorous, the children, especially Roseann, found a means, albeit unfulfilling, to make a small degree of contact with undemonstrative, distracted Edward O'Donnell.

If watching television had been a pleasant diversion before, now it became a solace for the motherless kids. Since Edward O'Donnell had virtually abrogated his parenting responsibilities, the children were left pretty much on their own to pick and choose what shows they wished to watch and how late at night they stayed up watching them. (Rosie remembers, "It was typical for us to sit in front of the TV for hours and hours on end. When other kids would be outside playing, we'd be inside watching the tube.") Roseann in particular became even more addicted to watching the tube, especially any program (such as Fred MacMurray's sitcom, *My Three Sons*) which featured a single-parent household as its premise. She could relate all too well to such onscreen situations. These shows were a lifeline. They helped her to cope with her unrelenting loneliness.

Later, when a new daytime TV soap opera, *Ryan's Hope*, debuted on ABC-TV in July 1975, Roseann became hooked, and it became part of her viewing regimen, along with her mainstay, *All My Children*. Because *Ryan's Hope* had an urban setting—New York City—Roseann found it very easy to relate to the program's plotline. She was particularly fond of actress Kate Mulgrew who was cast as the show's Catholic, virtuous heroine, Mary Ryan. In fact, when the plot eventually found Mary about to receive an oncamera marriage proposal from another character, Roseann couldn't bear the thought of missing one episode of this especially fascinating storyline. Since these were the days before the now common VCR, the imaginative youngster devised a scheme to remain at home near the TV set that pivotal Monday. By contorting her breathing into a heavy wheeze and groaning about her imagined illness, she convinced her distracted father that she had a touch of bronchitis. Thus, she was permitted to stay out of school that day. This ruse went on for a solid week, by which time Mary Ryan was altar-bound.

With no available adult to set guidelines at the O'Donnells and having already triumphed with her gambit of playing hooky from school, Roseann looked for other ways to take impromptu personal holidays from school. She remembers ". . . me and my sister would cut school on the day of the Academy Awards. We'd go to the store, buy all our favorite foods, make dinner, get dressed up, do our hair. I mean, we saw all the movies nominated, we'd make predictions, then sit there and scream and yell all night."

In addition, Roseann's obsession with theater-going continued apace. If she couldn't persuade a relative or a friend's parents to treat and/or chaperone her on such a trek, she'd hoard her allowance money (and the extra amounts she earned by her extensive rounds of neighborhood baby-sitting). When she had saved enough, she'd sneak off to a Saturday matinee at the Westbury Music Fair on Long Island or, later, into Manhattan for an afternoon performance of such musicals as *Pippin, Best Little Whorehouse in Texas, Bubbling Brown Sugar, Ain't Misbehavin'*, etc.

One of the youngster's most compelling experiences was attending a performance of Bette Midler's very offbeat Broadway musical showcase, *Clams on the Half Shell* (1975). Roseann was so captivated by the highly talented, campy/trashy entertainer that it led her to deciding that she ". . . wanted to be her. I didn't want to be like her. I wanted to be her." Roseann saw in this new idol a huge talent who didn't mind using unorthodox approaches to get ahead in show business, including playing on her own unconventional looks. Like Barbra Streisand, Bette Midler would become an important role model and icon for Roseann.

Meanwhile, despite having "discovered" Bette Midler, Roseann's passion for Barbra Streisand only increased. For one thing, continuing to be such a devout Streisand fan was a means for the Long Island girl to keep alive memories of her dead mother, the latter having been such an avid Barbra booster. In fact, Roseann began to fantasize that, somehow, she might engineer a meeting between Streisand and her widower dad and that the two would marry. Imagine having your idol for a new mother!

As the weeks and months tortuously passed following Mrs. O'Donnell's death, Roseann found herself seeking emotional consolation outside her immediate family. As it happened, dollops of it came from next door where her best friend, Jackie Ellard, resided. "I lived at the Ellards' house: 22 Rhonda Lane. Jackie Ellard's mom really took me under her wing; she was really maternal in a non-intrusive way. I was raised at the Ellards' house. I ate dinner there four nights a week." (Regarding this generous neighbor, Rosie would remark not long ago: "Every year, I send a Christmas card to Jackie's mother, Bernice, and I tell her all the Ellard-esque things that I have in my house: I have an electric knife that cuts the meat thin. And Tupperware with the right kind of lids. . . These were all things that the Ellards had that I always wanted. And I'm so happy to be able to have an Ellard-kind of house for my son. Because the Ellards provided me with safety and the feeling of being nurtured, things I didn't have in my own house.")

When not being the unofficial domestic head of the O'Donnell household or attending school classes or burying herself in hours of TV watching, or stuffing herself with junk food, Roseann burned off excess energy in athletics. "I was a tomboy who played sports every single day: basketball, baseball, field hockey, touch football, kick ball, hide-and-seek, kick the can, running bases. . . ." Later, she would coach brother Timmy's softball team and, in high school, would play softball. In college, she would be the short stop on the campus team.

Another means of emotional escape and release for Roseann was to maintain a diary. "Like most kids I tried to keep a journal. I got one at Christmas, by January 5th it was over. I lost the key. Later, I actually found the journal I kept in the 6th grade—I guess I was about 12 years old. . . . I had written it in code, because I was afraid somebody would find it. Like, 'Today went to 692 and I told them about 44.' As an adult, I'm reading this and like what am I talking about? I had no clue."

• • •

It seemed each year brand-new situations arose which tore away at the fragile continuity of Roseann's life. For example, when she was thirteen, she got her first period. It was a telltale sign that her childhood—so tied to her mom—was now a thing of the past. Because she had no mother or older sister to turn to for a medical explanation, practical advice or sympathetic understanding, she confided reluctantly in her flustered dad. He took her to the local supermarket to purchase sanitary pads. Seemingly oblivious to her potential embarrassment, he proceeded to brag to every friend whom he encountered there about Roseann's change of life and her "special" necessary purchases. (Later, Roseann would distill this traumatic episode into a comedy bit for her stand-up act. However, at the time it happened, it was far from amusing for the highly sensitive teenager.)

Another illustration of her changing life occurred when she began junior high in the fall of 1974. She had to get used to a new public school in Commack, classrooms filled with unfamiliar faces among both her teachers and classmates. Thankfully, one instructor there took a special interest in the vulnerable yet rebellious Roseann. It was Patricia Maravel, her math teacher. Mrs. Maravel not only gave the girl special attention during class, but, after school, did her best to provide Roseann with a focus and a sense of receiving maternal love. Pat had a tremendous impact on the impressionable girl and her example would encourage the teenager, for a while at least, to consider teaching as a possible career goal alternative to becoming an actress.

Now, thanks to her considerate teacher and to Roseann's next-door neighbor, Bernice Ellard, the twelve-year-old had two surrogate mothers! Every year since that time, Rosie has sent each of the two women Mother's Day cards and, in connection with Pat, has become the godmother of her two children.

Having adjusted to her new school environment, Roseann soon evolved into the class clown, maintaining only a thin edge between being considered funny or disruptive in the classroom. By the time she entered Commack South High School on Scholar Lane in September of 1976, O'Donnell admitted that because she had "no guidelines or boundaries" at home she and her siblings were "pretty wild, with little respect for authority." As she further explained to reporter Gail Shister of the Knight-Ridder Newspapers in May 1996: "I never did what anyone told me."

As time went on, as a gawky, overweight teen with no guiding parental presence, Roseann developed an even stronger disdain for authority. As she has said, "I always felt I knew more than them. I got away with that attitude because I was funny. I was lucky I wasn't prone to getting into trouble. I was a kid prone to succeed." She further detailed, "I never rebelled in traditional ways. I didn't smoke or drink or have sex. I just went to comedy clubs at 15 [onward] and told everyone I was going to be a comedienne."

Rosie has described her high school as being ". . . a suburban refuge. We didn't even have greasers there." She admits that she hung around with a tight group of Catholic girlfriends and that "I never saw a Protestant person until I went to college." She continued with her sports: ". . . I played softball and volleyball and tennis and basketball. A regular tomboy jock girl and proud of it."

However, as much as Roseann wanted to be "one of the kids" in high school, there were too many differences in her life from their norm to make such a goal realistic. For example, at home she was essentially running the household and functioning as a mother figure to her siblings. One neighbor of the O'Donnells at this time would detail for a supermarket tabloid in July 1996: "She was raising her own brothers and sister—yet she always found time to put on a clown outfit and entertain the local kids. . . . There were about 28 little children in the neighborhood, and she baby-sat for almost all of them. They just adored her."

Then too, few if any of her schoolmates were as "devoted" to theater-going as Roseann, who thought nothing of cutting classes on a Wednesday to catch a Broadway matinee. According to her, "I would memorize the theater directory, and I'd tell all the ushers at the theaters that I was going to be a star." She admitted that occasionally she'd steal cash from her dad's wallet to pay for the Long Island Railroad ride into Manhattan and to buy standing room for Broadway shows like *The Wiz*.

One of her favorite song-and-dance shows proved to be *They're Playing Our Song* (1978) with Lucie Arnaz and Robert Klein. Not only did Roseann revisit the popular musical several times, but after the matinee she would frequently go around to the stage door to collect Arnaz's autograph. Then she started writing letters to the actress (who was the daughter of Lucille Ball, another favorite of Roseann's). Arnaz, who sensed that here was a stage-struck, lonesome young woman rather than a potential stalker, graciously replied to her ardent fan's letters. In turn, Roseann was excited by these simple notes from a celebrity. Not only did she take them to school to show her friends (who were generally unimpressed), but she had the correspondence framed. (Years later, in August 1996, Lucie would appear on TV's *The Rosie O'Donnell Show* and guest and host would reminisce about the importance of those written exchanges.)

Besides playgoing on her own, Roseann frequently went to movies alone on the weekends. Then after the evening showing, she would appear late at friends' parties, eager to discuss the latest picture. According to the future celebrity, "I remember when I saw *The Deer Hunter* [1978] and was really excited about it, but they were like, 'It's only a movie, who cares.'"

Other emotional elements divided Roseann from her high school peers. According to one former classmate, Roseann ". . . was always smiling and making everyone laugh—yet she missed her mom and often the tears weren't far away. . . ." Then too, there was the matter of dating. According to another school chum, "I don't remember her ever having a boyfriend, even though she was very popular with the boys. The guys liked Rosie because once she came out of her shell, she was more than a match for them. She could throw a football, catch a baseball and curse with the best of the boys."

It was not that Roseann was unaware of or didn't think about sexual activity. It was just that her priorities were different from those of her fellow students. For instance, while reminiscing with *New York Times* reporter Todd S. Purdum in May 1994, Rosie recollected two of her hometown's better known landmarks—at least to the teenage population. One was the Commack Motor Inn. She described this establishment as, ". . . where they had mirrored ceilings over the beds." She further added: "That's where everyone in high school went to have their first sexual experience. Except for me. I was more interested in the Tiffany's Wine and Cheese Café (later changing its name to Legends), which was directly across the street, where you could get cheese platters and rent, like, Yahtzee and games to play at the table. And then, on our way out with our pitchers of sangria, we'd look to see if there were any cars in the Commack Motor Inn of kids we knew from high school." At Tiffany's, Roseann and her equally underage pals used faked IDs.

There possibly might have been other reasons why overweight, insecure Roseann had little or no apparent interest in dating during high school besides being self-conscious about her appearance. For one thing, she had no positive adult male role model at home to make the opposite sex seem appealing in a romantic and/or emotional way. Magazine writer Mary Murphy, who interviewed Rosie for the June 15, 1996 issue of *TV Guide*, took occasion in her article to analyze Rosie's past, revealing a person who, to this day, apparently still avoids romantic commitment via a standard female-male relationship.

Murphy writes of O'Donnell: "She describes an environment of concealment and fear, a childhood buffeted by conflict coupled with the negative effects of relatives' alcoholism. Which is one reason why, she says, she decided to adopt a baby [in 1995] rather than have her own child." Murphy quotes O'Donnell with saying, "I really had no ego investment in recreating myself. Nor did I feel the need to dive into my gene pool or go fishing there, because there is a tremendous amount of illness in my family, a tremendous amount of alcoholism."

Then too, a father still in denial about his wife's death and "closed" to the family, may very well have heightened Roseann's dislike or distrust of adult males in general. Verbal abuse on his part of any kind could have been devastating to his impressionable daughter.

Such abuse may very well have translated into Roseann's ongoing concern for victims of child abuse and battery. For instance, in discussing her pet theory that O.J. Simpson, the celebrity, was given preferential treatment in his Los Angeles criminal trial, Rosie argues, "And it's sad because if it wasn't O.J. Simpson, there's no way that he would be able to get away with it. . . . People are like, 'He couldn't possibly— there's no way. He's the Hertz guy. He couldn't do it.' It's the same thing—you know, little kids are abused by their parents. They can't really believe that their parents would be capable of such heinous acts."

On other occasions, when angered to speak out against those who claimed that rock superstar Michael Jackson could not possibly be guilty of the alleged child abuse, she retorts, "You know, they say that about priests. They say that about people's fathers and their brothers and the elementary schoolteachers and the soccer coach. They say it about every man who is accused of [child] molestation . . . Wake up."

• • •

By the time Roseann entered her final year at Commack South in September 1979, she had already held a variety of jobs including many stints of baby-sitting, being a day camp counselor one summer, employment as a part-time waitress, selling T-shirts, etc. At age seventeen, she'd devoted the summer vacation between her junior and senior high school years to working at the nearby Sears in their catalog return department. She disliked the regimentation of the 9-to-5 job, not to mention dealing with disgruntled customers.

Looking back on her "glory" year as a high school senior who was on the student council, Rosie has acknowledged, "I was Miss Do-Gooder." She elaborates: "I was Miss High-School everything. I was the prom queen. I was the homecoming queen. I was class president. I was class clown." Always the jokester, especially when it involves commenting on her own life, she adds facetiously, "And something else. . . . Oh, Most School-Spirited, which comes in handy in life. You never know when you might have to do a cheer." Since stereotypically, a school's Homecoming Queen is traditionally pretty in a conventional way, how did 5'7" Roseann, who weighed about 140 pounds under the best of circumstances, win such an accolade? According to one Commack South classmate: "Most of the girls at school were happy when she was voted Homecoming Queen. At least it wasn't a pom-pom girl or someone who was slim and beautiful . . . It was Rosie—who was just pretty funny."

Ever since Roseann had played Glinda the Good Witch in her second grade production of *The Wizard of Oz*, "I was pretty much in a play every year from then on." This held true throughout her high school years, where she was a member of the Drama Club (and among other activities played the drums in a school group). During her final semesters (1979-1980) at Commack South, there was one particular show in which she participated which would ultimately change the course of her life. "We had *Senior Follies*, which was sort of like *Saturday Night Live* skits about the teachers. . . . I did Gilda Radner, Rosanne Rosanna-Dana, talking about school apathy and I would impersonate her. And a local guy who owned a club in the area was a comic, and his little brother was in my year, and he asked me if I would come and do stand-up in his club. I said, 'No, I'm going to be an actress.' He goes, 'Why don't you try it?' So I tried it. . . ."

• 4 •

When I was a child, we lived in a house with no parental supervision, so all we did was watch television. And when you are a comedienne, you write what you know.

Rosie O'Donnell, August 1992

*A*t a very early age, Roseann had been instilled with a love and appreciation of show business by her doting, fun-loving mother. Once Mrs. O'Donnell recognized Roseann's affinity for performing comic one-liners, impressions, etc., she respected and encouraged her daughter's fast-developing fantasy of one day becoming an entertainer.

Almost from the start of this informal introduction to the performing arts, the imaginative and creative youngster developed specific career ambitions. As she spelled out to cable TV talk show host Al Roker in April 1995: "I actually wanted to be a Broadway actress because I grew up here in New York, on Long Island, I used to come to the city and see Broadway shows with my mom when I was a little girl. And that was my only sort of relationship with real live people who did this for a living. I'd see movies, but I never met them. I didn't know where they lived, who were they—but I'd come to see a Broadway show, I'd stand outside the stage door and I saw the people who had just done the show. So that was really my first love, was to be a Broadway star."

On another occasion, explaining how it was such a fluke that she became a stand-up performer, she said, "There are comedians who

30

watched Johnny Carson and thought, 'God, if only I could do a monologue.' I was never one of them. I always wanted to be an actress. Barbra Streisand was my hero, idol, god, queen. Also Carol Burnett and Lucille Ball and Bette Midler. I wanted the funny roles. I wanted to be Laverne, to be on *Happy Days*. Those were my dreams as a kid."

When Roseann was only fifteen, she, like several of her girlfriends, had already become veterans at using false IDs to gain admittance to comedy clubs in the vicinity of Commack. However, unlike her pals, Roseann was far more adventurous and daring, which was her way of hiding her shyness, loneliness and a persistent lack of confidence about her looks. Thus, in her efforts to divert attention from her assorted insecurities, she created a brash, aggressive posture which she punctuated with comic, ironic remarks. Next, add to this mix the surface maturity she'd attained from years of running a household and caring for her siblings. Then, stir in a pinch of typical New York-bred impudence and cockiness. Finally, season the package with a touch of Irish blarney (inherited from her dad), and you have the (apparently) brash Roseann O'Donnell of her mid-teens.

One of the hangouts for Roseann and her friends was the Ground Round Restaurant in Mineola, Long Island. It was a branch of the restaurant chain famed for its (higher-price) hamburgers and the habit of the bar-area customers throwing the shells from their complimentary peanut snacks onto the floor. At the Ground Round, Tuesday was open mike night in the bar area. On one of these evenings, O'Donnell accepted a dare, and competed in the amateur contest.

Rosie recalls, ". . . I was sixteen, and I looked like I was twelve, with this cute little haircut and big sweatshirt and sweatpants, and I was this little tough girl, and the audience—grown-ups like my parents' age—were like, 'Look at this little kid with chutzpah.'" She had no act, but, wearing funny sunglasses, did one-liners as well as material she had (unconsciously) tried out on friends and family over the years. To be sure, she was very amateurish, but so were the other contestants. Rosie won the $50 first prize. Flushed with victory, she thought "Wow, this is easy."

Giddy with success, Roseann wished that her so-supportive mom was still alive so she could share this triumph with her. Her older brothers were preoccupied with their own lives and, as for her dad, he wouldn't or couldn't be vocally responsive to her achievements. And, besides, all she needed to do to add to his growing misconceptions about her supposedly "wild" lifestyle was to point out that she was performing in clubs where they served liquor. It was bad enough that he was convinced that his high-spirited, unconventional daughter must certainly be part of the hippie generation, one of those addicted to the wicked weed. Adding fuel to Mr. O'Donnell's imagination about his daughter's supposed recklessness was the actuality that sixteen-year-old Roseann had already been in a car accident. One day while driving to the library, she clipped another car as she was parking her dad's Chevette. Any impulse to leave the scene unnoticed was checked by the fact that the driver of the other vehicle was still in his now-dented car.

Mr. O'Donnell's persistent belief that Roseann smoked grass frustrated her. Not only was she NOT a marijuana-user, but she'd never even smoked real cigarettes. Later in her career, her battle-of-the-generations situation would become fodder for her comedy act. Therein, she'd describe her dad as the type of suspicious, overprotective father who was always stationed at the front door when she came home at night. Typically, he'd be shouting, "You're taking, aren't ya! Oh, ye bunch of pot takers . . ." She would cap the sketch with: "He's an idiot, my dad. Kind of an idiot. I think they need to form Idiots Anonymous for people like my father."

Meanwhile, Roseann experimented with her comedy "routines" at a few other open mike nights at clubs in the area, sometimes fortifying her courage for the session with a few beers. According to O'Donnell, "I had no act at all. I hid behind a big pair of goofy glasses, pointed at guys in the audience and said things like, 'Nice shirt, pal.'" Other bits of her disjointed act included an impression of the video arcade game Pac-Man and other, equally mundane observations. She would punctuate her hopping from topic to topic with such transition lines as "OK. Yeah. So . . ." or "Right. OK. So . . ." More importantly, though, all this trial and error made the fledgling comic realize that she was experiencing a degree of fun and that, perhaps, she ". . . could make a living doing this [comedy thing] while, hopefully, getting seen as an actor."

Then, during her last year at Commack South High School, along came the job offer from the brother of a classmate who had seen her perform in the *Senior Follies*. After the show, he offered her a chance to appear at his restaurant/club—not at open mike night, but as a *paying gig*. Roseann accepted. Her first few (fumbling) attempts at this venue met with little audience enthusiasm. Per O'Donnell, "I didn't have any material, let alone an act, so I came off and blamed it on the audience."

By the third such time the audience gave her the proverbial cold shoulder, Roseann realized she had to put together a real act. But how? From what? To whom could she turn?

Once again, television came to her rescue. For years, the tube had provided a salve for her loneliness and her creative thirst. The world of TV shows had long been her substitute parents for teaching her about life. And now, the tube magically provided her with the answer to her latest dilemma. The day before she was to make her next stand-up club appearance, she happened to see a rising young comedian, Jerry Seinfeld, deliver his routine on TV's *The Merv Griffin Show*. His performance seemed pretty funny to Roseann (as it had to the television studio audience). Being a quick study with dialogue, she made full mental notes of Seinfeld's act.

The next evening, O'Donnell made her scheduled stage appearance. Instead of her usual semi-trite raucous quips, etc., she launched loudly into the very organized Seinfeld material, which began with: "You know, I was on my way over here tonight and the car broke down. I opened up the hood and [I say to myself] what am I looking for? A big on-off switch?" And so it went, with Roseann regurgitating Seinfeld's well-honed routine. And, being a natural-born mimic, Roseann was easily able to make full use of Jerry's effective cadence and delivery style. The smooth material worked almost as well for her as it had for Seinfeld. She virtually killed her club audience!

Winding up her spot, Roseann left the stage, dazzled by the audience's enthusiasm. She had succeeded and it hadn't, after all, been that hard. However, her joy was short-lived. What followed would remain forever etched in O'Donnell's mind. "I came off stage . . . and these guys came from all sides, real threatening like, and said, 'Where'd you get those jokes?' and so I told them. I told them I'd heard Jerry Seinfeld do them on *The Merv Griffin Show*. When they told me I couldn't do that, that I had to do my own material, I was crushed, devastated. I mean, I didn't have any idea how to go home and make up my own jokes."

It was a taxing job for the deflated Roseann to absorb this lesson in professional ethics. In truth, in her innocence, it hadn't occurred to her that it was a no-no to borrow baldly another comic's material. In her naiveté, she argued back that "A joke's a joke. It was on TV." As for the need to write her own jokes (since she certainly couldn't afford to hire others to do so), her angry retort was, "Well, forget it! I'm not doing this!" In her amateur's logic, Roseann reasoned, "When you're an actress, they don't ask you to write the movie." In short, recalls the slick comic pro of today: "I was so mad. I was 16 and I thought they were ridiculous."

Time took its course. Once she got over the hurt, humiliation and fury at being so chastised by her peers, she began considering the wisdom of the unsolicited warning from her exasperated colleagues. As such, she decided to heed the advice so often given to fledgling authors: "Write about what you know." She began searching her life for any nuggets of humorous events that could be mined for her act—anything that the audience (mostly her father's age) might relate to and appreciate. Eventually, she fastened on her years at Catholic school as inspiration for her material. Expanding upon and/or exaggerating the harsh discipline and strict rules of such an upbringing became the core of her new, self-written act. It was a frame of reference, she decided, with which the predominately Irish Catholic club patrons could relate. And so, armed with new routines which also contained self-deprecating humor, she began to make other comedy club appearances on Long Island at The Round Table, The White Horse Inn, etc.

With the exuberance and determination of youth, Roseann juggled her hectic schedule of high school, helping out at home, baby-sitting for hire and performing comedy club gigs whenever opportunities arose. As she has detailed, "It was pretty good for a kid, on the whole. You could make $10 at each place, and you could hit four, five a night. If you emceed, you got $15 a night."

As the months passed, she decided that it would be less pressure to be an emcee rather than to be just one of the endless procession of comics taking their brief turn in the line of fire in front of the live mike. Being the host allowed her to be more herself. It also saved O'Donnell from having to create continually new extended material beyond her patter for introducing the act and/or, occasionally, for jibing the audience. These evenings at the clubs proved to be marvelously educational for Roseann: "I watched every comedian and saw what they did. They'd take an experience from their life that was relatable. They put the humor into it and presented it to the audience, who would go, 'Oh, yeah, I've done that.'"

Looking back at this apprenticeship period, Rosie acknowledges, "Luckily, I started at 16. When you're that age, you have such a huge ego that you think you are the best thing in the world. That narcissistic immaturity served me very well, because when they didn't laugh—and they shouldn't have laughed, because I wasn't funny—I thought to myself, 'Well, this audience stinks!' I had that huge, impenetrable self-confidence that only a child can have. When I was 28 and had been on the road for ten years, I couldn't believe I had walked onstage and performed with no material. In hindsight, it's frightening to me. At the time, it wasn't frightening. It was empowering."

On the other hand, years later, in retrospect, a more mellow Rosie would allow that being so career-oriented so young had a negative impact. It caused an imbalance in her life. She regrets ". . . missing out on a lot of the things that your average 17-year-old does. Every single weekend of my life from the time I was 17 until now I've been in a nightclub or a comedy club. . . . It's never being out with friends on New Year's Eve—it's being in a club with 300 strangers. I was working nearly every holiday and every weekend. . . ."

• • •

Meanwhile on June 22, 1980 at 4:30 p.m. Roseann O'Donnell, age eighteen, who was an over-achiever in extracurricular activities and class popularity if not in academics, graduated from high school. The majority of her fellow seniors (in a class of 553 students) had little real idea of what career paths, if any, they'd take in life. Such was not the case with boisterous, gregarious Roseann, the perpetual jokester who couldn't get enough of Broadway shows, the latest movies or a heavy-duty regimen of television. "Everybody knew what I was going to do," she has said. "On the yearbook, they'd write, 'Say hello to Johnny Carson when you're a big star.'" While she was anxious to get started with her acting career (not stand-up comedy) in show business, she decided that a college education—especially one that offered theater arts courses—couldn't hurt her chances at making good in the industry.

Although Roseann did not have the requisite high grades or aptitude test results to make her an appealing candidate to some institutions of higher education, she possessed other very desirable traits: she was a personable, well-rounded student, with lots of high school activities (drama club, sports, etc.) and popularity achievements (senior class president, homecoming queen, etc.). So, if she wasn't up to the standards of any of the Ivy League colleges (which were out of her financial reach anyway), she still had a choice among many very satisfactory schools which would accept her and which, very importantly, offered her a financial scholarship.

After narrowing down the options, Roseann decided to attend Dickinson College, a co-ed institution founded in 1773. It offered degrees in Bachelor of Arts and Bachelor of Science, catered to a multi-ethnic student body, and prided itself on the small size of its classes, usually averaging 18 students. This college is located in the lush countryside of Carlisle, Pennsylvania. Carlisle, once a colonial frontier village and now the seat of Cumberland County, is situated in the south central part of the Keystone State, 189 miles southeast of Pittsburgh, and 22 miles southwest of Harrisburg, the state capital. Carlisle is also home to the Dickinson School of Law, the U.S. Army War College, and, as well, the renovated Carlisle Theatre, an art deco movie house built in 1939.

For Roseann who had never lived away from home, Dickinson was an ideal choice. It was far enough away (232 miles), but still close enough for a bus or car trip (approximately 4 hours) back to Commack whenever necessary. As she prepared to embark on her college life, she certainly must have had mixed feelings about leaving the nest after so many years of being "in charge." However, at the same time, this move would permit the eighteen-year-old the luxury of focusing on just one person for the time being—herself. Whatever ambivalent feelings she may have harbored about her father or "deserting" him now that her older brothers were already high school grads and on their own career tracks, she was comforted that her sister and younger brother remained at the Rhonda Lane home to help out their still-single parent.

By September of 1980, Roseann was one of the 1,700 or so students enrolled at Dickinson which boasted an 85-acre main campus with an additional 18-acre recreational area nearby. Roseann roomed at Drayer Hall situated between College and Moreland streets, due north of South Street. Drayer was a traditional all-women's residence hall, housing 180 students within its long corridored confines. There was an elevator to reach the higher floors and, in the lobby, a well-appointed lounge which featured a grand piano.

Part of Roseann's weekly activity at college was to work in the administration office, a requirement of her work-study program which provided for her student loan. There, she soon felt at ease with the friendly office co-workers. And she thrived in gym classes and sports (especially softball). However, it was a different story when it came to academics and fulfilling the basic requirement courses. (Students at Dickinson did not declare an academic major until the end of their sophomore year.) She felt out of her depth scholastically and it made her persistently uncomfortable. As she would confide to reporter Hilary De Vries in 1994, "It was a school for people much smarter than me." To escape the weekly grind, Roseann and her dorm roommate would often take the two hour-plus bus trip into Philadelphia, where they'd check out the sights, including hanging out at some of the South Street clubs.

Between working on campus, doing sports and trying to find ways to further her future show business career, Roseann subconsciously gave low priorities to cracking the books. As a result, she ended her freshman year with a 1.62 (or D-) average. She had done so badly that there was no point in her returning there the next fall. If this fait accompli upset her (or her family) at the time, in later years she harbored no resentment against Dickinson College. In fact, in August 1996, on one of the early episodes of the first season of *The Rosie O'Donnell Show*, three of her full-time co-workers from the administration office at Dickinson College were in the audience. One of them, Dotty, was picked to be the audience-member-announcer for that episode's opening and when Rosie appeared oncamera to start the proceedings, she chatted animatedly with her once office mates.

Never one to accept failure, Roseann was determined to give college another try. This time she chose a far bigger school (14,000 undergraduates). It was located in Boston, Massachusetts, the state's capital and a major hub of higher education. (During the school year well over 120,000 students attend colleges and universities in this metropolitan area.) She picked and was accepted by Boston University which was renowned for its theater arts department. She auditioned for the program with a scene from *Hello, Dolly!* (Having many times seen the Barbra Streisand film version of the Broadway musical hit, O'Donnell was well equipped for her audition. She had easily mastered every dialogue bit and nuance in the test scene.) As a result she was given an acting scholarship to Boston University.

So, once again when summer ended, Roseann left home and Commack, this time headed to heavily urban and very cosmopolitan Boston. There she matriculated at B.U. with its mass of high-rise campus buildings stretching along and about Beantown's Commonwealth Avenue. In contrast to Dickinson where she had been a small fish in a compact pond, now she was a minnow in a big ocean school of academic fish. With a goodly percentage of the student body living off campus and the campus itself integrated into a sprawling metropolitan city, the university offered Roseann far less structure and supervision than had her prior college.

With this freedom and accessibility, Roseann found time to catch all the new movies, see plays on their pre-Broadway tours and make the round of comedy clubs that had sprung up around Boston. At B.U., there was always so much to do—especially when one was *not* fascinated by textbook study. In fact, she also did a few stand-up comedy engagements, including the time she was asked to fill in for another comic at a suburban Boston comedy forum.

As part of her B.U. work-study program, Roseann was employed in a college-operated video arcade. Hardly anyone ever came to the facility. To make her work shifts pass faster, O'Donnell played the games herself. Breaking the rules, she used the eight quarters school officials gave her to feed the machines. Years later, on her TV talk show, O'Donnell would discuss her long-ago "borrowing": ". . . they were always short $2.00 . . . they thought no one would steal $2.00, but I did. I did 'cause I used the quarters to play the games . . . Geeze!"

For some students at B.U., it must have seemed a long, long time between September and February. However, in the relatively short space of those six months, Roseann both began and ended her academic stay at Boston University. Years later, she would wisecrack on national TV that she was kicked out of B.U. because she couldn't get up in time for her 7 a.m. movement class. On other occasions, she has admitted the more painful reality. The event that triggered her separation from the university happened in one of her theater arts courses in which she was exploring her potential as an actress—both serious and comic. If she thought she had a flare for comedic timing, her professor obviously disagreed and took occasion to dress her down in front of all the other course students. Rosie has recalled, "He told me the part of Rhoda Morgenstern [the sidekick played by Valerie Harper on one of O'Donnell's most cherished TV sitcoms, *The Mary Tyler Moore Show*] had already been cast and that I would never make it as an actress." Roseann was so humiliated by the adverse experience and angered by the teacher's sarcastic judgment that she quit school.

Having already struck out twice with academia, O'Donnell finally accepted in early 1982 that she must stop postponing the inevitable. It was time to take her act—whatever that might be—on the road—wherever that may be.

· 5 ·

*I never had something to fall back on because I was never going to
allow myself to fall back. I would hear, 'Get something else in case,'
and I'd go, 'No.' If there's a net, you'll fall. And chances are if there's
not, you're not going to get off that rope. You have to know in your
heart of heart, 100% sure, that you're going to succeed, in order to do
it.*

Rosie O'Donnell, July 1993

Roseann O'Donnell reached her twentieth birthday in March
1982. She had prematurely concluded her college years, and
was again back home in Commack, Long Island. Once more
she was mired in her father's household—and this time without an
educational career path or a job at hand. It was embarrassing to her
ego and stifling to her long-cherished dreams of Roseann the star.

Now that push had come to shove, she saw no other option than to
plow ahead with jump-starting her career in the entertainment field,
however best she could. Other women her age might have considered
marriage or a more typical office or retail job as the next step for an
unemployed college non-graduate. Not Roseann! She intended to fulfill her childhood dreams of entering professional show business, no
matter what. Even if there had been a family member who could, or
would, advise her on life options at this critical point, it's unlikely that
the determined young adult would have listened. She was confident in
her destiny if not her methodology.

Years later, Rosie would look back and reflect, "I never wanted to be a
stand-up comic. . . . My goal was always to do *Oklahoma!* or *Gypsy*. . . .
My idols were Chita Rivera and Liza Minnelli, and Lucie Arnaz." So if
this fledgling actress wanted to be Broadway's next Ethel Merman or

Barbra Streisand, why did she now pursue a career in stand-up comedy? For one thing, her (sub)conscious sabotaging of her college education also cut short her chances to take college-offered acting, dance, voice, etc., classes—all necessary training to embark successfully on auditions for stage roles. For another, Roseann was realistic enough to appreciate that she lacked any of the extra gimmicks (professional credits, conventional good looks, contacts, etc.) to get ahead on the stage. Without these attention-getters she could be stuck forever in casting call hell. She might easily spend years of frustrating, hard effort making the rounds of Broadway agents and auditions and never find any real acting work. That much she knew.

Relying on instinct she determined that performing professionally—even if it was comedy at the crummiest club—could provide her with the needed exposure and lucky breaks. Certainly, such miraculous situations had occurred in the careers of her show business role models, so why not for her. Thus, for O'Donnell doing stand-up was not a heart's desire but a calculated means to an end.

If Roseann "had" to enter the ranks of professional stand-up, she couldn't have picked a better time to do so in the United States. Stand-up comedy was then a happening thing from coast to coast in North America. But such had not been the case even twenty years earlier. Back in 1963, there was only *one* showcase club in the entire country for up and coming comedians. This was Manhattan's the Improv, recently opened by a former advertising man, Budd Friedman, and his singer wife, Silver. The Improv's methodology of featuring new and raw talent was in sharp contrast to nightclubs which generally booked only established acts and employed comics, if at all, as the opening act for featured singers, etc. And, by the early 1960s, thanks to the competition of free television and other lifestyle changes, the number of nightclubs left in America had vastly diminished.

During the Improv's first two years, they had no cover charge. The New York club also did not pay the fledgling comics, based on the theory that the operation was a testing ground for unseasoned talent. Even when the club began to charge customers a fifty cent admission, the comedians were still not paid. Once the establishment got its liquor license, its profit line increased and comics began to hang around much more frequently. If it was a house rule not to pay the performing comics, there was no policy against giving the entertainers free drinks. Meanwhile, about the only site where rising comics could get paid ($30 a weekend) to work out the kinks in their act was at Pips in Brooklyn.

As for the then existing Village clubs like the Champagne Gallery, they mostly booked singers and musicians.

In 1975, Budd and Silver Friedman divorced. She continued the New York City forum and he relocated to California. By that point, Budd estimated that the New York Improv had presented 10,000 new acts, many of which were comics and singers (such as Bette Midler). In addition, this establishment was the training ground for such future stand-up greats as David Brenner, Bill Cosby, Robert Klein, Freddie Prinze, Jimmy Walker, *et al.*

Once in Los Angeles, Friedman opened the LA Improv which competed for business with another local comedian showcase, the Comedy Store, started three years earlier in 1972. The latter operation was founded by Mitzi Shore and her then husband, comic Sammy Shore (they are the parents of 1990s comedian Pauly Shore), in conjunction with comedy writer Rudy DeLuca. Among the future funnymen stars who worked at the Comedy Store in its early days were David Letterman, Richard Pryor and Robin Williams. Mitzi Shore bought out her partners the next year and also had a policy then of not paying the talent.

Back in New York, in the mid-1970s, two other important showcase havens for comics opened their doors. They were Catch a Rising Star and the Comic Strip, both of which also had a no-compensation plan for comics. Meanwhile, up in San Francisco, the Holy City Zoo sprung up and this small club did the unique thing by paying for stand-up comedy acts! On a good night a comic could earn as much as $75 a show there. It was not bad money then for doing what one loved and for getting paid to learn on the job. However, this pay-the-acts trend did not catch on elsewhere.

Beyond the opportunity of testing new material and presentation, another major perk for comics gradually occurred at the Improv, the Comedy Store, Catch a Rising Star, etc. With their rising reputation, these establishments began to become places where performers could be spotted by talent bookers and, in turn, be invited to perform on one of the national TV talk programs such as *The Tonight Show with Johnny Carson*. This change inspired an increasingly larger number of (new) comics to perform, without salary, at these clubs. At the same time, it also was a magnet for more and more audience members who hoped to witness up close the humor of jokester stars in the making.

In 1979 an amazing thing happened in the world of live stand-up comedy. A group of comics, realizing that Mitzi Shore's Comedy Store was grossing an estimated $2.5 million yearly, banded together as "Comedians for Compensation" and struck the club. This strike led to nasty situations on the picket lines, defections among the pickets to the enemy camp for fear of reprisal blacklisting once the strike was over, etc. Eventually, a compromise was worked out with comics—even newcomers—being paid a minimum of $25 a set.

The LA Improv saw the handwriting on the wall, especially after a mysterious fire ruined part of the club. Friedman began modestly paying its talent. On the East Coast, a planned stand-up comics' strike was circumvented and a payment schedule for performers was worked out. Thereafter, comics pressured the few showcase clubs in other parts of the U.S. to institute a salary arrangement (often a percentage of the audience admission charge).

When the bi-coastal strikes ended and the comedy clubs found they could still be very profitable even after paying the performers, a new trend developed. Promoters around the country began to book (young) stand-up talent into the hinterlands, often taking over fading saloons, dance halls, etc., for the showcases. As the comedy club industry mushroomed, the number of such spots jumped from approximately 10 in 1980 to close to 300 paying showcases by 1986.

Thus, by the early 1980s, it was possible, by careful planning, scrimping and effort, for a stand-up comic to make a living in his/her chosen profession playing the comedy club circuit. And, after all, these gigs could lead to cable TV work, especially on HBO or Showtime which found stand-up comedy to be an inexpensive, easy way to package/present entertainment for its viewers, whether it be a solo act or a taped edition of an evening at a particular comedy club. Then there was the potential of a stand-up comedian becoming enough of a "name" to secure work in occasional feature films as fast-rising Paul Reiser was already doing.

• • •

Now that Roseann had convinced herself to embark full force on the world of stand-up, she sped into operation. She took comedy and improvisational acting classes whenever she could afford the fees. To earn her way, she accepted emceeing gigs—usually on Long Island at such spots as the Eastside Comedy Club, Chuckles, Governor's, etc.—and began networking, hoping to win similar master of ceremonies jobs or stand-up comedy assignments on the road. If it required embellishing her resume "credentials" with a fictitious engagement here or there, so be it.

The Road! It sounded so glamorous, especially to anyone hand-cuffed to a tedious 9-to-5 office job, or, for those stuck at home day-in, day-out as an unappreciated homemaker. However, Roseann quickly learned the reality of the road. As she has described, "You fly to some city you don't know and some stranger picks you up. You drive to this condo in the middle of nowhere. There's mildew on the shower curtain and a lock on the phone because the comic who was there last week ran up the bill. And it's what I did for years."

On another occasion, she would paint an equally bleak picture: "Back in the early eighties, along the East Coast, stand-up was just burgeoning. All the comics would share a condo. You'd arrive in town and they'd have a kid come pick you up in a used Vega or Toyota with a door that didn't close. You'd have to get in on the driver's side and climb over his lunch from Hardee's. All of us would be scrunched in the back seat, and he'd take us to this filthy condo where we would all live for a few days, with the sheets that have to be shaved because they had little bumps on them . . . rotten leftover take-out food in the fridge. Very disgusting."

All this was definitely disheartening. However, Roseann was young, resilient and determined to make her mark. So she coped as best she could. However, there was even worse in store for her: "The other comics were much older. They'd pick up women at the bars, bring them home, have sex in the rooms [of the same condo apartment "suites"] next to mine. I was like 20 and totally freaked out from hearing these noises through the walls. I put the dresser up against the door. Everybody was doing drugs and drinking. And I was just this [naive] little girl on the road, scared in her room." Roseann found her own way to cope. She began drinking, not just a nip here and there, but "a lot." As she has explained, "Instead of going back to the motel to be awake and afraid, I would stay and drink with the waitresses after the show and try to get sleepy."

Beyond ALL of this—and THIS was a lot—O'Donnell had to deal with YET ANOTHER major problem . . . gender discrimination. It was an "established" show business axiom that club or even TV audiences (especially males) would not tolerate the female counterpart to the typically aggressive, abrasive, sometimes foul-mouthed male comic. Before the 1970s, the majority of the *few* women who did a form of a stand-up act used "dumb" routines in the tradition of Gracie

Allen or Marie Wilson. A departure from this heritage came in the 1960s when Totie Fields, Phyllis Diller and Joan Rivers made their mark in (night)clubs and on TV. However, even then, convention demanded that they hide their intelligence or acerbic observations behind a mask of self-deprecation. As such, their acts included poking fun at their weight, looks, or roles as subservient housewives.

There were also such rarities as Elaine May and Jackie "Moms". Mabley. May, in tandem with partner Mike Nichols, made sharp social observations unfettered by self-disparaging jokes. Mabley (1894-1975), an African-American, created a stage image as a feisty grand-motherly type who wore outlandish outfits and often performed with-out her false teeth. Mabley mixed social satire and ribald humor in her decades of performing on the black (comedy) club circuit. Another comedic trend-breaker who rose to fame in the late 1960s on TV's *Rowan and Martin's Laugh-In* was Lily Tomlin, who featured sharp, smart satire. Finally, fortified by these pathfinders and changing social mores, a new type of frank female comic burst on the scene in the 1970s and early 1980s. These assertive exponents included Whoopi Goldberg, Sandra Bernhard, Elayne Boosler and Judy Tenuta.

When Roseann hit the road in the early 1980s, there were ". . . about eight women doing stand-up at that time. There were so few women, we were never booked together on a show. If we were, they called it 'Women's Comedy Night.' Like it was a big deal." In particular, she recalls one club owner saying, "You're the third woman we've had, and the first two sucked. If you stink, we're not hiring any more." That remark staggered Roseann: "That's a lot of pressure, isn't it? The respon-sibility of my entire gender ever performing there again? I'd be told, 'Most women comics suck, but you were all right.' It was horrible."

Roseann had learned from her experience as a surrogate parent at an early age, as well as playing traditionally male sports, etc., that, if given the opportunity, she could tackle most tasks or jobs that a man did. Thus, being a semi-pioneer in the field of women's stand-up was daunting but not insurmountable to her. In fact, she's admitted, "Well, I think that it was an asset for me when I started. It was such a rarity to have a female comic performing at all in a comedy club live that it helped me get noticed. I think that if I was a male comic . . . it would have taken me a lot longer to perhaps get to a certain level."

As a result, Roseann, who lacked the confidence or connections to be booked into a New York City club, found herself increasingly out-of-town for short stints. In those days the circuit included such landmarks as the Comedy Connection (Boston), Garvin's (Washington, D.C.), the Comedy Castle (Detroit), the Comedy Club (Cleveland), Zanies (Chicago), the Holy City Zoo (San Francisco), the Laugh Stop (Newport Beach, CA) and the growing chains of Punch Line and Funny Bones clubs that had begun in Pittsburgh, PA and Atlanta, GA respectively. It proved to be a grueling existence of, in Roseann's own words, ". . . traveling alone on dark roads in cars that seemed to have a death wish and living in seedy, club-provided accommodations."

In these apprentice years, Roseann was not a practitioner of the Joan Rivers' school of comedic self put-downs. Instead, she gravitated toward what she termed "observational humor through characterization." Her role models were Whoopi Goldberg, Lily Tomlin and Robin Williams. Her rationale for this performing choice was ". . . I could show casting people that I could act as well, because my goal never was to be Johnny Carson. It was always to be more Carol Burnett."

O'Donnell soon established performance guidelines. She determined that she was never to say anything in her act about another individual that she wouldn't say to that person's face. She disagreed with those comedians who believed that ". . . it doesn't matter what you say, as long as they laugh. That the fact that someone laughs justifies the hateful, hurtful comments that you make. And I don't think that that's a valid reason." For O'Donnell, "The end does not justify the means." On the subject of political correctness, outspoken Roseann had her own viewpoint. She felt that it ". . . has no place in art. I think that you have to live the truth of whatever it is that you're doing, whether it's painting or—whatever the truth is for you. . . . I try to stay true to what I believe, and if I think something's offensive, I won't do it."

Roseann's out-of-town club engagements were a shopping list of learning lessons for her. At one stopover, she was dubbed with a new professional first name. It happened when the audience had mistaken her full name for "Rosanne Rosanna-Dana," the popular character created by Gilda Radner on TV's *Saturday Night Live*. When O'Donnell came on stage, the disappointed customers booed her. Thereafter the emcee christened her "Rosie," a name which stuck onstage as well as off. And there was, of course, the occupational hazard of coping with every comic's worst nightmare—the heckler in the crowd. Rosie learned by trial under fire, including having to fend off a paroled, hard-edged convict in one Texas comedy club.

Rosie soon developed a thick protective skin against jibing audience members. She devised effective—if crude—put-downs to handle such messy situations. A few of her favorites were, "The next time you come to a comedy club, stop at a drugstore, buy a condom, and put it over your head. If you act like a dick, you might as well dress like one." Another was, "When I wanna hear from an asshole, I'll fart."

Now that she was a working professional, Rosie could not but hope that her father would come out of his emotional shell to acknowledge at least her career. Perhaps he might even attend her stand-up engagements when she performed on Long Island. However, these changes in behavior never came about.

Speaking of this ongoing situation in 1994, the best she could offer about the still-hurtful lack of rapport was, "I assume my father is proud of me. He really doesn't say very much. I've done stand-up comedy since I was 16, and I think he's been to three shows in fifteen years. It's not really a great track record. . . . He's not really into discussing his feelings." By this point, Rosie had been in one form or another of therapy counseling since she was 18, trying to better deal with her unresolved feelings about her parent and her childhood traumas which had snowballed into emotional pitfalls in her adulthood. However, as late as mid-1996, she would confide to *TV Guide*'s Mary Murphy that she was "by no means done yet" with the exploration of her emotions.

If father and daughter living in proximity for years had done nothing to mend the ever-widening gulf between them, the stalemate would be "resolved" in the coming years. By then, Edward O'Donnell had been a widower for well over a decade. Eventually, he met a woman named Mary and they married circa 1986. (As with most events in Rosie's life, this provided fresh grist for her comedy act and media interviews. Some of her commentary about the nuptials included: "They got a Saladshooter. That's really appropriate for a 60-year-old man. Dad just can't get enough of shooting radishes all over the kitchen.") Soon thereafter, Edward would retire from the Grumman Corporation aerospace plant (which, due to the sagging defense industry, was already cutting back drastically on its work force). Later, he and Mary moved to the Raleigh-Durham area of North Carolina.

Even after he and Rosie lived so far apart, Edward O'Donnell would still remain an integral part of Rosie's stand-up act. However, she has cautioned, "The father I have in the show is a lot nicer and a lot more approachable than the father I had in reality. My father in reality is not the affable Irish leprechaun." As for her stepmother, Rosie would admit that, to a degree, she got along with Mary because ". . . she wasn't raised in our family and didn't know the rules, so she's communicative."

In 1982, The Eastside Comedy Club in Huntington, Long Island had been in operation for three years. It was founded by Richie Minervini and its acts were now booked by Rick Messina. In the years to come, Messina, a one-time bartender, would become an increasingly important nationwide booker of comedians. It was tradition in most such clubs to be closed on Monday when, following the weekend rush of business, audience traffic would be light. Messina decided to form an improv group, much in the tradition of Toronto's and Chicago's Second City troupes. He put out the word that he was having auditions for the to-be-formed Laughter Company.

Rosie was a frequent performer at Minervini's Eastside Comedy Club in its and her early stand-up comedy years. (She would later say of Minervini, "He gave me the breaks and took me under his wing. If it wasn't for him, I probably never would have done stand-up comedy.") Being aware of the tryouts, she showed up for the auditions. Among the 65 or so other hopefuls was Vinnie Mark, who had grown up in Massapequa, Long Island and who was then in the first year of (community) college. He and Rosie, who were the same age, developed an immediate rapport. It also turned out that they both had had experience with improv (which is far different than an organized stand-up routine) in acting classes. As the tryouts continued they found themselves among the rapidly diminishing number of finalists as the talent pool under consideration decreased to its final number. When the ordeal was over, the Laughter Players consisted of Peter Bales (also the group's director), Dave Hawthorne, Jim Meyers, as well as Vinnie and Rosie.

A routine quickly developed for their weekly Monday night show. The group, who often individually had their own gigs to perform on the weekend, would arrive at the Eastside Comedy Club about 3 p.m. on Monday and rehearse for three hours. Then they'd break for a snack and be back in time to go on at 8:30 p.m. for the two-hour show. After the improv segment, the troupe showed their stamina by doing individual stand-up gigs for the audience. Their payment for the whole night consisted of a small flat fee which they split among themselves.

Because Rosie and Vinnie were the least experienced of the improv troupe, they were given the straight lines to deliver, while the other more experienced members would provide the sketches' punch lines. Under the best of conditions, it was a tough gig. Matters weren't helped when some Monday nights a few rival comics (who had not been selected for the troupe) would be in the audience and razz the troupe. (Some years later, by which time Rosie was emceeing and producing a weekly national cable comedy showcase, these same hecklers sent in audition tapes asking O'Donnell to put them on the lineup. She had not forgotten their earlier bad behavior and never booked them for *Stand-up Spotlight.*)

As time wore on, the Laughter company reduced its ranks to a quartet when Jim Meyers dropped out and was not replaced. In late 1983, the group was among the improv talent in the New York area who auditioned at NBC-TV in Manhattan for an upcoming hour-long weekly improv comedy show that the network was casting. They arrived at the appointed time, and found themselves auditioning in front of a panel of judges. Only after the audition did the two older, tense members (Peter Bales, Dave Hawthorne) of the Laughter Players explain to the still-relaxed and loose Rosie and Vinnie, the facts of life. The key judges at the session had been the upcoming series' producer, Lorne Michaels (the creator of the seminal TV show, *Saturday Night Live*), and established comedian/writer Buck Henry, the latter scheduled to be part of the new program's troupe.

As it turned out, none of the Laughter Players made it to the final cast of NBC-TV's *The New Show* which debuted on January 6, 1984 and, due to poor ratings, was off the air as of March 23, 1984.

Meanwhile, the Laughter Players continued their weekly stand at the Eastside Comedy Club, now on Wednesday evenings instead of Mondays. Increasingly, owner/booker Rick Messina would have weekend work for Rosie and Vinnie (on a package deal) out of town, especially in the tri-state area. At any one time they might have a weekend job in a club in Buffalo, or perhaps at the Comedy Cabaret in Trenton, New Jersey, or the Comedy Cabaret's other location in Wilmington, Delaware. Typically, Rosie and Vinnie each received $110 a performance.

By now, it was clear to Mark and the others that Rosie possessed that special drive and aggressiveness needed to propel her up the professional ladder. Recalling those fledgling days together, Vinnie especially remembers three qualities about go-getter Rosie. With her booming voice she never really needed a microphone to reach the back rows of a club audience. She also had made a crucial self-discovery. As she was fond of saying, "I can take mediocre material and sell the shit out of it." Thirdly she knew how to network.

Once she began at the Eastside Comedy Club there was no holding Rosie down. If anyone mentioned a name of a possible contact anywhere in the country, she was immediately on the phone giving the person a hard sell about her talents. On the surface at least, she was unrelenting and fearless. When comedian/actor Shirley Hemphill (star of the TV sitcom, *What's Happening!!)* saw O'Donnell perform at the Eastside Comedy Club, she made it a point to say hello to Rosie and to compliment her on her comedic skills. Rosie, in turn, was quick to follow Hemphill's suggestions regarding ways to smooth out her stage act and how to better network within the industry for more prestigious stand-up assignments.

But even a goal-oriented workaholic like Rosie O'Donnell could occasionally almost slip up. One night in 1984 after performing her stand-up shtick at a Long Island comedy club, a youngish woman said hello to Rosie and inquired, "How'd you like to be on *Star Search?*" Being an avid TV watcher, Rosie was certainly aware of this new but already very popular nationally syndicated television talent show. It was hosted by Johnny Carson's talk show sidekick, Ed McMahon. A somewhat cynical Rosie responded with, "Oh yeah. Sure." The clubgoer then told Rosie her name. She was McMahon's daughter, Claudia.

· 6 ·

Stand-up comedy is like boxing, because it's a combative art form. If you're not trained and you go in the boxing ring, you're going to get the crap kicked out of you, no doubt about it, because the other guy is trained. With stand-up, it's the audience, because they know you can deliver a good punch and if you don't have it and aren't in shape, they're going to beat up on you.

Rosie O'Donnell, November 1994

*I*n the early years of television, nasal-twanged, ukulele-playing Arthur Godfrey had enjoyed a ten-year-run (1948-1958) with his *Arthur Godfrey's Talent Scouts*. Every Monday night from 8:30 p.m. to 9:00 p.m., "scouts" would bring front and center before the television cameras their latest discoveries to perform before the national TV audience. Winners were selected by an audience applause meter. Many of the contestants were young professionals-in-the-making hoping that nationwide exposure would launch their careers into the major leagues. Among the many "discovered" on the program *before* they became really popular were Pat Boone, Rosemary Clooney, the McGuire Sisters, Johnny Cash, Patsy Cline, Steve Lawrence, Tony Bennett and thirteen-year-old Connie Francis (playing an accordion).

Twenty-five years after *Talent Scouts* expired the format was revived, this time on a big glossy scale. Veteran TV announcer and spokesperson Ed McMahon was signed as the host of this hour-long *Star Search*. (Until that time, Ed was best known as Johnny Carson's overly convivial second banana on *The Tonight Show*, the individual who announced nightly at the start of the proceedings, "And hereeeeeeeee's Johnny.") *Star Search* debuted in national syndication in September of 1983. The format featured hopefuls in each of several categories: male vocalist, female vocalist, musical group, TV spokesmodel, stand-up comedian, actor, actress, etc. Each week there was a different panel of talent agents and producers as judges who selected the winner in each category. At the end of each season, there would be quarter- and semi-final playoffs with a victor being picked eventually in each category. In the process, cash prizes permitted a winning contestant to amass a total of as much as $100,000. At the height of its popularity, there were an average of 20,000 applicants per year hoping to make it to the *Star Search* stages, but, in any given season, only 160 contenders were chosen.

During the show's dozen seasons on the air, the competition categories would be altered, the program would move from its point of origination in Los Angeles to Orlando, Florida and, in the fall of 1994, MTV veejay Martha Quinn would join McMahon as co-host on what was then called *Ed McMahon's Star Search*. Among the many future notables who made their mark on *Star Search* during the series' long run were comedians Kim Coles, Rick Ducommun, Jenny Jones, Martin Lawrence, Dennis Miller and Sinbad; country rock group Sawyer Brown; singer Sam Harris, and such future TV actors as Brian Bloom (*As the World Turns*, *Smokey and the Bandit*), Ami Dolenz (*General Hospital*), Joseph Gian (*Hooperman*) and Amy Stock (*Dallas*).

Meanwhile, back on Long Island at the comedy club, the patron quickly proved to skeptical Rosie that she was indeed Ed McMahon's daughter, Claudia, and that she was among the program's many talent seekers. Now convinced, O'Donnell quickly accepted the offer to make a further taped audition which, if successful, meant she would be flown to Los Angeles in the fall of 1984 to compete on the actual show. She passed the preliminaries and was soon off to the West Coast, even though some of her family and friends thought it was a waste of time because, they assumed, she could never hope to win against the stiff competition on the show.

Once in California, O'Donnell promptly made her debut *Star Search* appearance. As was true in the comedy clubs of the early 1980s, there were still relatively few female stand-up comics performing their craft on television. So brash Rosie, with her pronounced New York accent and heavy-duty surface confidence, and that cascade of long curly dark hair, was a novelty. She beat the rival humorist in her initial round on the program. In the show's brief history to that time, she was the first woman contestant to win in the comedian category. Thereafter, she was the champ in her classification several weeks in a row, and each time she succeeded, she earned another $3,500 in cash.

It was a heady experience having such successful and recurrent national exposure. She had always hoped one day to perform on *The Tonight Show* and if she couldn't be joking and chatting on the air with Johnny Carson, then having a similar opportunity with Ed McMahon, Johnny's sergeant-at-arms, was a workable substitute. Moreover, Rosie was living another long-cherished dream. She was finally in the Mecca for all movie-lovers—Hollywood. Like any devout tourist, she now could stand in the cement footprints of film stars at Grauman's Chinese Theater on Hollywood Boulevard, scout out the Vine Street Brown Derby hoping to catch a glimpse of a movie luminary going in or out of the landmark restaurant, take the Universal Studios tour, explore Disneyland in Anaheim, etc.

However, all was not completely joyful for the enthusiastic contestant from Long Island. Being on a tight budget and wanting to save as much money as possible to finance her career, she stayed at a cheap Hollywood hotel not far from the TV studio where *Star Search* was taped. Most of her meals were not glamorous power meetings at the trendy Polo Lounge at the famed Beverly Hills Hotel. Instead her dining out generally consisted of quick hot dog meals grabbed solo at a burger stand close to her rather shabby hotel. Most of the time—especially in the evenings when there were few touristy things to do—she was quite lonely.

Moreover, there was behind-the-scenes friction at *Star Search*. Sam Riddle, the show's chief producer, didn't cotton to Rosie's in-your-face personality. He told her, as if it was a major discovery, that she really needed to lose weight. Further undermining the young woman's confidence, he insisted, as O'Donnell would vividly recall nearly a decade later, that she "... was way too tough to ever make it in Hollywood." (Years thereafter, by which point Rosie had found fame, she would snipe back publicly at him and his career prognosis.)

One of the perils a stand-up comic faced on *Star Search* was that several consecutive victories on the program had a downside, that of quickly running out of good material to perform before the cameras and the show's judges. At the ripe age of 22, Rosie fell victim to this plight. In the semi-finals she lost to fellow comedian, the slightly older John Kassir. (He would go on to a lengthy career in stand-up comedy, as well as acting on the stage and, more recently, providing the voice of The Cryptkeeper on HBO-Cable's *Tales of the Crypt* as well as in the 1996 movie, *Bordello of Blood*.)

During the break in time between the taping of her preliminary rounds and the semi-finals on *Star Search*, Rosie returned to the East Coast. She was astonished at what a few appearances on national television could accomplish. Not to say that she didn't expect adulation from her Commack, New York friends and from some members of her family. And there were her Laughter Company pals at the Eastside Comedy Club in Huntington, Long Island, where she was still performing when she was in town. However, she was taken by surprise whenever she went shopping at a mall. There, while strolling along the crowded plazas, she'd frequently be stopped by people, asking the same question, "Didn't I see you on *Star Search*?" Others smiled and gave her a thumbs-up sign for future *Star Search* victories.

This first real taste of popularity was obviously exciting for Rosie. It also reinforced her long-cherished belief that she could really become a star someday, even if it meant more years in stand-up until she was discovered for bigger things.

Soon the time came for Rosie to return to Los Angeles for the semifinals. On that elimination round of *Star Search*, she lost to John Kassir, departing that playoff with a $1,500 consolation prize. (A few years later, on April 4, 1987, O'Donnell would return to *Star Search* for its *2nd Annual Star Search to Stardom Reunion*.)

After losing the big money on *Star Search*, Rosie came back to New York. It was to be a short visit. With her accumulated TV winnings of over $15,000, O'Donnell had already decided to relocate permanently to Los Angeles. She reasoned, "If you want to surf, you have to go to the water." She was convinced that if she was situated in the heart of film and TV production, sooner or later she'd get her big break. So enthusiastic was Rosie about her potential that she suggested, then begged and finally chided her improv troupe cohorts to make the West Coast move along with her. However, they each voiced a checklist of reasons for remaining which necessitated their remaining for the time being on their more comfortable home turf. Not so for Rosie who had no parental or romantic ties to keep her New York-bound.

Once again in Los Angeles, Rosie rented a furnished studio apartment in a humble part of Hollywood. Next, she splurged and had her teeth crowned. After all, she didn't want those movie close-ups, about which she had so long fantasized, to be marred by crooked teeth. Once that cosmetic task was accomplished, she made the rounds of comedy clubs and bookers, all the while waiting for the phone to ring. Her attitude was, "Well, I did *Star Search*. Now everyone in Hollywood has seen it and—I'm gonna wait." And wait she did, to no avail. What

O'Donnell had not reckoned on at the time was that while *Star Search* was quite popular in many parts of America, the Ed McMahon TV showcase was looked down upon in the film capital. The industry rated the show as being too unsophisticated a production to warrant it being considered an immediate launching pad for bright new talents. Besides, ultimately, O'Donnell had not been a season winner in her stand-up category.

Frustrated by the lack of offers, she haunted the Los Angeles comedy clubs, especially the Improv where she eventually became friendly with the club's owner, Budd Friedman. However, she couldn't get herself booked at the Improv. At the time, there was too much competition—too many hot young comedians who were as aggressive as Rosie and who had killer material to throw at club audiences. Besides, it was still a case of the old boys club. Few female stand-up comics were allowed to perform at the major venues.

Eventually, Rosie did get a gig, it was in Detroit at the Comedy Castle. Because of her *Star Search* credentials she was made the headliner, a career first for her. There were three comedians performing nightly and, as the "name," Rosie went on third. However, she couldn't connect with the audience. In her own words she was "tanking." What made matters worse was that the comic who preceded her on the bill, a Detroit fellow, was slaying the crowd. When Rosie came on she was an anti-climax to the hot young male comic. When he saw what was happening, he talked with O'Donnell and graciously agreed to switch positions in the lineup. The change in presentation order was a lifesaver for Rosie, for if she had been canceled, word would have gotten around in the small world of stand-up comedy and her career might have been damaged irreparably. Over the years the good-natured comic, who went on to national fame in clubs, TV, films and bookwriting never mentioned the incident. That is, until he was a guest on *The Rosie O'Donnell Show* and the host herself recited on-air the facts of how modest funnyman Tim Allen had once saved her career.

• • •

There followed a disillusioning period for Rosie at the end of which she finally had to admit the need to regroup. Friends and family members urged her to come back East. Instead, she took advantage of an offer from a woman friend in Arizona and moved to Phoenix, where the two shared an apartment. Scorching as the desert environs were, it was not the kind of high temperature O'Donnell wanted. She needed to be part of the red-hot show business climate.

Upon returning to Los Angeles, she still found the right doors not opening. "Time and time again, people told me to quit, that I was too tough. I was too New York. I was too heavy. But I didn't listen to them. I thought, 'You're all idiots!'" With her savings fast dwindling, she had few other options beyond going back out on the road.

Over the next months, Rosie had a scattering of playdates up and down the West Coast, especially in the San Francisco area. She also did her comedy gig at a Lansing, Michigan venue as well as in Detroit for the same booker. Occasionally her *Star Search* pedigree earned her an engagement at a more prestigious site, such as when she, along with two other comics, performed fourteen shows a week at the Comedy Stop at TropWorld in Atlantic City. (Among O'Donnell's many other appearances there would be on May 13-19, 1991, when she was joined by fellow comics Joe Mulligan and Frank Del Pizzo.) In addition, there was the December 28-30, 1989 stint when she was the opening act for The Temptations singing group at Trump Plaza in the New Jersey gaming capital. She also told jokes onstage at the Improv at the Riviera Hotel in Las Vegas. Through the ups-and-downs of these jobs, she constantly honed her craft, becoming a far more polished technician.

One thing her brush with *Star Search* fame did NOT accomplish was to insure that she received pay equal to that of male comedians on the club circuit. Rosie remembers, "At this one club, I became friendly with the woman who did the books. . . . She said, 'There must be a mistake here. It says you're only getting seven hundred dollars to head-line. It must be seventeen hundred, right?' I was getting less than half of what the men would get."

Occasionally, when back East for a gig, she'd perform at the Eastside Comedy Club with her friends the Laughter Players. Now, when she was doing comedy in greater New York City, she'd stay at inexpensive Manhattan hotels. As before, whenever she needed to relax, to fill time or to stave off loneliness, she had the comfort of her life-long TV addiction. She recalls being glued to the tube ". . . where one station used to run three *Mary* [*Tyler Moore Show*] reruns in a row. I used to sit there laughing out loud, thinking, 'They're going to hear me laughing in this room all alone and they're going to come and get me.'"

Back in Los Angeles in 1986, Rosie found herself occasionally on the same bill with Dana Carvey, the 31-year-old Montana-born come-dian who already had had recurring parts on two TV series: *One of the*

Boys (1982) and *Blue Thunder* (1984). As Carvey would demonstrate when he was a very amusing guest on Rosie's TV talk show a decade later, part of his popular act then involved the use of a guitar and his gift for improv comedy. He'd have audience members feed him bits of biographical information which he would turn immediately into humorous song lyrics, which he would then sing while plucking on the guitar strings.

One evening toward the middle of 1986, Rosie was again on the same bill with Carvey, this time at Igby's Comedy Cabaret, a popular comedy site owned by Jan Maxwell Smith and located on Tennessee Place in West Los Angeles. Before the sets began that night at the horseshoe-shaped theatre with its 165 seats, the buzz was out that important industry personnel would be in the popular club that evening. Word had it that NBC network honchos were coming to catch Carvey's act, as they were considering adding him, along with several other new regulars, to the lineup of comics on *Saturday Night Live.*

For a change, the grapevine was indeed correct. The executives who dropped by Igby's included Brandon Tartikoff, the wunderkind head of NBC network programming, and *Saturday Night Live* executive producer Lorne Michaels. They were impressed by Carvey's abilities and decided that, yes, he would be a good catch for the new season of *Saturday Night Live.* While waiting to pay the bill, Tartikoff accidentally saw Rosie performing her comedy material. The 36-year-old president of NBC Entertainment was immediately taken with Rosie's brassy demeanor. As was his wont, it prompted a sudden brainstorm. She might be just the jolt of energetic talent needed to recharge one of his faltering NBC sitcoms. Another person in the Tartikoff party, executive producer/director Hal Cooper, agreed.

After Rosie completed her stand-up routine, Tartikoff introduced himself to her and mentioned his casting idea. She vividly recalls, ". . . I said to myself, 'Yeah, right! Come on. He's not going to do that. That's the kind of story you read in a Hollywood newspaper'." However, Tartikoff was very serious indeed about his job offer.

The show in question was *Gimme a Break.* It had debuted on NBC-TV on October 29, 1981. It was based on a deceptively simple comedy premise: a widowed, middle-age Caucasian police chief with three growing daughters hires a zaftig black woman, the best friend of his late wife, to be housekeeper in his increasingly unmanageable household at 2938 Maple Lawn Street in the fictional California town of

Glen Lawn. Before long, the portly, sassy Nell Harper and the rotund
Chief Carl Kanisky are engaged in a never-ending battle of wills.
Weekly each tried to assert his/her authority in the household for the
greater good of all.

This half-hour comedy starred Nell Carter, a 4'11" rotund bundle of
energy who had galvanized audiences in the hit Broadway musical
Ain't Misbehavin' (1978) and won a Tony for her forceful presence.
When she recreated her much-praised performance for a 1982 TV
special, she won an Emmy. Her co-star in *Gimme a Break* was journeyman actor, Dolph Sweet, a gruff, burly performer who was a veteran of
such daytime soaps as *The Edge of Night* (1967-1968) and *Another
World* (1972-1977). On the nighttime drama series *The Trials of
O'Brien* (1965-1966), he'd played police Lieutenant Garrison.

Gimme a Break was in many ways derivative of the old radio and TV
series, *Beulah,* which on radio had featured, among others, Hattie
McDaniel, and on the tube had starred Ethel Waters and then Louise
Beavers. Like its predecessor, *Gimme a Break* was about a black woman
working for a white family whom she takes to her heart. The new sitcom was very sentimental and obvious. However, it was harmless and
occasionally sparkling fun, especially when Carter's spunky character
broke into song or went off on one of her I'm gonna-be-good-to-
myself binges. The program never made it to the top 25 shows in viewers' ratings during its first season (1981-1982), being always beat out
by the likes of *The Jeffersons, Three's Company, One Day at a Time,* etc.
However, *Gimme a Break* was sufficiently popular to be renewed at the
end of its premiere year on the network lineup. Thereafter, it sailed
along for the next three seasons comfortably ensconced on the NBC-
TV schedule. En route, additional recurring characters were added to
the program: John Hoyt as Grandpa Kanisky, Joey Lawrence as a six-
year-old orphan, Joey, who comes to live in the household, and Telma
Hopkins as wisecracking Addy, Nell's good friend.

Disaster hit *Gimme a Break* on May 8, 1985, when Sweet died of
cancer, a few weeks short of his sixty-fifth birthday. There was much
conjecture among NBC executives and viewers alike whether the show
could survive without his presence. After all, as the duck out of water,
he'd been the primary catalyst in the ongoing storyline tug-of-war over
what was best for his offspring. Without him, who could loving but
unpredictable Nell do battle with week to week? To whom would she
prove episode by episode that she was indeed the well-meaning, if
often juvenile, surrogate mother of the clan?

During the 1985-1986 season of *Gimme a Break*, the scripters tried to solve these problems. After acknowledging the Chief's death and his being mourned by all, the storyline incorporated a new man (Jonathan Silverman) into the household by having him wed the middle Kanisky girl (Lauri Hendler). However, already wearing thin, the show seemed baldly anemic without the stabilizing presence of cantankerous Chief Kanisky. Thus, by the end of the fifth season, NBC, along with the show's executive producer/director Hal Cooper, had to make a decision. Either they had to call it quits with the show or revamp the format yet again. They chose the latter which is when Brandon Tartikoff happened to spot 24-year-old Rosie onstage at Igby's doing her comedy thing.

During the course of the next several weeks, Tartikoff's people met with Rosie's people (i.e., her agent) and a deal was struck. She would join the cast of *Gimme a Break* for the 1986-1987 season under the following guidelines. She would appear in a guest-starring role on one of the show's first new episodes that fall. If she clicked with the viewers, as they believed she would, she would join the cast on a permanent basis.

Meanwhile network minds concocted a fresh premise on which to hang the sitcom's sixth season. With the three Kanisky girls now gone from the household (married, working or college-bound), Nell and Addy relocate to New York, the former to work at a publishing house, the latter to teach at a nearby college. Grandpa and Joey tag along with them to the Big Apple. The family nucleus was now comprised of Nell, Grandpa and Joey and they would soon inherit Joey's younger brother, Matthew (Matthew Lawrence), from the boys' irresponsible father. By now, the restructured household has moved into a Manhattan apartment building owned by a goofy landlord (new cast member Paul Sand). He, in turn, happens to operate El Gaspacho, a Spanish restaurant downstairs. As for O'Donnell, she was set to play Maggie O'Brien, a feisty dental hygienist from Boston, who moves upstairs of Nell's place. (Rosie would term her sitcom character as "Rhoda Morgenstern with an Irish accent.")

All went according to plan. When the resuscitated *Gimme a Break* returned to the airwaves—without much network fanfare—on November 19, 1986 in its Wednesday 9:30 p.m. time slot, Rosie was on hand as strong-willed Maggie, the smart-mouthed upstairs neighbor. The powers-to-be decided that O'Donnell was a useful new storyline character and exercised their contractual right to extend her appearances through the rest of the season.

Under ordinary circumstances, Rosie should have been jubilant by this juncture. Her years of dreaming, striving and maneuvering had put her just where she wanted to be—on a prime time TV network series. It was everything she had hoped for all those years when, as a toddler, she had sat transfixed in front of the family TV and had imagined herself up there on the little screen entertaining a world of home viewers. An additional reason why she should have been happy was that she was now earning very decent money on a regular basis. With some of that largess, she'd purchased a sharp beige RX-7 car to drive about town. Nevertheless, there were several things which spoiled O'Donnell's jubilation.

For one, the enthusiasm and dedication she expected to find on the sitcom set was generally missing. By now, the series' long-time regulars were satiated with their shallow characterizations and the repetition of silly plotlines (no matter how cleverly the scripters tried to disguise the episodes' lack of originality). Besides, the veterans on the show sensed that these recent desperate measures to revitalize the program wouldn't postpone the inevitable (i.e., cancellation) by too many more months.

Adding to Rosie's discontent was the Nell Carter situation. She and Rosie should have had a lot in common. Nell had done Broadway musicals; Rosie loved song-and-dance shows and hoped to do one herself in the future. In 1979, Carter had played a character named Ethel Green on the daytime TV show, *Ryan's Hope*. That soap opera had been one of Rosie's favorite programs. And to make their potential connection even stronger, Nell had even been a celebrity guest on the first season (1983-1984) segment of *Star Search*. However, Carter had no affinity for cast newcomer Rosie. The reason might have been the pressure of Carter coping with a drowning series, or it could have been that her ego was bruised upon realizing that she was no longer able to carry the show herself. Or perhaps, it was disenchantment with the younger, less heavy Rosie who was getting too many laughs on camera compared to her.

Whatever complex set of reasons Carter had at the time, she would not address O'Donnell off camera on the set by her real name. O'Donnell pointed out to *Newsday* reporter David Friedman in 1988, "Nell always called me Maggie [O'Brien] and I don't think it's because she's into the Stanislavsky method." With such negative vibes surrounding her, and the mixed feelings of the other "old-timers" on the show toward any "newcomers," O'Donnell never felt part of the cast during her run of episodes on the by-now creaky vehicle. (Years later, on the October 30, 1996 edition of *The Rosie O'Donnell Show*, Nell Carter would be an on camera guest. By then, having survived severe health problems, a career decline, etc., a very restrained Carter now "remembered" being very happy to have worked with Rosie on *Gimme a Break*. In fact, she claimed it was she, having seen O'Donnell on *Star Search*, who suggested the stand-up comic join the aging sitcom. The apparently quite nervous Carter also mentioned that by the point Rosie joined the 1986-1987 TV series, she (Nell) was burned out from too many seasons on the show. As such, Carter insisted on Rosie's TV show that she was relieved to have another cast member on hand who could and did get audience laughs on the fading *Gimme a Break*.)

Adding to Rosie's discomforts on the sitcom set was the stress due to her efforts to stop drinking. (One acquaintance at the time would recall that Rosie had a fondness for drinking quickly three or four beers then having a chaser shot of Jameson's Irish Whiskey.) Years later, Rosie would confide, ". . . when I moved to L.A. and got on a sitcom, a friend of mine said, 'You drink too much, and you've had a lot of alcoholism in your family.' I was so mad. I said, 'Are you implying that I'm an alcoholic?'" O'Donnell adds, "She was a therapist, this friend, and she said, 'I just think you have a problem.' So I stopped drinking totally for 5 years, just to show her I could. And I think it's good that I did, because if I had continued along the way that I was, I seriously feel that it would have become a problem for me."

Meanwhile, *Gimme a Break* struggled on as its ratings further declined. In March 1987 it was switched from its Wednesday night berth to Tuesday at 9:00 p.m. It didn't help matters. The network finally canceled the series and its final first-run episode aired on May 5, 1987.

For Rosie, the professional wounds created by this series flop were far greater than those she had suffered earlier on *Star Search* when she lost the comedy playoffs. Her agent and friends repeatedly told her that it wasn't her fault that *Gimme a Break* had died. On the contrary, they reasoned, she'd added much-needed spunk and humor to the floundering comedy—more so than the other newcomers on the series' final season: Matthew Lawrence, Rosette LeNoire, or especially Paul Sand, in the embarrassingly silly role of the daffy landlord.

However, strong-minded, highly sensitive Rosie would not be consoled. She would later admit to *US* magazine that it was ". . . the most crushing blow of my career. My goal was to be on a sitcom; then I got on this show in its last year and people weren't ready to be there. I thought I've climbed this mountain and there's nothing there."

O'Donnell would remain in a professional funk about *Gimme a Break* for well over a year. Then fate intervened and gave her career another needed boost.

• 7 •

I don't think that comedy comes from pain, but I think that it comes from being able to interpret what it is you've been through and put a slant on it because you're forced to. If you don't see the pain in something, I don't think you can see the levity. It's both sides of a coin.

Rosie O'Donnell, June 1994

*E*ven a highly career-oriented individual like Rosie O'Donnell—so determined, so enterprising—has low points in which her confidence and drive wanes. Such was the period after *Gimme a Break* went off the air in the spring of 1987. Up to that point, she'd been convinced that being featured on a network television sitcom—a major achievement in itself—would have paved the way to her ultimate goal, that of being in the movies. But it didn't. She blamed herself that her TV series exposure hadn't pushed her career immediately to the next desired level. Pondering her future in the entertainment business, 25-year-old Rosie was full of gloomy predictions about the uninviting prospects ahead. She and her agent sought work where they could find it, which mostly meant more stand-up gigs on and off the road.

It also didn't help Rosie's faltering confidence to be offered uninspired TV work. The choices were as unpromising as, for example, playing the sister of very stocky Mindy Cohn (Natalie Green on *The Facts of Life*) in a spin-off from that waning sitcom. Rosie's sagging spirits were further impaired by her feeling that, according to own high standards, she wasn't really making it professionally. As a benchmark, she judged her accomplishments to date against such fast- and ever-rising female comics as Roseanne, Carol Leifer, Rita Rutner, Paula Poundstone and Judy Tenuta. Each of them were breaking out of the comedy-on-the-road rut with more appealing show business options. It wasn't that O'Donnell was jealous of her fellow women comedians. That wasn't in her nature. Rather, she felt that in comparison to her female peers in the world of stand-up, she wasn't moving up the career ladder fast enough or dramatically enough to suit herself.

Being so focused on MAJOR success, O'Donnell downplayed her actual achievements. It wasn't self-evident to her that, gradually and mostly on her own, she'd already moved up several notches in the highly competitive world of entertainment. It didn't satisfy her that now, thanks to her slicker act and her credentials (i.e., *Star Search*, *Gimme a Break*), she was now an increasingly viable commodity in the relatively narrow field of stand-up comedy. It didn't soothe her ruffled ambitions that these days she was no longer rejected when she wanted to perform at such major show spots as the LA Improv or to have her comedy gig at one of the clubs be included on tape for *An Evening at . . .*, *Comedy on the Road*, etc., which were staple fare on such cable networks as HBO, Showtime and Arts & Entertainment. A few years earlier, O'Donnell would have been thrilled by her current status of legitimacy in the stand-up community. However, now she expected more of herself and, as an intensely goal-oriented person, she was dissatisfied with her slow progress.

As before, when Rosie was unhappy, she overate, especially now that she didn't have to look "fit" for her canceled TV series. Junk food was still one of her best friends. Over the years, since beginning her various on-again, off-again therapy sessions, she would gradually accept the connection between calorie over-consumption and her state of mind. As she would acknowledge in the years to come: ". . . if it was simply about food, nobody would be overweight. It's about all the emotions connected to it, and why you do it, and why you need to disguise yourself to feel safer or—you know, it's—I mean, it's years and years of therapy, and it's a lifelong struggle, and not necessarily to be thin, but to be at a place where you can, you know, feel your own body and yourself connected to your body. And I think the heavier you are, the more disconnected you are from feeling. And that's the reason that I, at least have used food to, you know, kind of get away from myself."

Further on the subject, Rosie has admitted, ". . . I've always sort of had 20—up to—between 20 and 50 pounds to lose, you know? And I go up and down without really noticing, which is really where the illness part of this whole thing comes in because when I am at my thinnest, I will look in the mirror and see the same person at the fattest. And I never can tell what weight I am until I put on clothes."

•   •   •

Budd Friedman, owner of the LA Improv and other similar night spots, not only knew a great deal about the comedy business from his many years of showcasing stand-ups in his clubs, but he was the producer of *An Evening at the Improv*, an hour-long television program seen on A&E Cable since 1985. As such, he had a lot of inside knowledge of what was going on in the cable TV business. It was he who alerted Rosie that MTV was looking for a female comic to become a veejay on its cable network. (The veejay is the oncamera host who provides commentary between each shown music video.) Having by now recovered her career stamina and enthusiasm, she maneuvered an audition for this job based in New York City.

O'Donnell appreciated that exposure to a new audience—such as the with-it MTV crowd—could only increase the likelihood of her moving up to the big times. She would explain, "I needed a change, a new challenge. I saw it as an opportunity to let a lot of people know me and to be distinguished from the many female comics who were working the circuit."

Besides, if Rosie was back East she could spend more time with her sister Maureen, now living in New Jersey. The latter, having attended Providence College and gone into banking, had married and had a daughter. Although Rosie had no time or inclination for marriage herself, she had a strong maternal instinct, enhanced by her childhood years of tending to sibling needs. It would be great, Rosie decided, to get to know her months-old niece firsthand. It was part of her new priority to be more a part of her siblings' lives.

Buoyed by a fresh sense of purpose, Rosie arranged to be auditioned for the MTV position. It was an opening coveted by many who saw this as a wonderful chance for national exposure, besides bringing in a steady paycheck. As it developed, O'Donnell's MTV tryout was one of those tests which appear unstructured and unfocused, but actually does provide a quick means of assessing an applicant's basic on-the-air aptitude. Rosie remembers, "MTV put me in front of a camera, turned it on, then asked me which rock star I want to be locked in an elevator with, and what we'd talk about." O'Donnell's answers were Tina Turner and her own new cosmetic dental work. Neither these responses nor her oncamera appearance on the test tape sold Rosie to MTV. She reasoned, "I wasn't hip enough, the traditional thin, young, heavy rocker."

Nevertheless, Rosie's MTV audition was not a waste. It proved to be another instance of O'Donnell's almost uncanny knack of turning a given situation into an opportunity to (1) sell herself, (2) make friends, (3) network on the spot and (4) sell herself some more. It was a methodology that came naturally to her and one which she would refine over the years. If her salt-of-the-earth looks and Irish Catholic wholesomeness were non-threatening to others, her brash New York-style toughness had a way of pushing business conversations on to useful new areas of discussion. Such was the case with her meeting with MTV officials.

After rejecting Rosie for its veejay spot, MTV executives gave Rosie a tip. She was told that VH-1 (Video Hits One), their sister cable channel, might have work for her. That network, begun in 1985, was less hip, more middle-of-the-road and catered to a 25 to 40-year-old marketplace. Under its current president, Ed Bennett, it was undergoing a format change. VH-1 was moving away from stodgy, marshmallow-type videos (Barry Manilow, Kenny Rogers, Julio Iglesias, *et al*). They intended to partake more of the cutting edge without overlapping too heavily on MTV's franchise. As such, they required on-air veejays to introduce their lineup of top-40 rock 'n' roll videos. O'Donnell applied, was auditioned and hired. Her new assignment began in April 1988.

Her job duties required Rosie to perform two-minute introductions that led into the music videos which were aired in chunks of time slots seven days a week. The job demanded a person who could ad-lib chatter that would amuse or inform the viewer, but definitely not distract people from staying tuned to the next video. O'Donnell's spots were pre-taped in clusters and then inserted into the programming at the appropriate points. For someone with several years of stand-up and improv experience, the seemingly daunting task was surmountable. It also helped that O'Donnell knew a great deal about rock music and listened to much of it on her own.

When asked by *Newsday* how she liked her new line of work, Rosie admitted, "VH-1 is perfect for me right now. I get to talk about my life, my weight, Whitney Houston's ego problems, Linda McCartney's off-key singing, my sister's baby, whatever pops into my head." On the other hand, she acknowledged, "The hardest part is not having an audience. I never know if I'm going over. There's a lot of insecurity in a job like this." In an interview with the *New York Times*, she further elaborated, "My first week, I was terrorized. Stand-up comedy is an interactive art form; it's presentational. Try to do stand-up with no audience; it's nearly impossible. My goal as a veejay was to make the cameramen laugh, to give me something to play off."

The best thing about Rosie's career move was that VH-1 was available in more than 30 million homes throughout the United States. It meant a lot of professional exposure for O'Donnell and that included a great many viewers who had never been to a comedy club in their lives. It was a wonderful way for her to expand her recognition (and fan) base. However, there was a downside. Rosie has always been a quick study who is constantly looking for the next creative challenge. Therefore, the essential repetitiousness of her on-the-air activity eventually became tedious.

In addition, there were the clashes with VH-1 producers who decreed that for each on-the-air introduction, Rosie should reintroduce herself to home viewers. She thought this ridiculous, especially since her clips were aired so many times each and every day. It prompted her to exploit her outrageous streak. One time she would say, "Hi, I'm Kiki Dee" or "Hi, I'm Chaka Khan" or whatever singer's name came to mind. One day, O'Donnell, a long-time enthusiast of the kitschy *The Brady Bunch* TV sitcom and its cast of actors, popped out with, "Hi, I'm Florence Henderson." Not long afterward, she received a call from Henderson's manager who claimed that Rosie was using his client's name to promote her own show. The matter was resolved and O'Donnell promised the producers that she'd stopped doing that. Sure! Yeah, right!

Although Rosie's VH-1 was time-consuming and, at times, exhausting, it did not prevent or restrict her from continuing with her increasingly lucrative stand-up gigs. Already in the 1987-1988 TV season, she'd been on Showtime Cable's *Comedy Club Network*, an hour show taped at comedy clubs around the country. Then on March 26, 1988 she was seen on the cable special, Showtime's *Comedy Club All-Stars*. This 60-minute production, hosted by stand-up comic and TV star Harry Anderson, featured the six best of the 92 comics who'd appeared on the network's *Comedy Club Network*.

Among those reviewing *Comedy Club All-Stars* was John Voorhees (*Seattle Times*). He decided, "If these are the best, then the state of stand-up comedy in the U.S. is in a sad state indeed. . . . With the exception of Tom Parks, none of the six seem capable of creating what might pass for a comedy routine. Instead, we get a lot of one-liners as the comics jump from subject to subject and nearly all focus on the same topics: sex and their own teeny-tiny lives. None exhibit anything that might pass for wit or comic insight. . . . Monica Piper and Rosie O'Donnell are the most amusing. . . ."

By mid-1988, plucky Rosie—thanks to her continuous TV work—was considered a "name" in the comedy club arena, one who could be expected to draw in the customers. She appeared Wednesday, July 13 through Friday, July 15th at New York's Catch a Rising Star, the stand-up landmark located at 1487 First Avenue. One of the many who caught her act there was *New York Post* reporter Bill Ervolino. He described her as a "fast-talking charmer with a snappy delivery and energy to spare." He judged, "Throw in a master's degree in pop culture—O'Donnell generously peppers her material with kitschy images—and you have an act that virtually crackles with laughs, whether she's recalling an unpleasant trip to her dentist ('I grabbed his little mirror—the one that looks like you ripped it off the side of Barbie's Country Trailer . . . ') or describing some creepy lizard she saw at Disneyland ('All the Japanese tourists started screaming, 'Godzilla!' and running for Magic Mountain.')." In the reporter's opinion, "O'Donnell mugs a bit too much—repeating one particular facial expression over and over—and there are times one wishes she would give us a little more from her heart and a little less from her TV set. . . . "

The next month, mid-August 1988, O'Donnell worked onstage at the Chicago Improv. Three comedians appeared on the bill but Rosie was the headliner. Once again, a goodly portion of her act was geared to TV trivia. There were her riffs on *The Brady Bunch* and *The Partridge Family*, and later her rap versions (set to recorded music) of the theme songs to *The Beverly Hillbillies* and *Gilligan's Island*. Her session also included a routine about cockroaches with strong attitude, leading her into vocalizing bits of *West Side Story* with the insects as gang members. And not to be overlooked were her jokes revolving around her "Irish immigrant" dad. The *Chicago Sun-Times* weighed, "At her best, she poked fun at some of the crotch-grabbing macho of certain New York types. But O'Donnell wants more, she told the audience. She wants to address social issues someday."

In 1989, VH-1 again reassessed its programming lineup in relationship to what MTV already offered as well as to the ever-changing profile of VH-1's target viewership. This review led them to once more alter their programming format. The switch, which took place over the subsequent months, would lead to the elimination of its video jocks in favor of short-form (half-hour) one-on-one specials with such artists as Anita Baker, Harry Connick Jr, Melissa Etheridge, *et al*. Other changes included adding a batch of weekly and/or nightly shows, hosted by past/present pop talent. Soon there would be actress/former rocker Ellen Foley presenting the Top 21 music videos each week and ex-Herman's Hermit singer Peter Noone hosting *My Generation*, a nostalgia fest. With all these changes at VH-1, Rosie realized she'd soon be without her daily TV forum and her paycheck. (One of the options she explored but ultimately rejected at the time was to co-host a daily wake-up radio program on New York's WQHT.)

Damage control was always one of Rosie's strong points. Not waiting for the ax to fall, she analyzed her situation, came up with some ideas and then requested a get-together with management at VH-1/MTV. At the meeting, she suggested a new project, one that would hopefully fit in with their fresh programming philosophy. Her concept—certainly not original—was to host a weekly half-hour series of stand-up comedy which would feature two well-known comics as well as one up-and-coming new talent. The decision-makers told her they'd get back to her. After much prompting from her, they did. Thanks to her enthusiasm, persuasive abilities and tenacity, they eventually agreed to letting Rosie not only host the new project, but be its executive producer—that is, if they approved the test shows which she had to find a way to package on her own.

These pilots for what became *Stand-Up Spotlight* were taped at Rascal's in West Orange, New Jersey, a long established stand-up venue. Rosie knew the management there, which led to her getting favorable terms for putting together the tapings, which were accomplished with a production crew working on spec. Always very organized and methodical in dealing with her own career, Rosie carried over these qualities into her new capacity as the show's executive producer.

Stand-Up Spotlight met with management approval. The one basic change to the concept was the decision to switch the program's point of origination after the first thirteen segments. It was decided to thereafter tape the shows on the West Coast at the Ice House in Pasadena, California. That venerable showcase had begun life as an ice house or meat locker for a nearby Army barracks in World War II. In 1960, Bob Stane, who had previously operated the Upper Cellar coffee house in San Diego, turned the premises into a comedy forum. It soon gained a reputation as an ideal site because, within the club's layout, not one of the 200 seats was further than 25 feet from the performance stage. Steve Martin, Lily Tomlin and Tommy Smothers were some of the notable comics who performed at the Ice House in their (and its) early years. Later, A&E Cable launched its long-running *Comedy on the Road* there, and the establishment was also used for USA Cable's *Up All Night* starring Rhonda Sear for on-location taping.

Stand-Up Spotlight debuted on VH-1 cable at 8 p.m. on Sunday, November 19, 1989. It proved popular enough with viewers and inexpensive enough to please management. Every day Rosie, efficient, quick-thinking and always with clipboard in hand, learned something new about being an efficient producer. Before long, she had the situation under control, and, in the process, learned to cope with the spectrum of problems involved in booking stand-up talent. As the show gained momentum and popularity, Rosie began receiving scads of audition video tapes from comics all over America. From these, she selected the new talent needed to fill out the bill of a given show. Typically, she remembered her old friends, fellow comics such as Vinnie Mark of Long Island and Rick Ceifer of Boston, with whom she'd worked the circuit over the years. She insured that they had opportunities to appear on *Stand-Up Spotlight*. And just because she might be more in the limelight at the moment than an old pal or former co-worker, she never presented herself as being on a different level than they. She always took an interest in the other person. Rick Ceifer, for example, recalls appreciatively the rapport he's had with Rosie, which never changed, no matter who was having good times or bad times. For years she'd nagged Ceifer to take more of an interest in how he dressed and always wanted to take him shopping at trendy men's clothing shops. This friendly concern did not diminish now that she was a TV producer.

Several segments of the series would be taped in a condensed time frame and then aired and re-aired over a seasonal cycle. Part of O'Donnell's duties included making sure that the talent arrived on time for the tapings, that each person rehearsed the logistics of his/her allotted time on stage for the camera crew, etc. Backup comics were available in case a performer canceled at the last minute or a scheduled entertainer did not follow the established guidelines for guests on the show. Rosie certainly knew what it was like to be a stand-up scratching for that big break, coping with a love-hate relationship with an audience that either could be subdued with a killer act or could turn thumbs down on an act that was bombing. As such, she did her best to put her guests at ease. As a show of appreciation, she insured that each talent—whether an established act or a newcomer—received a VH-1 fleece white robe and VH-1 embossed travel bag. Such niceties on Rosie's part were a rarity in the world of stand-up.

One of the prime benefits of *Stand-Up Spotlight* for Rosie was that, like her VH-1 veejaying, it gave her and her slightly acerbic comedy tremendous exposure to a wide level of home viewers. (By then, VH-1 was available in over 36 million households.) As the host who opened each show by coming on stage from the back of the seating area, O'Donnell had the opportunity to wear more varied and flattering wardrobe. Her emceeing duties on camera enhanced her posture of self-confidence, her ability to banter or parry with the audience, and to exchange witticisms with her on camera guests. As a result, thanks to *Stand-Up Spotlight*, Rosie, with her increasingly earthy humor, broadened her industry visibility and audience appeal. It was excellent preparation for what lay ahead.

· 8 ·

I always thought I would get on a sitcom and eventually do films, because I have specific goals, which is how I run my life. I tried to take steps that I thought would get me there. In show business, there's no one way to get where you're going. People have to cut the jungle with their own machetes and hopefully reach their destination.

Rosie O'Donnell, November 1994

*P*rofessionally, 1990 was shaping up well for Rosie. She continued to executive produce and host *Stand-Up Spotlight* for VH-1 at the Ice House in Pasadena, California. She was teamed with fellow comedian Bill Engvall in a half-hour cable television special, taped at the Comedy and Magic Club in Hermosa Beach, California. That show aired on Showtime Cable on June 2, 1990 to favorable audience response. She was also increasingly in demand to perform at charity fund-raisers and she was a willing volunteer, especially for cystic fibrosis and causes which dealt with children.

Constantly on the go, Rosie was back in New York City in March 1990, where she celebrated St. Patrick's Day by performing at her old stomping-grounds, the Eastside Comedy Club in Huntington, Long Island. She was back on the East Coast again in July 1990. She performed a scheduled gig at Manhattan's Caroline's Comedy Club. With a wealth of experience in the field and the pre-recognition factor of her high visibility on cable TV, Rosie had little trouble winning over the crowd. She had learned a very important rule of thumb that was essential for survival with mercurial customers who at one minute would applaud the comic in the spotlight and the next would shove him into a hot seat with their constant heckling and/or stony silence. The sim-

71

ple but difficult to execute key was ". . . you alter your act no matter what audience. You feel out an audience and you kind of go with what it is."

While in New York Rosie agreed to appear on Sally Jessy Raphael's syndicated TV talk show. The episode, which aired on July 27, 1990, was entitled "Funny Ladies" and featured five female comedians, all of whom were veterans of playdates at the city's key forum, Catch a Rising Star. Earnest, bespectacled Sally opened the show with the statement: "I believe that the women you're going to meet are the hottest, the funniest female comediennes in this country. These are our pick hits and we will stand by them." The panel was composed of Susie Essman, Rosie, Carol Siskind (a regular on *The Tonight Show*), Carrie Snow (host of *Comedy Tonight* on PBS-TV) and a bulky performer who went by the stage name of Pudgy.

Rosie more than held her own with her peers as Raphael jumped from topic to topic:

Dating: "Yeah, my stepmother's always giving me dating advice you know. . . . Like, 'Honey, sweetheart, if you give the milk away for free, he's not going to buy the cow.' And then you say, like, 'Thank you, Mary. What do you want me to do, buy a big bell, put it around my neck, graze in a field somewhere.'"

Dieting: ". . . you go once a week, you have six days on your own to deal with your 200 optional calories. Sally, that's 200 calories, any way you like them. Didn't work. You know what I would do, for my 200 calories, I would have two lite beers, which is legal, but after two beers, who cares about Weight Watchers, okay. . . . Two beers, I'm at some diner going, 'Can I have a Twinkie salad, please.' It didn't work for me."

Life on the Road: "You know, generally, if you work in a nightclub, it's not really a lot of fun to go to clubs. Or, when we're on the road, we spend all our time in restaurants, so going out to dinner doesn't thrill me."

Rosie was always eager to give co-workers a plug. She took such an opportunity during the *Sally Jessy Raphael* program that day when she pointed out and introduced comedian Jeanette Farber who was seated in the studio audience. Jeanette was one of those who contributed jokes for O'Donnell's four minutes of emceeing chores on each segment of *Stand-Up Spotlight*.

• • •

With Rosie now contracted by VH-1 to produce and tape 26 additional entries of *Stand-Up Spotlight* before the end of 1990, she decided it was high time to make a real commitment to her new roots in California. Tired of living in rental apartments, condos, etc., she bought a home. With California real estate still very pricey—this was before the recession and the real estate market fallout—O'Donnell quickly discovered that she could not afford to buy in swanky Beverly Hills, Bel Air or even in the Hollywood Hills. Instead, she shopped for a house in the nearby San Fernando Valley. The area had long been a joke with the wealthy and trendy who considered "The Valley" a cultural wasteland and crinkled their noses at the fact that in the summer, the Valley is 5 to 10 degrees warmer than property closer to the Pacific Ocean. However, the prices were far more reasonable there.

O'Donnell picked a compact (1,518 square foot) two-bedroom house in Studio City, which was approximately fifteen minutes from West Hollywood and even closer to the adjacent spread of film and TV studios situated in Studio City, Universal City and Burbank. Built in 1940, the Cape Cod-style house at 4116 Bellingham Avenue was on a quiet side street in a comfortable residential neighborhood a few blocks from Laurel Canyon which transverses the Valley north to south and Ventura Boulevard which cuts across the Valley east to west. Rosie paid $415,000 for the property which boasted a two-car garage, but no swimming pool and only a small yard.

Once a new homeowner, Rosie decorated the place in a mixture of the British brand frilly and working class functional. She made sure there was ample room to display her assorted collections. They were not of Wedgwood china or Franklin Mint collectible plates, but rather a mixture of fast food emporium premium items (such as McDonald's Happy Meals figures). Rosie was very proud of her self-decorating and too down-to-earth to be concerned that her abode was in "The Valley" or that she hadn't used a professional interior designer to whip the premises into proper shape.

In fact, as her career fame increased, she initially and proudly invited reporters to her home to conduct interviews with her. She soon rued that impulsive decision. Later, she would recall some of these ego-deflating experiences. "It was like the reporter who saw my house and said [snidely that] it looked like Laura Ashley. I created the house I wanted as a kid—matching curtains to the couch. I said to her, 'Where did you think I lived? A garage with tools?'" Another time, she snapped to a journalist who cited the disparity between her tough demeanor in public and her softer side at home, "I mean, is it so shocking that I'd have floral pillows in my house?" Meanwhile, having learned her lesson with the media, she thereafter conducted most of her interview sessions at restaurants. A frequent spot for this chore was Art's on Ventura Boulevard in Studio City. This was the delicatessen famed for its motto that "Every Sandwich is a Work of Art." It was one of O'Donnell's favorite hangouts.

Perhaps the severest critic of Rosie's home-decorating style came from the brother of one of her new-found celebrity friends. The individual was Christopher Ciccone, the brother of Madonna whom O'Donnell became friendly with in 1991. One day, Christopher visited Rosie at her Studio City place. Not one to mince words, he announced, "If you're going to do Laura Ashley, why don't you really do it? This is tacky trash." Stung to the quick at the time, Rosie would later have a change of heart about the caliber of her home decoration. She vowed to Madonna, by then a close pal, "I promise I will not decorate with Laura Ashley again."

• • •

In the 1990s, production costs for Hollywood studio product kept escalating higher (to around $30 million for an average major release), while financiers' willingness to gamble on original creative properties declined further. Always eager to find pre-sold concepts that would be sure-fire box-office hits, moviemakers turned increasingly to the once rival medium of television for their "inspiration." As Nickelodeon Cable's Nick-at-Night was constantly proving anew, TV viewers, especially aging baby boomers, were entranced with reruns of classic and not-so-classic sitcoms and other types of old television series on the tube. So, it was reasoned, why not bring some of these series to the big screen? The gimmick had been mined before in Hollywood on an occasional and not generally big-budgeted basis: *Dragnet* (1955), *Our Miss Brooks* (1956), *The Lineup* (1958), *Munster, Go Home* (1966), *The Muppet Movie* (1979) and *Dragnet* (1987). However, these were sporadic ventures compared to the onslaught during the 1990s. These films included *The Addams Family* (1991), *Wayne's World* (1993), *The Coneheads* (1993), *Dennis the Menace* (1993), *The Beverly Hillbillies* (1993), *Maverick* (1994), *The Brady Bunch Movie* (1995) and *Sgt. Bilko* (1996).

During this barrage of 1990s theatrical film adaptations of TV shows, one such entry got very much lost in the shuffle. It was *Car 54, Where Are You?*, a movie completed in 1990. However, it didn't find release—and limited at that—until early 1994 because its distributor, Orion Pictures, had fallen on hard times. The company was going in and out of bankruptcy, causing several of its finished features to sit on the shelf for years after they were made.

Car 54, Where Are You? was based on the half-hour, black-and-white sitcom created by Nat Hiken (*Sgt. Bilko*) which ran on NBC-TV for two seasons (1961-1963). It was a predecessor of the lame-brained cop comedy formula used later in the *Police Academy* and *Naked Gun* movies. The show starred pop-eyed Joe E. Ross (Officer Gunther Toody) and horse-faced Fred Gwynne (Officer Francis Muldoon) as bumbling, oddball members of the 53rd precinct in a run-down section of the city. They were literally a Mutt and Jeff team, with Toody being short, stocky, nosy and a corner-cutter, while Muldoon was tall, taciturn and a stickler for the letter of the law. Much of the action of the slapstick-filled weekly episodes was set in the precinct locker room or in the partners' patrol car.

In the late 1980s, film producer Robert H. Solo latched onto the concept of translating *Car 54* to the big screen and Orion Pictures agreed to distribute the comedy. To direct the venture, Solo hired Bill Fishman who came from a background of music videos and who had guided the motion picture *Tapeheads* (1988). That well-regarded satirical comedy had starred John Cusack and Tim Robbins as two wannabes trying to make it on the Los Angeles music scene.

Ideally, it would have been a casting coup if the original two stars from *Car 54* could have appeared in the upcoming film. However, Joe E. Ross had died in 1982 and Fred Gwynne (a noted stage actor) was more interested in doing showy dramatic screen roles, such as his parts in *The Cotton Club* and *Ironweed*, than in rehashing a slapdash property from decades ago. So, to fill their shoes, Fishman and his casting people hired John C. McGinley to play Francis Muldoon. McGinley was a journeyman actor who had supporting roles in many movies (e.g., *Wall Street*, *Talk Radio* and *Suffering Bastards*). As his cohort, Gunther Toody, the producers and director turned to croaky-voiced David Johansen who had founded punk rock's original glam band, the New York Dolls. After that glitter rock band had folded, he developed a solo career as Buster Poindexter. The reasons for hiring Johansen were that he vaguely resembled Joe E. Ross and that the movie's original concept encompassed having the Toody character perform several songs in an assortment of styles, including rap. For nostalgia sake, two veteran members of the 1960s TV series' cast were rounded up for the new release: Al Lewis as Officer Leo Schnauser and Nipsey Russell as law enforcer Anderson, who in the new storyline would be the precinct's captain.

Where the filmmakers showed a then unappreciated perspicacity was in the selection of the other performers. Each of them, fairly unknown or underrated at the time, have since gone on to far more major careers in TV: Daniel Baldwin (*Homicide: Life on the Streets*), Jeremy Piven (*Ellen*) and Fran Drescher (*The Nanny*). When it came time to cast Toody's put-upon but loving wife, Lucille, the decision-makers were torn. Some of the executives wanted a "name," especially if she was to sing musical numbers. Rock music's Cyndi Lauper was an initial consideration. Then another name came into the discussion: Rosie O'Donnell.

The casting people had seen her on VH-1 and thought that with her built-in New York accent and tough-but-sweet demeanor she would be a natural for the role. She was contacted in Los Angeles and she came in for a reading. Bill Fishman remembers not being impressed by her audition. She just wasn't coming across in the part. Within days thereafter, she recontacted him and persuaded him to give her another chance. At the new reading, she was much more lively and savvy. It convinced the director that he wanted her for the part. However, Orion Pictures thought otherwise and it was a battle of wills before she was finally okayed by the front office for the role. Finally, Rosie's long-cherished dream was coming true. She was going to be in the movies!

As an economy measure, the movie was filmed on location in Toronto, Canada, with only establishment shots accomplished in New York City. Production got under way on August 27, 1990 and lasted for two months, winding up on October 26, 1990. The storyline for the hopefully goofy movie was simplicity itself: Brooklyn police officer Gunther Toody's partner, Leo Schnauser, is retiring. The inept Gunther is assigned a new co-worker, rookie Officer Francis Muldoon, a straight arrow who is overzealous in his clumsy efforts to fight street crime. Meanwhile, the city's district attorney dispatches a key witness, Herbert Hortz (Jeremy Piven), to the 53rd for protection. Since his testimony could send mobster Don Motti (Daniel Baldwin) to prison, Hortz is put behind bars for safekeeping. When attempts are made on his life, Captain Anderson (Nipsey Russell) stashes Hortz in the trunk of Tooty's car for the time being. Bumbling Gunther, after a night on the town with his amorous wife, forgets that the witness is stuffed into his car trunk. Later, three prostitutes steal Toody's car and wind up in Coney Island. There with Motti's hoods fighting the men in blue, the hectic showdown—which includes a frantic Tunnel of Love ride—occurs. Also caught up in this episodic melee is Velma Velour (Fran Drescher), a blondized, curvaceous tootsie who has a yen for men in uniform and who takes a shine to naive Muldoon.

Production was hardly under way when director Fishman found he had to spend as much time fighting fires with the Orion management (who were, in turn, coping with huge financial reverses). As such, Fishman had too little time to spend rehearsing and coaching a movie newcomer like Rosie. He already had enough on his hands in trying to convince the distributor that Rosie's costuming and makeup should both be flatteringly played up, not low-balled for cheap laughs.

Thus, O'Donnell had to sink or swim mostly on her own during the filming. Self-preservation was second nature to O'Donnell and she did her best to make the shoot a learning experience both on- and offcamera. By observing the others perform she acquired the rudiments of screen acting. Because the movie's tone was exaggerated slapstick and a lot of the action was fleshed out almost spontaneously on the set, Rosie's improv background proved very useful. At nighttime she would join cast and crew members for dinner and relaxation as they analyzed the day's work and went over the next day's scenes.

As the weeks progressed, Rosie became increasingly disillusioned by her maiden filmmaking experience. She would reflect later, "I thought I was going to get in a film and it was gonna be the greatest thing. I was gonna be working, working, working. Most of it is waiting, waiting, waiting you know." She also outlined another frustration in her crossover from live performing to film work: "I'd do a funny thing and I'd want to look at the cameramen and see if they were laughing. You know, I was tempted to look around, 'Is anyone getting this?' But no one can laugh, so it was very hard to make the change."

Filming wrapped up on October 26, 1990 and everyone returned to Los Angeles. By then it was no secret that Orion Pictures was running out of money. Fishman would later quip that he first knew the picture was in trouble when Orion stopped validating his parking during post-production. "Then, they took our desks away. Next thing I knew I was trying to finish the film by asking friends of mine, 'Hey, can I use your song in my movie! I can't pay you anything but if it comes out, I'll give you a ticket to the premiere.'"

As the weeks and then months dragged by, it seemed *Car 54* was doomed for oblivion, especially after Orion Pictures filed for bankruptcy. At first, Rosie was disappointed and then increasingly upset that her maiden movie should be so jinxed. However, as more time passed, she reconsidered—especially after she made other more structured, well-produced features. Meanwhile, it had become a joke in Hollywood that *Car 54* (like the other frozen Orion Pictures products of the time) was a picture that never was. Rosie soon was of two minds about her work in the capsized project. When she was being considered for future screen projects, the question of her screen experience came up, which, of course, presented a problem. Should she or should she not bring up *Car 54*, and should she or should she not suggest to the casting people that they screen clips of the still-unreleased movie.

As of July 1993—by which time a great deal had changed in Rosie's life—she could joke on NBC-TV's *Today* show: "I did a sex scene, actually, in my first film that wasn't released. Maybe that's the reason [*Car 54, Where Are You?* wasn't released]. Gratuitous nudity. I don't know. I mean, I don't really have a problem with it." Later she would say she felt the movie "had no heart" and that it made her really hungry to be involved in a creatively involving movie project.

By this point, Orion Pictures had come out of Chapter 11 bankruptcy and was making noises about releasing their batch of shelved movies. Then there would be a period of silence. Finally, in early 1994, Orion actually set a release date for *Car 54*. Actor Daniel Baldwin, an unofficial spokesperson for the cast, told the media, "It seems very funny that in all this time none of the actors was ever informed of what was going on with the movie. We heard nothing. . . . Now they need us, and suddenly, we're expected to be at their beck and call." Asked what he thought of the film he answered diplomatically, "It's funny, because it's so zany. But not a movie I would make today."

Director Bill Fishman was equally annoyed by the manner of the sudden release. It was tough enough that Orion had cut way back on the post-production budget and then had later reedited the film with its own cutter. However, now they were dumping the property onto the market without a proper send-off. Even worse, Fishman counseled the distributor that they had scheduled *Car 54* to open in the same period as a major studio film which was geared to the same moviegoer demographics. Fishman was told he was wrong, but sadly, he was correct. The "other" film was Jim Carrey's *Ace Ventura, Pet Detective*. The latter film was a blockbuster, while *Car 54* sputtered to a relatively quick ignominy. (*Ace Ventura* grossed over $72.2 million in domestic release, while *Car 54* dropped out of the U.S. box-office charts after two weeks, having grossed an anemic $1.17 million.)

If moviegoers on the whole didn't bother with *Car 54*, unfortunately the critics found time to see the mildewed, dated product. Paul Birchall (*Los Angeles Reader*) warned, "Some things, like wine and cheese, improve over time. However, this entirely ghastly update of the quaint 1960s television series . . . isn't one of them." He sympathized, "Usually talented performers like [Nipsey] Russell, [Rosie] O'Donnell, and [Jeremy] Piven have reason to be as embarrassed as they look on screen." *Entertainment Weekly* rated the film a "D-" because "This loud, garish update of the campy '60s sitcom is a brainless floparooney. The annoyingly cartoony David Johansen (that voice—stop it!) and the unamusingly dorky John McGinley star . . . Other talent flailing away: Rosie O'Donnell (in her first movie role) as Lucille Toody, . . . " The *New York Times*' Janet Maslin pointed out, "Its humor can perhaps be gauged by the fact that the director, Bill Fishman, manages to insert an obscenity into the title phrase, and that Officer Gunther Toody's familiar cry of 'Oooh! Oooh!, is now used in a sexual context. . . . As Gunther's wife, Lucille . . . Rosie O'Donnell is used mostly for one-note hollering, in crass domestic scenes that play like [a movie by cult director] John Waters without the taste."

The trade papers were equally unresponsive to this mishmash filled with anal-fixated humor and such bedroom riposte as "Your nightstick is poking me!" to which a character replies, "My nightstick is on the table." The *Hollywood Reporter* chided, "Among the players, Johansen devours the most scenery, closely followed by [Al] Lewis and Rosie O'Donnell. . . ." *Daily Variety* voted thumbs down: "Crude, virtually laughless and aimed at a target audience that's probably never heard of the source material. . . . Johansen—an odd choice for the lead . . . and Rosie O'Donnell, as Mrs. Toody, perform at such a shrill level they're nearly unwatchable. . . . "

Both before and especially after *Car 54*'s delayed release, Rosie did her best to erase her debut film from memory. As soon as newer and better credits allowed, she removed it from her background fact sheet whenever job searching. When asked why she'd done that—which should be pretty obvious to anyone who's seen the picture—she snapped, "It was so bad they held up releasing it. You think I'm going to lead off my resume with that?" On other occasions, she closed the discussion on this combination screen debut/screen failure with "I didn't know what I was doing."

· 9 ·

I wanted to be either Barbra Streisand or Joe Namath. I couldn't figure out which. . . . I wish I could be a professional athlete but I knew that there's no sports that women could play professionally except golf, which I hated, and tennis, which I wasn't good at.
                                    Rosie O'Donnell, September 1996

*I*n baseball, it's three strikes and you're out. No ifs, ands or buts. In Hollywood, you're as good or as bad as your last (or current) project. So how was Rosie scoring according to the rules of the show business game? *Gimme a Break*, her TV series of one year had expired and her first feature film, *Car 54, Where Are You?*, was in limbo. That was bad. Thankfully, however, on the plus side, Rosie was earning points for her continuing assignment with the successful *Stand-Up Spotlight* (which would later win a Cable ACE Award nomination). This gave her two positive credentials on an ongoing series: (1) executive producer and (2) host/emcee. The fact that *Stand-Up* catered to a youngish TV viewing audience was also to the good. Thus, for the present, Rosie was okay by Hollywood's standards.

It certainly didn't hurt Rosie's industry status to be featured in a *TV Guide* article in August 1991 devoted to five up and coming comics. Besides Rosie, the write-up focused on Pauly Shore, Taylor Negron, John Leguizamo and Tommy Davidson. According to Jane Marion, the author of the piece, "In a crowded field of comics, here are five fresh faces you won't forget."

In addition, by the time this *TV Guide* spread appeared, Rosie was already participating in a new major film project. It was *the* one that

81

would prove to be her springboard to fame. And, interestingly enough, she owed the lucky break to her love of sports.

• • •

Contrary to most people's beliefs, professional league baseball in the United States has not always been a man's sport. Back in the 1940s, with so many men being drafted for military duty in World War II, the shortage of players threatened to close down many of the minor leagues. The fallout could have extended to the major leagues. However, Phillip K. Wrigley (the owner of the chewing gum empire and the Chicago Cubs baseball team) and a few other business partners spearheaded a drive to create professional women's baseball teams. The concept was they'd play in competition against each other's squad in what came to be known as The All American Girls Professional Baseball League. The experiment proved sufficiently popular to last not only throughout World War II, but even after the GIs had returned home once peace had been reestablished. The women's league, which at its high point would expand to ten teams, continued in operation until it sputtered out in 1954.

By the late 1950s, the innovative women's league was fast being forgotten. However, in 1958, the group was inducted into the Baseball Hall of Fame in Cooperstown, New York. The publicity surrounding this occasion led to several print articles about this unique squad of players. It also prompted Kelly Candaele (whose mother, Helen Callaghan Candaele St. Aubin, had been one of the league's star players) and Kim Wilson to produce a documentary film. This 1988 movie, titled *A League of Their Own*, featured Helen, her ball-playing sister and many other alumnae from those halcyon days.

It was a *Boston Globe* article on the subject that led Hollywood film producers Bill Pace and his partner, Ronnie Clemmer, to attend the upcoming annual reunion of League members in Ft. Wayne, Indiana. There, these former players, now in their mid to late sixties, played nine holes of golf and participated in a three-inning ball game. Pace and Clemmer were so intrigued by the potential of turning this unusual sports story into a feature film that they soon negotiated the screen rights to the League's unique history. Meanwhile, another moviemaker had become aware of the subject matter and had flown to Cooperstown, New York to discuss the situation with Hall of Fame officials. Upon learning that Pace and Clemmer's production company,

Longbow Productions, controlled the screen rights, the newcomer filmmaker had to strike a deal with Longbow.

This new participant on the baseball project had been born Carole Penny Marsciarelli in the Bronx. She had followed her older brother, Garry, to Hollywood, where he had gained prominence as the producer/writer of TV's *The Dick Van Dyke Show* (1961-1966). When Garry packaged the sitcom, *The Odd Couple* (1970-1975), he gave his sister, now a divorced mother with a child, a small recurring role on the show. It certainly beat her previous secretarial occupation. Later, when he created *Happy Days* (1974-1984), his sibling, Penny, had a guest role on this hit TV show. She was cast as spunky, lower class Laverne De Fazio, with her pal, Shirley Feeney, being played by Cindy Williams. These two comical characters were quickly spun off into their own TV series, *Laverne and Shirley*. The hit sitcom ran from 1976 to 1983, making major stars of Cindy Williams and her on camera teammate, Penny Marshall. By then, Penny—she of the endearing Bronx whine— had tired of acting and decided to turn her attention to directing. Her debut feature was *Jumpin' Jack Flash* (1986) with Whoopi Goldberg, followed by *Big* (1988), a major success featuring Tom Hanks.

By the time Penny became involved in the women's baseball project—to be called *A League of Their Own* like the earlier documentary—she already was very busy professionally. She was producing/directing the drama *Awakenings* (1990), starring Robert De Niro and Robin Williams, so it was decided she would "only" produce the sports movie while David Anspaugh (*Hoosiers*) would direct. Jim Belushi was contracted to play the drunken former major league player who is hired to coach the girls' team.

At this point, Twentieth Century-Fox had a tentative agreement to distribute *League* if name stars could be found for the lead roles of the two ball-playing sisters. On the other hand, Penny thought the parts should be played by (relative) unknowns. She finally capitulated to the studio's wish list of Demi Moore and Daryl Hannah for the key assignments. However, by the time filming was projected to actually start, both Moore and Hannah were busy elsewhere. Twentieth Century-Fox put the project in turnaround, canceling it despite a nearly $5 million investment.

Now deeply committed to the project, Penny took *League* to Columbia Pictures which was distributing her *Awakenings*. A deal was struck regarding the new venture. Alan J. Pakula (*All the President's Men*, *Sophie's Choice*, etc.) would direct and Debra Winger would undertake the pivotal lead role. By May 1991, Winger was honing her ball-playing skills in preparation for the start of the shoot. However, by May 18 she was officially off the project. Some attributed her departure to her perfectionist nature which made her seem a holy terror from the viewpoint of many filmmakers. Other industry observers said that she was upset by the news that Madonna was likely to be cast in the picture as one of the ball players and that Winger was fearful that the Material Girl's presence would move the storyline focus away from her. Not long after Winger left, so did director Pakula. Thereafter, it was decided Penny would direct the picture. Geena Davis was quickly hired to replace Winger. Filming was to get under way on July 10, 1991 in the Midwest. Already, the publicity generated by all these turns of events gave the project high visibility even before the first foot of film had been shot.

During the months of intense pre-production in the spring and early summer of 1991, Marshall had cast the other, less crucial roles in the picture, most of which were the women ball players on the various league teams. Being a stickler for detail, Penny intended to hire only those actresses who looked comfortable performing on the ball field. Word filtered down within the movie industry that there were several available roles for athletic performers in *League*. Suddenly there was a rush of Hollywood actresses deserting Rodeo Drive shopping for warm-up sessions at batting practice centers.

One of those who heard about the *League* casting call was Rosie's agent. As O'Donnell remembers, "They needed somebody who could throw from third to first. Somebody told Penny Marshall that Rosie O'Donnell goes to batting cages every day, so I got a call." Then, in turn, Rosie's agent spoke to her about the casting call. "He asked me if I could play baseball and I said, 'Yes, I can.' I knew there was no other actresses in Hollywood who could lay down a bunt as good as me."

The next step ". . . was really funny," Rosie would recall. "They had about 200 women about 10 times in a row go down to USC [University of Southern California in Los Angeles] and audition with each other. And they filmed us on video hitting and running and throwing and catching. And it was really funny to see all these actresses who had never played baseball who had lied to their agents and said 'Oh, yeah, I can play.' Like, you know, these really thin Barbie doll-like women. And I'm like 'Honey, hold the thin end of the bat, OK? Good luck. . . . Be careful out there.'"

Coach Rod Dedeaux and his assistants monitored these special try-outs at USC's Dedeaux Field. Rosie easily survived this elimination round. Rosie has said, "When I read the script, I thought, 'If I don't get this part, I'll quit show business.' If there's one thing I can do better than Meryl Streep and Glenn Close, it's play baseball." As events progressed, O'Donnell met and read for Marshall. Penny was already familiar with Rosie's stand-up work, having seen her on TV. After Rosie was hired, Marshall would comment, "The part was originally for a hot, sexy girl, but I liked Rosie so much we changed the story to suit her. She can make anything funny."

Rosie was now a member of the *League* team, joining such other cast performers as Jon Lovitz (the cynical talent scout), Lori Petty as Geena Davis' sister and David Strathairn (a league co-founder). Tom Hanks, whose screen career was still reeling from a tremendous flop (*Bonfires of the Vanities*, 1990) was signed to be the down-at-his-heels team manager. He took over from previously assigned Jim Belushi who was now busy elsewhere. (Hanks had earlier worked with Marshall on the movie *Big*.) To make this production more of a family affair, Marshall hired her brother, Garry, to play Walter Harvey, the chocolate king, who founded the league. Penny cast her real-life daughter, Tracy Reiner, in a supporting role. (Tracy was the product of Marshall's first marriage, but bore the surname of Penny's second husband, actor/director Rob Reiner, whom Penny later divorced.) Also participating in the cast was Garry Marshall's daughter, Kathleen.

Then there was the role of Mae Mordabito, a secondary but potentially showy role. Penny and her casting people were in negotiation to have Madonna take the assignment of the ex-taxi dancer pal of O'Donnell's character. Signing sexy, outrageous, hugely popular Madonna would be a coup that would guarantee the picture lots of potential ticket buyers. By this juncture, Rosie had become chummy with her new boss. One day, Penny informed O'Donnell that it was now hopeful that Madonna would finally come aboard as an onscreen ball player. Suddenly, out of nowhere, the nasal-twanged Marshall advised unsuspecting Rosie, "If she likes you and she likes me, she'll do the movie. Be funny."

To say the least, this was putting a great deal of pressure on Rosie. In fact, O'Donnell was so "petrified" of meeting the superstar, let alone convincing her to join the *League* team, that she had diarrhea for two hours before their scheduled chat. As Rosie recalls the now famous meeting, "First of all, *Truth or Dare* [a revealing backstage/performance film about Madonna] had come out three weeks before and I felt an affinity for Madonna. Both our mothers died when we were little, and I love water bottles, just like her. I went to see it with my friend Mike and he said, 'Maybe one day you'll work with her,' and I lit into him. I said, 'You are such an idiot. I am a comedienne, and she's a pop goddess!'"

Here is one account of their first conversation:

ROSIE: Hello, I have a vibrator.
MADONNA: Panasonic?

And a friendship was born.

Another time, Rosie would recall a bit differently her introduction to the pop song idol, "The first thing I said [to Madonna] was 'Hi, my mom died when I was little, too.' And from that moment on we were friends."

Whichever way the meeting actually transpired, Madonna joined the cast of *A League of Their Own* and was paid a hefty salary. (Ironically, the song "This Used to Be My Playground" Madonna would specially record for use as a background vocal, ended up not on the soundtrack album because Madonna was under contract to a rival label, Warner Bros. Records.)

• • •

It was decided to shoot *A League of Their Own* on location. Part of the filming would be accomplished at Chicago's Wrigley Field where the actual Girls League had sometimes played competition games during the 1940s and early 1950s. The rest of the movie was to be leased in Evansville, Indiana, a smallish and somewhat quaint Midwestern town which boasted of its 5,600 seat, 1915-vintage Bosse Stadium. To gain the town's cooperation, the production was to pay a daily rental fee, sponsor a new stadium scoreboard and make a $20,000 gift to the stadium. In addition, the moviemakers would provide all the free food the volunteer extras (for the stadium crowd scenes) could eat, acknowledge both the field and town in the movie's credits, etc. Other sequences were to be filmed in nearby Huntingburg and New Harmony. A few pickup shots—where the female ball players board—were to be shot at a private home at Fifth and Main street, in Henderson, Kentucky.

By the time Rosie joined the 120-member cast and crew for the start

Courtesy of Annette D'Agostino.

The former O'Donnell family home on Rhonda Lane in Commack, New York.

Courtesy of Seth Poppel Yearbook Archives.

Rosie O'Donnell and fellow student actor in a production of *Witness for the Prosecution* at Commack South High School.

Class of 1980—Commack South High School.

Courtesy of Photofest.

As dental technician Maggie O'Brien on the TV sitcom
"Gimme a Break" (1986-1987).

Courtesy of Photofest.

Rosie O'Donnell as blue-collar worker Lorraine Popowoski on the TV series "Stand by Your Man" (1992) with fellow cast members. Bottom row: Rick Hall, Sam McMurray, Melissa Gilbert-Brinkman. Back row: Rosie, Miriam Flynn.

With (left to right): Ann Cusack, Anne Elizabeth Ramsay and Madonna as patriotic professional baseball players in *A League of Their Own* (1992).

As friend and newspaper editor boss of Meg Ryan (left) in
Sleepless in Seattle (1993).

As determined assistant district attorney Gina Garrett with co-stars Richard
Dreyfuss (center) and Emilio Estevez (right) in *Another Stakeout* (1993).

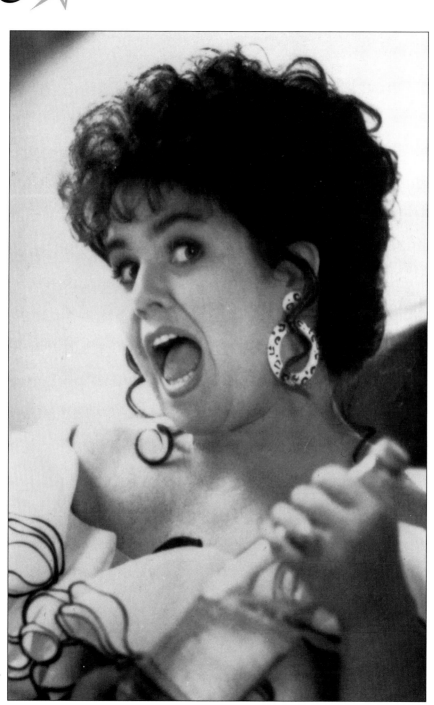

Courtesy of Photofest.

As bubbly Lucille Toody in *Car 54, Where Are You?* (1994).

As Rizzo, leader of the Pink Ladies, with co-player Jason Opsahl in the 1994 Broadway revival of *Grease!*.

of work in Chicago, she had an unintentional surprise for director Marshall. Penny had requested that O'Donnell lose at least twenty pounds by the time the shoot got under way. Rosie had responded with, "Oh sure, Pen. No problem." However, came the day of reckoning:

MARSHALL: You didn't lose any weight.
O'DONNELL: I know. Surprise.

If Rosie had lacked the needed discipline before filming, Penny intended to do something about the performer's expanding waistline now. Says O'Donnell, "The first time we got to the [baseball] field, they said, 'Okay, two times around.' I said, 'Around what? Are you kidding me?'" As for doing the requisite laps, the comedian recounts, "They were coaching me, holding doughnuts, saying, 'Come on, Rosie, you can do it.' It was a nightmare."

Ironically, as filming continued, Rosie *gained* weight. As she has explained, "I had fantasies at the beginning of the movie of . . . becoming a lean, mean fighting machine—120 pounds of sinewy muscle. However, that didn't occur because there's this thing on movie sets called craft services which is like an 80' table with every kind of fattening carbohydrate they can find and that is put on the table free as much as you want and constantly from the time you get on the set at 5:30 a.m. until you go home at 10 p.m. Complete with hot dogs and sandwiches and twizzlers and doughnuts and Pop-tarts and cookies . . . and need I go on."

Making *A League of Their Own* proved to be a daunting task in many respects. From hindsight, Marshall shrugs her shoulders and whines "Who knew? I didn't know." She was referring to a host of production problems on location. These ranged from the constant 120° temperature to the over-sized, hungry mosquitoes hovering around the playing field. In a real baseball game, the spontaneous plays between opposing teams are only guided by the rules of the sport and each player is an in-shape professional athlete. In contrast, for the film, the cameras were set in particular positions to capture needed specific footage at a given time by particular players, all of whom were women who were non-pros and not always in tip-top shape.

As Tom Hanks assessed the situation, "There were a lot of constraints. We . . . were hampered by the smaller mitts, the '40s mitts. For the most part, the real stuff happens in little tiny moments, and you put those moments together for the movies. These girls are not going to go off and play big-time ball anytime soon." Rosie cites, "It was really tough because we had specific shots that we had to get. So the pitcher had to get the pitch over the plate, which was a tough thing to begin with because it's a regulation-size field, and the batter had to hit it to a specific spot, the person on second had to field it right and throw it to first. And so it was very monotonous."

One of the other complications on the set was that with a squad of female performers in key acting assignments, there came that time of the month when, as Marshall said, "Everyone gets a little testy at the same time." Fellow cast member Tracy Reiner remembers, "I somehow came back with Rosie's period schedule. Not only would we all get it at the same time, by the middle of the movie—we switched schedules, and I was thinking, 'It's the 12th, I've never gotten my period on the 12th in my life!' And Rosie's saying, 'Hey, that's mine!'" For the record, O'Donnell insists, "I didn't really keep too close track of everyone else's periods, to tell you the truth, I mean, that was used as an excuse a lot of the time for people fighting with one another. And I'm thinking, 'God, didn't that go out in 1970 with Gloria Steinem and Bella Abzug?'"

On one hand, Geena Davis would come away from this picture saying, "I found it an incredibly bonding experience. I think adversity breeds bonding. And because of the difficulties in shooting a movie like this, and being all the way from home and everything, we all really got along together and supported one another. It was a very friendly, comfortable nice atmosphere. I think women are good at that kind of thing, really supportive."

Tracy Reiner has a different take on making *League*: "We all have big mouths. I have a big mouth. Lori's got a big mouth. Madonna's got a big mouth, Rosie's got a big mouth. You know, we all talk, we express ourselves. . . . Geena was kind of a recluse; she was in her trailer all the time, did things on her own all the time." This was in line with Rosie's memory of the shoot: "It's hard to avoid the petty fights, and they definitely occurred. And anyone who tells you they didn't is lying. Actresses on the whole are an insecure breed, myself being one of them. And there were little cliques that formed and unformed, and then new ones formed. And *this* one was mad at *that* one because she didn't get invited to the slumber party. We all reverted to our adolescence, because we were locked with one another for 22 weeks, working six days a week."

To complicate matters further, Penny Marshall was, according to Rosie, the type of director who would shoot and reshoot a scene until she thought it was just right, no matter how many takes it required. "It was 'Do it over, do it over!' A million takes. On the whole, 99 percent of it [i.e., the filming] was 'Get this specific play, get this hit, get this reaction, get this throw.'"

The repetitious, tedious (re)filming before any given scene was completed was very difficult on the actors. It was even worse for the locals stuck in the broiling, humid weather with unfriendly airborne insects always on the attack. Once the initial novelty wore off of being part of a Hollywood film with big film stars, it was a major challenge to keep the volunteers at the stadium on a given day, let alone insure they'd return in sufficient numbers for the following weeks ahead.

One gambit for keeping the crowd interested was providing the unpaid spectators with free food. However, there were only so many hot dogs, junk food snacks and soft drinks the extras could consume while diverting themselves between takes. Marshall found an impromptu solution for the lull-time while her crew lined up the next shots. She walked over to Rosie and said, "Go do something." An assistant then handed O'Donnell a microphone. "So for 30 minutes," Rosie recalls, "I'd be singing *The Brady Bunch* theme and doing stand-up for 5,000 extras. When Geena [Davis] or Tom [Hanks] was not too busy, I'd go, 'Ladies and gentlemen, here's Tom Hanks!' And Tom would come out and do something. And then I'd go, 'Oh, you want to hear from Madonna, do you? *Madonna!*' Everyone participated." During some of the down time, they'd play "Stump Rosie." In this game, the extras would shout out the name of a TV show and Rosie, microphone in hand, would sing it.

On other occasions, while shooting in Evansville with 5,000 extras hanging around, O'Donnell would belt out "Like a Virgin" and the Material Girl "would come running out of the dugout and tackle me." Sometimes Rosie and Geena would amuse the onlookers with trivia contests regarding TV commercials.

According to Geena Davis, "We'd do goofy stuff. My favorite thing to do was to sing 'Bohemian Rhapsody,' which nobody knew, because it's such an old song. And I happen to know *all* the words to 'Bohemian Rhapsody.' And so we would sing this at the top of our lungs—Rosie knew the words too, and a couple of other people...." Davis also recalls, "For some reason, I got obsessed with *Jesus Christ Superstar*... and I guess as a distraction from the heat and the hours and the tensions on the set, I got all interested in making everybody mount this production of JCS. Every morning in the makeup trailer, I made everybody practice, and I cast everybody in parts. We were going to do *Jesus Christ Superstar Goes Hawaiian.*"

Hanks remembers, "We'd always end up being bored out of our heads and start entertaining the crowd somehow with bat-balancing competitions, or we would spell out 'Evansville' with our bodies. . . . We had puppet shows going on over the dugout walls. Geena kept writing musicals and performing them kind of extemporaneously, usually with snippets of dialogue from the actual movie. I'll tell you, some of the hardest laughing I've done on a movie set was in the dugout waiting for some shot to be lined up, with the entire team there."

• • •

Relations between the cast/crew of *A League of Their Own* and the Indiana locals had to be very accommodating to succeed with the endless days of takes and retakes at Bosse Field. All the time, there were opportunities for clashes between the stars and local sensibilities off the set, especially during the evenings and weekends.

Despite efforts to establish immediately an atmosphere of cooperation with the townsfolk, things went amiss even before the first day of shooting in Evansville. Columnist Bill Zwecker had appeared on Joan Rivers' TV talk show and mentioned that when Tom Hanks was asked if he was excited about his pending on-location sojourn in Evansville, he'd said, "Well, no. I'm sure Evansville is a nice town, but it's certainly not going to have all the excitement Chicago has." This unfiltered recitation of Hanks' actually innocent remark didn't sit well with Indiana folks. However, it was only the tip of the iceberg.

When Rosie and the others arrived in Evansville (population approximately 127,000), the film's production office provided them with a hospitality packet which pinpointed the city's attractions. It underscored that the legal age of (sexual) consent in Indiana was 18, but that one had to be 21 to buy alcohol or to be present when it was consumed. There was a long list of houses of worship, grocery shops, health food stores and even the name of a local masseur. As far as night life went, the kit detailed 20 possibilities which fell into 3 categories: clubs, bars with style and dives. It also noted adult bookstores and a nearby gay bar. The "Best Bets" section listed 44 restaurants and 17 pubs.

Tom Hanks and his actress wife Rita Wilson and their children were provided with their own rented house on five acres with a pond. Geena

Davis, Madonna and a few of the others had their own individual headquarters. The remainder were allotted quarters in nearby motels, etc. Rosie, a veteran of life on the road, easily adapted to the new surroundings. "There was a mall, a movie theater, and a McDonald's. I was fine." She also noted, ". . . we'd see every movie. We even paid to see *Cool as Ice* [a bomb starring Caucasian rapper Vanilla Ice], so that tells you how the summer was." For cast member Lori Petty, after working six days a week, she—like most of the others—would go out on the town on Saturday night, no matter how worn out she might be. The usual activity was to head to a nearby dance bar and "let it all hang out."

However, for the Material Girl who had dyed her hair jet black for the movie, life in Evansville was a far different story. According to Rosie, "But somebody like Madonna, who spends half her time in Europe, eats only at the best restaurants—that's not going to be an entertaining place for her to go." So the pop diva found her own diversions. Said Hanks, "There was one gay bar that, uh became a hangout for the, uh—you know, Madonna found it." Then there was the onslaught of paparazzi drawn to tracking Madonna's every move, to photograph every out-of-town male visitor who appeared at the doorstep of her rented home outside of Evansville. The traffic included such notables as rapper Vanilla Ice, major league ball player Jose Canseco (reportedly on hand early one morning to give her baseball tips), etc.

However, the final straw for conservative, civic-minded Evansville locals occurred after Madonna left town. During filming, none of the citizenry could recollect that she'd ever gone out of her way to chat with any of the natives, unless it was while ordering food or making a purchase at a store. Then along came the published issue of *TV Guide* which contained Madonna's response to being asked how she'd liked Evansville. Her too spontaneous reply was, "I may as well have been in Prague." These words won the singer NO friends in Evansville. Rosie, by now Madonna's official champion, would insist later, "Her comment, which I think was grossly misinterpreted by the people of Evansville, really wasn't meant as a slight." This remark was generally taken with a grain of salt by everyone.

Even usually congenial Hanks had a few scrapes with the locals. On one hand, he admitted of his Evansville stay: "We loved the place. We loved going to the Dairy Queen and getting a chocolate cone on Thursday nights." On the other hand, there were limits to his mingling with the public. For example, there was the time a man drove a tractor up to his front door, hauling thirty or more people in a hay ride. He was miffed when Tom declined to come along. Eventually, during the shoot, Hanks had to hire security guards to keep the public from ringing the doorbell to ask if they could take a picture with him. Such behavior on his part, earned the actor a reputation with some locals of not being neighborly. In fact, he acknowledged, "Every now and again, people would drive by and flip us the bird."

During the shoot (which would end on October 30, 1991), Rosie had to get used to Madonna's peccadilloes, as well as accommodate herself to the idiosyncrasies of the other cast members. However, one particular incident stuck out in Rosie's brain from her weeks of making this motion picture. It occurred while the cast was filming in the Windy City at Wrigley Field. During a stretch of downtime, Rosie spotted Robin Knight, one of the other onscreen ball players, stooping down to gather little chunks of dirt off the pitcher's mound. She was packing these "treasures" in Ziploc bags to take home. O'Donnell says, "I thought she was on crack, I'm thinking, 'What the hell are you doing?' She's like, 'It's Wrigley Field, man!' I guess for me it would be like being in Bette Midler's dressing room." It reminded O'Donnell that it's all a matter of how you look at things and what are your particular passions in life.

· 10 ·

Well, I said on one interview that she [Penny Marshall, director of
A League of Their Own*] was the queen of the retake, and she was*
angry. She's like, "Rosie, I don't do retakes. I do coverage, coverage."
That's what she does. We'll shoot it from this angle. We'll do it like
10 times. "OK, moving in, moving." You know, so she shot every
scene from every conceivable angle that—that you could do it. But
actually, it's very beneficial because you end up having a lot of
opportunities to do the same scene over and over again and she has a
lot of film to work with to edit it together for a final product.

Rosie O'Donnell, July 1992

*O*n *Car 54, Where Are You?* unfavorable circumstances had
combined to turn the filmmaking process into relative
chaos. For Rosie and the others, it had been more of a game
of survival rather than one of skill. In contrast, the making of *A League
of Their Own* was an extremely positive experience. This time Rosie
was part of a Class A production with solid professionals both in front
of and behind the cameras. In particular, she was working for a well-
respected director, Penny Marshall, who also happened to be a childhood idol because of Penny's TV sitcom acting days. Explained Rosie,
". . . I'm such a huge *Laverne and Shirley* fan that I know all these little
trivia facts about Laverne and Shirley, like Boo-Boo Kitty, a stuffed
animal, and how she used to drink milk and Pepsi. And I would quote
lines from *Laverne and Shirley* to her, which she found amusing on
some level, I think."

O'Donnell also confided to her new-found mentor that she wanted
to learn to direct one day herself. "So," according to Rosie, "Penny, in
her nasal New York accent, would command, 'Comere. See what I'm
doin' heah? I'm makin' a dolly shot 'cause we wan' movement. See why?
Dat's why.'" When the fledgling screen player asked Penny what she
knew about various camera lenses, the latter responded, "What lenses

schmenzes? You hi-ah the D.P.[director of photography] ta know dat. You don't gotta know dat. You gotta know what's funny."

What also pleased O'Donnell about her current film director was that Marshall gave her space to develop her characterization. On *Car 54*, the novice actor had been too much in awe of the filmmaking process to appreciate the give-and-take that should exist between the director and a cast member. Too often on that first movie venture, the insecure newcomer had been left to her own devices and had frequently substituted bravado for technique in padding out her one-dimensional role.

By the time of *League*, Rosie was far more confident and relaxed about making movies. By absorbing the filmmaking process, she'd come to understand the requisites for making on camera time count to make her presence stand out on the screen. She had come to appreciate the advantages of moviemaking over being a comedian performing solo in front of a club crowd. As she now realized, "When you're a stand-up comic you have all the power and all the control. You're the writer, the editor, the director, the performer. And that feeling of an ensemble [on a film set] is really very welcome, and it also takes a lot of the pressure off you. And you're able to say somebody else's words in a way that someone else tells you to say it in clothing that someone else chooses."

There were, however, other important moviemaking lessons that O'Donnell had yet to accept. With the constant takes and retakes on *League*, she had ample opportunity to learn and acquiesce. For example, on *League* she still found herself waiting for an audience response after delivering a funny line. As Rosie later said, ". . . being a stand-up comic, you do something, you get it back. It's an interactive art form. . . . I'd do a joke and I'd look around. She'd go [imitating Penny Marshall] 'Cut! What are you looking for?' I'd go, 'Nobody's laughing.' She, like [again imitating Marshall's inimitable voice] 'It's a movie! They're *not* supposed to laugh!' So that was tough, to get used to. . . ."

On another level altogether, unlike many others on this sports picture, O'Donnell knew she could handle the athletic requirements. ("Well," she would tell *NBC Today* in June 1992, "I was pretty good. You know, I'm one of the few women on the team who could throw from third to first without a lot of ice on my shoulder after the game.") Her talent on the baseball diamond gave her an advantage over most of the other actors. As such, she was able to focus largely on her acting performance, not on masking deficiencies in her ball playing. This gave Rosie a huge sense of self-confidence, and, in turn, brought respect from co-workers. Nevertheless, O'Donnell concedes to having learned a few new tricks about ball playing. For example, one day during practice, Pepper Davis, a former Girls League player, was on hand to coach the actors. "I was in batting practice," Rosie would describe, "and I'm hitting away, and Pepper said to me. 'Rosie.' I go, 'Yeah?' 'Move your right foot.' 'Which way?' 'Point it up, point it up.' So I move my right foot, honestly, an inch forward. Oh my God—boom! You know? And she just nodded and walked away."

O'Donnell's self-assurance was further buoyed by the fact that it was she to whom everyone turned when the extras needed to be entertained during the endless breaks between takes. It was also O'Donnell, in contrast to most of the others, who didn't treat Madonna with awe and goddess-like respect. Instead, salt-of-the-earth Rosie was the Material Girl's pal and equal both on screen and off. These elements earned her esteem points with both cast and crew.

Additionally, on the Indiana location, Rosie grew to better understand why she'd been hired. It went far beyond her expertise with a baseball mitt and bat. She came to realize that Penny had seen in her fellow comic a natural instinct for what was funny. As Rosie worked further on this production, she accepted more fully that her knack for delivering a comic line was an integral reason for her being on *League*. With such encouragement from Marshall, O'Donnell was relaxed enough to exploit her well-honed timing in snapping out comedic dialogue. As a result, this filming experience was a far cry from *Car 54* where she'd been a too-willing pawn in a slapstick celluloid cartoon.

Originally, in *League*, Rosie's Doris Murphy, the third basewoman with the mouth of a truck driver, was a small part in the overall ensemble. However, that wasn't the case by the time the project finished at the end of October 1991. Her character emerged with additional screen time in colorful bits that would make Rosie stand out and be memorable to moviegoers.

When asked later if she'd ad-libbed a lot on this movie, Rosie answered, "A lot. Thanks to Penny, who trusted my comedic instincts. She would just go, 'Rosie, do something. Put the camera on Rosie at third base. Just react. Action.'" O'Donnell also claims that a lot of time when Marshall would ask the cast to do this or that unassigned bit for the camera, Rosie would volunteer. She jokes now that she was the only one of the cast who could understand what Penny was saying.

In particular, O'Donnell recalls one scene on the bus where Doris is comforting a perplexed teammate. Originally this *League* sequence was relatively brief. However, after they'd shot the scripted pages that day, Penny told Rosie to continue onward, to ad-lib. So O'Donnell talked and talked—saying anything that came to mind that seemed even vaguely appropriate. Finally, after ten minutes of this improv in front of the rolling camera, Penny screamed "Cut!" The drained O'Donnell yelled back, "About time!" To which the director replied in her famed nasal drawl, "Well, I wanted to see what you would do. . . . I let you go. Maybe I'll use it."

• • •

In *A League of Their Own*, set in the Midwest during World War II, candy bar magnate Walter Harvey (Garry Marshall) sponsors an all-female version of professional baseball. He hopes to save the sport which has been disrupted by so many players being drafted into military service. Later, gruff baseball scout Ernie Capadino (Jon Lovitz) scours the U.S. to find candidates for the ballpark auditions to be held in Chicago. His marching orders are to find women who are proficient at the game but who are also "easy on the eye."

On an Oregon farm, Ernie finds a stellar player, Dottie (Geena Davis), whose GI husband (Bill Pullman) is fighting overseas. She is recruited along with her spunky younger sister, Kit (Lori Petty). En route back to Chicago, more candidates are added to the potential roster. These include raucous Doris Murphy (Rosie O'Donnell), a former dance club bouncer, and the promiscuous Mae Mordabito (Madonna). The latter is Doris' friend, and she had been a taxi dancer at the establishment owned by Doris' dad.

In Chicago, Dottie, Kit, Doris, Mae and several others—including homely Marla Hooch (Megan Cavanagh)—are hired to play for the Rockford Peaches. They are made to attend charm school, wear baseball uniforms that have short skirts and exploit their feminine pulchritude. It is hoped that the novelty of (mostly) attractive women playing ball in fetching outfits will be enough to perk the public's interest and develop a loyal following. (One of the team's ballpark mottoes is "Catch a foul—get a kiss!") Their reluctant coach, tobacco-chawing Jimmy Dugan (Tom Hanks) is an ex-major league player with bad knees who has become an alcoholic.

Eventually, Dugan whips the team into a slick squad as the action builds to the crucial World Series games between the Peaches and the Racines. The focus is on various team members—especially Dottie and

Kit, who are rivals on and off the diamond—as they cope with personal aspirations and problems. Meanwhile, Dugan comes to appreciate that women athletes can be as good as their male counterparts. An epilogue, set in 1988 in Cooperstown, New York, finds the surviving alumnae of the All American Girls Professional Baseball League reuniting to celebrate their delayed induction into the Baseball Hall of Fame.

The sibling rivalry of Geena Davis and Lori Petty's characters provides the major storyline in *A League of Their Own* and their interaction receives most screen attention. However, because Tom Hanks was the movie's chief box-office attraction, he was permitted to make his truncated on camera time count heavily. One of his more memorable scenes occurs in the squad's locker room. There, his inebriated character has perhaps the longest urination sequence in the history of Hollywood pictures. His other big pay-off moment comes when he confronts a weeping outfielder (Bitty Schram). Incredulous at such sissy behavior, even from a woman, the macho ex-home run king screams: "Are you crying? There's no crying in baseball!"

If the "no crying" bit would prove to be a major highlight of the movie, O'Donnell's Doris Murphy (her number on the team is #22) has an ample share of camera-stealing scenes. Actually, it's Doris who ultimately utters the film's most memorable line of dialogue and one that has become a treasured sound byte of the 1990s. It occurs as provocative Mae Mordabito suggests that it might be good for stadium attendance if she lets her uniform become unbuttoned. She inquires of the others, "What if my blouse pops open and my bosom is exposed?" The unvarnished, unimpressed Doris snaps back: "You think there are men in this country who ain't seen your bosom?" Another killer moment for Doris occurs as she and other Catholic teammates wait in line at church to enter the confessional where Mae is currently enumerating her misdeeds. Moments before the priest emerges in a cold sweat from the confessional, a thudding sound is heard within the confessional. Doris wisecracks, "That's the second time he dropped the Bible since she's been in there."

• • •

As the mid-1992 opening of *A League of Their Own* drew near, Columbia Pictures' publicity machinery went into overdrive. As part of the promotional hoopla, there were tie-ins with Major League Baseball cards, Baskin-Robbins ice cream and, among many others,

Rosie's *Stand-Up Spotlight* employer VH-1. The latter cable network presented a glimpse of the film on their program, *Flix*. Meanwhile HBO-Cable and other outlets aired a promotional short subject entitled *The Making of A League of Their Own*. Penny Marshall even appeared live on June 27, 1992, on the Philadelphia-based QVC (Home Shopping) Network to promote the sale of licensed merchandise (T-shirts, crew jackets, baseball caps, etc.) bearing the movie's logo.

Director Marshall and key cast members hit the road to push their screen venture. When straight-shooter Rosie was asked what she thought of the completed movie, she responded, "Well, it's weird. It doesn't feel like a real movie to me because I'm in it. The first time I saw it, all I saw was myself. And every time I was on the screen, like, I looked down. And the second time I saw it, it was like, 'Oh, this is a fun movie.' Jon Lovitz is so funny, oh, Geena, then me, you know. So it sort of becomes not like a real, regular film."

Although the citizens of Evansville, Indiana had hoped the world premiere *of A League of Their Own* would occur in their home town, they would have to be satisfied with a follow-up "premiere" which was distinctly non-star-studded. Instead, the expensively mounted feature debuted with special events in late June 1992 in both New York City and Los Angeles. The Big Apple gala was a charity fund-raiser screening and party held at Tavern on the Green. The Los Angeles version took place at the Academy of Motion Picture Arts and Sciences on Wilshire Boulevard with a party afterward in the facility's parking lot. Tickets for the fund-raiser (a benefit for the Westside Children's Center) sold for $250 a piece. It entitled the guest to hot dogs, popcorn and peanuts, all served by waiters in T-shirts that were emblazoned with "There's no crying in baseball." Penny Marshall may have left the West Coast proceedings directly after the screening and Madonna may not have been in attendance at all. However, enthusiastic, Rosie O'Donnell was very much present at the festivities as were Geena Davis, Jon Lovitz, Garry Marshall and other cast members.

At the post-screening get-together, Rosie was as excited as any fan off the street to meet the milling celebrities which included Martin Short, Teri Garr, Richard Lewis, Harvey Keitel, Albert Brooks, Sally Kellerman, directors Barbet Schroeder and Irwin Winkler, and many other notables. (Madonna was not at the gala because of recording commitments in New York City.) At one point, O'Donnell spun around to a nearby reporter, unable to contain herself about having just spotted actress Christine Lahti in the celebrity crowd, "Oh, I'm a huge fan of hers. Can you introduce me? On second thought, don't. She'll think I just want to meet her so she'll say something nice about my movie."

With *A League of Their Own* blessed by its official premieres, it was time to unveil this $50 million picture for public consumption. A standard practice before a big-budget movie is released is for industry sources to predict how the movie will do at the all-crucial box-office. In forecasting the financial outcome for *League*, *Premiere* magazine wondered in print, ". . . women's baseball didn't exactly work as a sport—what makes 'em think it'll work as a movie?" There were also other nay-sayers. For example, Peter Keough of the *Chicago Sun-Times* pointed out, "[Penny] Marshall doesn't hesitate to make fun of women who don't conform to the traditional standards of female beauty, such as Marla Hooch a homely superstar, who's the butt of some cruel humor until she puts on a dress and lands herself a husband."

Keough also underscored, "As for sexuality, it's limited to Madonna showing her knickers in a roadhouse [dance] scene. And though lesbianism was not uncommon in the leagues, according to Lois Browne, whose book *Girls of Summer* [1992] was used as a reference source for the film, in Marshall's *League* it's the love that dare not speak its name." Remarks such as this drew the ire of Rosie who was already proving to be a most willing, attention-grabbing asset when promoting the film around the country. She lashed back against critics who condemned the movie's soft-peddling of touchy issues. Per Rosie: "Anyone who obsesses about whether any characters were gay, and whether they should be, should perhaps attend an ACT-UP meeting instead of a press conference because that's not really what this film was about."

Jami Bernard (*New York Post*) judged, "Personally, I don't care whether the actresses can 'really' play or not. *A League of Their Own* is a warm, funny comedy, with a snappy script. . . ." For Roger Ebert (*Chicago Sun-Times*), ". . . the movie has a real bittersweet charm. . . . What's fresh are the personalities of the players, the gradual unfolding of their coach and the way this early chapter of women's liberation fits into the hidebound traditions of professional baseball." Vincent Canby (*New York Times*) rated it "one of the year's most cheerful, most relaxed, most easily enjoyable comedies. It's a serious film that's lighter than air, a very funny movie that manages to score a few points for feminism in passing." Canby also observed, "Among the excellent supporting players are Rosie O'Donnell." *Daily Variety's* Todd McCarthy decided, "To anyone with a taste for old-time baseball, seeing the small, antique parks and being reminded of a time when the game was played with a purity of intent will represent a distinct pleasure all its own. . . . Of the large cast, Rosie O'Donnell stands out as the brash smooth-fielding third basewoman. . . ."

It was Richard Schickel (*Time* magazine) who provided the most balanced assessment of Penny Marshall's latest effort: "If the people responsible for *A League of Their Own* had tried just a little harder to avoid easy laughs and easy sentiment, they might have made something like a great movie. As it is, they have made a good movie, amiable and ingratiating." In the same vein, Jon Matsumoto (*LA Village View*) complained, "One is introduced to a number of potentially colorful but underdeveloped characters such as Rosie O'Donnell's sarcastic Doris and Madonna's 'All the Way' May [sic]. They crack one-liners and few details of their personal lives are revealed. But one never really grows to understand or care about them. Most of them seem like caricatures."

As always, the public was the final arbiter on whether *A League of Their Own* would succeed or not financially. The essentially gentle PG-rated movie which celebrated sports for the sake of sport, became a blockbuster hit in a summer full of big macho action thrillers. It went on to gross over $107 million dollars in domestic release. It even spawned a TV sitcom adaptation which aired briefly on CBS-TV in April 1993. Penny Marshall served as executive producer for the half-hour show, a few of the episodes were written by Babaloo Mandel and Lowell Ganz (who did the original screenplay), Tom Hanks directed one of the installments, and Garry Marshall recreated his role as Mr. Harvey. The other parts were all recast. Carey Lowell, Christine Elise, Katie Rich and Wendy Makkena took over the roles that had been played in the original by, respectively, Geena Davis, Lori Petty, Rosie O'Donnell and Madonna.

Meanwhile, the net result of the motion picture was to boost the stock of everyone connected with the whopping success. Being one of the most visible and vocal of the onscreen participants (with her loud, New York-accented hollering), Rosie raked in an important share of the critical and public adulation. As a direct result, it boosted her standing in the film community. She now had that most coveted of all things in the movie business—a major hit film. (Later, Rosie would be nominated for an American Comedy Award in the Funniest Supporting Female—Motion Picture category, a prize she lost to Kathy Najimy of *Sister Act*.)

But if there was general agreement that Rosie O'Donnell was now on the Hollywood fast track, there were still some who didn't appreciate her movie success. For one there was her dad who couldn't even bring himself to acknowledge to her that he'd seen her movies to date. For another, there was her sister Maureen's child. As Rosie confided on national television, "Well , my niece is four years old and she thinks I'm in *Beauty and the Beast* [1991]. She doesn't understand. Every movie she's seen is animated. So she tells everyone, 'This is my Aunt Rosie. She's in a movie, *Beauty and the Beast*. She's the beast. . .'."

· 11 ·

Coming to know and love her [Madonna] as a human being brought me to a different awareness of what that kind of media image does to someone.

Rosie O'Donnell, March 1994

*W*ebster's New Collegiate Dictionary defines a friend as "one attached to another by affection or esteem." That certainly has proven to be the case with Rosie O'Donnell and Madonna Louise Veronica Ciccone, the latter better known as Madonna. For her part, the mega-millionaire pop diva has said of Rosie, "I cannot explain the mystery of what happens when you become best friends with someone. I can only say that we are tortured by the same thing, we laugh at the same things, and I love her madly!"

On television's *CBS This Morning*, (July 9, 1992), O'Donnell would explain why she and Madonna had almost immediately bonded when they first met. According to Rosie, there ". . . were a lot of similarities in our lives. My mom died when I was a little girl, as did hers, and I'm named after my mom, as is she, and [we both have] large Catholic families. . . . So within the first 10 minutes I sort of told her my life story and we became friends shortly thereafter."

Madonna was born in Bay City, Michigan on August 16, 1958. Her first-generation Italian-American father, Sylvio "Tony" Ciccone, was a design engineer for the Chrysler/General Dynamics Corporation. He was a strict Roman Catholic as was his wife, Madonna (who, in turn, had inherited that name from her mother). Little Madonna was the third of four children born to the Ciccones. In late 1963, when she was five, her mother died of breast cancer. Thereafter, Tony Ciccone moved his family to Pontiac, Michigan and Madonna, who at one time thought she would become a nun, now coveted something more immediate—she wanted to be black because all her friends were African-American.

In 1966, Tony Ciccone married the latest in a series of housekeepers, so there was immediate rivalry between Madonna and her stepmother, a situation not helped when the youngster found herself forced to be a live-in baby-sitter for her two new stepbrothers. Her chief dream now was to "escape" from her home life. When she was fourteen, she met dance instructor Christopher Flynn who introduced her to the world of disco dancing in Detroit.

After graduating from high school in January 1976, she enrolled—thanks to a dance scholarship—at the University of Michigan where Flynn was a professor of dance. She quit after a year and, in the late summer of 1978, she relocated to New York City. To survive, she worked as a waitress and modeled (often in the nude). In 1979 she appeared in a softcore pornographic film (*A Certain Sacrifice*). Thereafter, she was briefly part of the Alvin Ailey American Dance Theater's third company.

Thanks to her newest boyfriend, musician Dan Gilroy, Madonna was introduced to the world of rock 'n' roll. He taught her to play the guitar and drums. Except for a few months in Paris as a backup singer for a minor disco star, Madonna remained with Gilroy. They lived together and she performed as a vocalist/drummer in his group, Breakfast Club. When that relationship ended, she formed her own band, Emmy. This was replaced in 1982 by a new band, Madonna, which specialized in funkier rap music. Her latest "boy toy," Mark Kamins, a club disc jockey, showcased her demo recording of "Everybody" at Danceteria, the trendy Manhattan musical night spot where he worked. Such exposure led eventually to a recording contract for Madonna with Sire Records. In mid-1983 her debut album, *Madonna*, was released, followed by *Like a Virgin* (1984). Both albums had a great impact on audiences everywhere.

By April 1985, Madonna had had several singles on the top music industry charts both in the U.S. and Great Britain. That same year, her debut mainstream feature film, *Desperately Seeking Susan*, was released. The low-budget comedy was a hit and proved that the singer was an above competent actress. The next month, she was on the cover of

Time magazine, and embarked on her first concert tour. On her 27th birthday (August 16, 1985) she married actor Sean Penn. Within short order, the couple dominated the tabloid newspapers, at first with accounts of their wedded bliss, then with recitations of Penn's explosive nature ignited by jealousy of any man who paid too much attention to his spouse. By mid-1986, the pair, who were now arguing violently in public, appeared in a limited run stage production of David Rabe's play, *Goose and Tomtom*. They also co-starred in *Shanghai Surprise* (1986), produced by The Beatles' George Harrison, which cast Madonna as a 1930s missionary (!) in China. The film was a big flop.

Madonna made more albums, did a Broadway play (*Speed-the-Plow*, 1988), won and lost a $5 million Pepsi commercial contract in 1989 because her first TV spot for the soft drink bottler was deemed far too controversial and yanked from the airwaves. Despite this setback, she had earned an estimated $43 million in the prior two years. She'd also filed for divorce from Penn in early 1989. She was only one of aging filmmaker Warren Beatty's love interests in the movie *Dick Tracy* (1990). However, off camera, for a spell, the couple was inseparable. Meanwhile, her albums, *Like a Prayer* (1989) and *I'm Breathless* (1990) were huge hits. After her Warren Beatty liaison ended, she became enamored temporarily with actor/model Tony Ward, who later appeared in such films as the gay *Hustler White* (1996). Ward was her co-star in the highly controversial (because of its bisexual fantasy sequences) music video of "Justify My Love." *Truth Or Dare*, a concert documentary filmed during her 1990 Blond Ambition tour was released in May 1991.

• • •

Within a short period after their first encounter, Rosie, 29, and Madonna, 33, became solid friends. As O'Donnell has pointed out, they shared a strongly Roman Catholic childhood background. They also had overlapping personality traits. Both were very outspoken, self-sufficient, highly motivated individualists who used their careers to establish their personal identities. Professionally, these two multi-talented performers had the knack of foreseeing upcoming show business trends. This led them (especially Madonna) to reinventing them selves and becoming mainstream innovators in their specialties. If Madonna was already an international superstar and pop icon, Rosie was already a nationally recognized name. Each talented woman also nurtured a strong ambition to become a successful movie actor. And, not to be overlooked, they both thrived on diet soda and candy.

Nevertheless, the duo also differed in many ways. (Rosie would once compare them as: "She's some exotic food, and I'm just a peanut-butter-and-jelly sandwich.") For example, Rosie used her mother's death as a shield to hide behind, while Madonna employed it as a battle scar in her fight to succeed. O'Donnell, at least publicly, was far more conservative than Madonna. Rosie did her best to keep her private life—if not her troubled childhood and family observations—private. In contrast, the chameleon-like singer exploited her on-the-edge romantic life publicly and thrived on breaking taboos everywhere. Amazingly, Madonna generally got away with her stunts and indulgences. (An executive for her recording label would observe once, "There almost can be no scandal when it comes to Madonna. She's so forthcoming. Like you're surprised that she did this? It's Madonna!")

Stocky O'Donnell was frequently embarrassed and professionally limited by the shape and size of her anatomy, except when she exploited her fullish figure in her comedy act. Again, in contrast, the highly sensual singer capitalized on her appealing body shape, and thought nothing of exposing her full anatomy for the "sake of art." While men had seemingly been of minor influence in the comic's professional (or personal) life, it was quite the contrary with the high-profile vocalist. The latter had gained a great deal of savvy and success through many of her romantic associations over the years.

The two women were opposites in several other respects as well. For example, in the early 1990s, O'Donnell was earning a very good living, but she was not in the whopping seven figures category of Madonna who had long been a multi-millionaire. As such, their level of extravagance in material things differed widely. Rosie lived simply in a functional, 1,500-square-foot two-bedroom house in Los Angeles' essentially unglamorous San Fernando Valley and rarely took pricey travel holidays. In fact, burned out on night life by years of stand-up comedy on the road, O'Donnell much preferred staying at home.

In contrast, among other residences, Madonna owned a 4,500-square-foot gated home in the Sunset Strip area of Los Angeles known as Birdland. In the fall of 1993, she'd put that house on the market for just under $3 million, having bought in 1992, a $5 million, 7,800-square-foot, nine-level Hollywood abode. (In the fall of 1996, Madonna would sell the multi-level Hollywood Hills home for about $5 million, having purchased for $2.7 million a more compact,

Mediterranean-style home constructed in the 1920s.) She was a world-hopper who enjoyed the plush life and cutting edge social scene wherever she might be. Rosie tended to dress plainly and preferred baggy jeans and blouses or pant suits—all of which played down her too full figure. In contrast, Madonna favored avant-garde, provocative garb which capitalized on her curvaceous body. As far as entertainment went, Madonna was not that keen on most TV programs, while Rosie adored the medium.

They were also unlike in the area of choosing and keeping friends. Rosie preferred long-lasting situations. Her roster of best friends includes her younger sister, childhood pals, as well as fellow comics (such as Vinnie Mark) from her stand-up years and friendships she developed through the course of her career (e.g., Fran Drescher, Penny Marshall, Madonna) and work-related travel. Many of her pals were female and their bonding was not (yet) a source of fodder for the media.

In comparison, Madonna has always found it easier to relate to men. Generally, women considered her too daunting an attention-grabber and a competitor for men, and as such, generally chose not to have her in their close circle of friends. Indeed, the singer was partial to a wide variety of men in assorted walks of life. Her pre-stardom years included a succession of men who were mostly musicians. Later she turned to actors-turned-directors Sean Penn and Warren Beatty. Further on there would be actor/model Tony Ward, outré basketball star Dennis Rodman, and still later, personal trainer, Carlos Leon (the father of her child born in October 1996). Through the years she has remained very close with her younger brother, Christopher, who redecorated her elaborate Hollywood home. One noteworthy non-male friend of Madonna's in the period before she met Rosie, was in-your-face lesbian comedian Sandra Bernhard. The status of the singer's and comic's highly visible friendship in the later 1980s caused endless tabloid speculation as to its full nature. However, that friendship evaporated amidst much extended public acrimony a few years later when Madonna devoted more time to another close friend, Ingrid Casares, who had earlier been part of Bernhard's social circle.

• • •

Having established a rapport with Madonna, Rosie recalls that not long after they met in 1991, Madonna invited her to her home to preview photos for her forthcoming book, *Sex*. According to O'Donnell, "She brought out some photos, and I remember thinking, Whoaaaa! I told her, 'Yeah those are your breasts and that's you naked, all right,' but she was talking about them as casually as I might talk about snapshots of my family at Thanksgiving." Rosie says that Madonna invited her to appear in the book, but that she declined: "Right, I'm going to be page forty-eight and page forty-nine." *Sex* would be published in 1992 at a retail price of $49.95 and came sealed in a Mylar bag along with a label reading "Warning! Adults Only! Besides containing a CD disc and a bound-in comic book, it was filled with revealing photos and not-so-cogent text defining the Material Girl's outlook on sex and her sexual fantasies. There were also bare-thread shots of several celebrities (Isabella Rossellini, Big Daddy Kane, Naomi Campbell) whom the singer persuaded to be lensed for the enormously successful project (which sold out its one printing of 500,000 in about three weeks).

Before long, Madonna and Rosie would frequently go out on the town together for dinner, a fund-raiser, a premiere, a movie or to a sporting event. Regarding their hanging around together, Rosie would recall to her singer friend, "I remember one of the first times we went out to dinner and I picked up the tab, and there was this look of shock on your face. I thought, I bet people don't do that for her often, but it's an awkward position also because most of the people I know in my life—besides you—don't necessarily have a lot of money, so I always . . . end up buying. I put down the credit card all the time and then I end up resenting it later. The more courageous thing to do would be to deal with it up front."

Soon it came time for Rosie and Madonna to join the cast of *A League of Their Own* on location in the Midwest. As Madonna would later admit to O'Donnell, "Meeting you was the best thing about doing that movie." She also added, only partially kidding, "If we had to do that movie again, I wonder if there would be a way to do it where we wouldn't have to play baseball out in the sun." When the singer once inquired what Rosie liked best about working with her, Rosie spit out, "I would say my initiation in the Bodyguard of America Society. Because becoming friends with you, working with you, I realize that I have a dual role in my life. I had this yearning to be a bodyguard, and finally, knowing you, I got to fulfill that dream."

During the making of *League* Rosie became the unofficial liaison between the super famous Madonna and the less lofty remainder of the cast and crew. Because the duo played pals in the picture, they had very similar shooting schedules, so they were always together. O'Donnell of the imposing physical presence, ran interference in keeping pestering fans away from the pop diva, who was petite by comparison. Describing her unofficial role as personal bodyguard to the Material Girl, O'Donnell has said, "Before I met her, I was always reading that Sean Penn was beating everyone up, and I thought that he must be a maniac. Now that I'm friends with her, I can understand—when we go out to the movies, and she's like 90 pounds and 5'3", and everybody loves to touch her—I find myself screaming at people, 'BACK OFF, MAN!' Like I'm a pit bull."

Then too, when Madonna grew a bit testy or too full of herself on the set, it would be Rosie who could bring her down to earth. She'd shout out an impromptu zinger or a tart observation, which would deflate the singer's temporary lapse into grandiosity. For example, Rosie recalls, "On the set Madonna had this boom box. Somebody threw a ball at it, and she goes, 'Hey! You break that, you're buying me a new one.' I said, 'Madonna, you have more money than most third world countries.'"

By knowing Madonna firsthand, Rosie was to understand far more fully the down side of celebrityhood. It led Rosie to perceive, "When you're the most famous woman in the world, people are going to write stuff about you. When I first met Madonna, we went out to dinner at this place called Topo Gigio. She and I and that's it. We had dinner, we had pasta, we had tiramisu. We got home at midnight. I'm watching the [TV] news the next morning in Chicago.

'Madonna flew to New York last night and had dinner with Donald Trump.'

"This was my first experience with the press announcing something that simply was not [true]. When you read something about Madonna you have to realize her kind of fame comes along once a generation. She's as famous as Elvis Presley: Elvis, Michael Jackson . . . You don't get much bigger than that. And who she is in real life has nothing to do with this image she has created which society seems to vent all of its frustrations on.

"Not to say that she's innocent."

When the filming ended and everyone returned to Los Angeles, most of the cast and crew went their separate ways, although there was talk of reuniting for a sequel. This was the accepted way of show business. During a filming you may get very tight with your co-workers, but once the project is over, your lives tend not to overlap at all until the next time you happen to work together. However, Rosie and Madonna continued their friendship. By now Madonna was calling Rosie by her frequent nickname "Ro" and O'Donnell would refer to the singer as "Mo." At one point, the close pals even thought of producing TV projects together.

It was astonishing to Rosie that whenever she and Madonna went someplace as simple as the mall or to a movie, there'd always be people crowding around and gawking at the Material Girl. (Unlike Madonna whom fans treated as a goddess on a pedestal, Rosie had a very accessible personae. When she was spotted in public—and this happened increasingly as her popularity grew—she would be greeted by her fans on a casual, equal-level basis.) Madonna took such massive adoration mostly in stride. However, for Rosie, who herself had never gotten over being star struck, it was a strange feeling to be gawked at—even if by association. As time went on, each of these women absorbed useful life experience information from the other. Madonna learned to not distance herself so much from her following. For her part, Rosie grew to appreciate that you can't be on a chummy first name basis with every individual who walks by and wants to say hello.

Thanks to Madonna, Rosie began to socialize more on the Hollywood scene, not only to have fun, but as a means of networking for future work. O'Donnell was not yet at the career stage where she was on everyone's A list or even B list for parties and functions which were always part play, part work. However, Madonna was considered a prized asset for any occasion, as her presence generated useful media attention. As a result, she was invited everywhere. Frequently, she would drag Rosie along. Quipped Rosie, "I kind of feel like the nerd on the JV [junior varsity] squad hanging around with the head cheerleader."

It was a new world for Rosie to be accepted now by the industry's movers and shakers, even if part of her allure was being Madonna's guest. If any of this—even by indirection—expanded Rosie's ego, one particular event got her feet solidly planted back on Earth. Madonna was invited, by Irving Lazar, a legendary Hollywood agent who has since departed, to an exclusive party at Spago's Restaurant in March 1992. It was Lazar's annual Oscar night bash where the famous gathered to eat, schmooze and watch the Academy Awards or come afterward to gossip and drink and nibble fancy edibles. Rosie recalls that she and Madonna stepped out of their limousine into the midst of the cordoned-off crowd of celebrity watchers. ". . . they were going crazy, and the paparazzi . . . are screaming, 'Madonna, Kathy, Madonna, Kathy.' They thought I was Kathy Bates. And it was in some paper, 'What was Madonna doing with Kathy Bates at the . . . ' And I'm like, you know, 'No, I'm the comedian. I just did a movie. . . .' So I got that for a while."

And when Rosie was away from Madonna, on the road doing stand-up gigs, etc., she found that her highly publicized rapport with Madonna had an effect not only on how audiences perceived her, but also on what she could talk about in her comedy routines. For a long time her riff had been based on her Irish working-class roots. However, that now had to change because of her celebrity status by association with Madonna. "What I lived for so long," Rosie has explained, "was the mall and normalcy. Now I do gigs and people scream, 'So what's Madonna really like?'"

On June 16, 1992, not long before *A League of Their Own* was released, Madonna was scheduled to promote the film on Arsenio Hall's late night talk show. The singer asked Rosie to accompany her to the TV studio and, in short order, O'Donnell found herself brought on stage to join the oncamera interview. During the telecast, Madonna turned a bit bratty and her peevishness extended not only to Arsenio but to Rosie herself. O'Donnell diplomatically tried to ignore Madonna's petulance. Nevertheless, at one point, the forthright comedian turned to an equally uncomfortable Hall and confided, "If she always acted this way, she wouldn't be my friend."

A few years later, Rosie could judge from the perspective of time, "I don't think she was being mean to me. I think she was just trying to keep her head above water. . . . It helped my career. She didn't have to bring me on. But she did. And I was thankful. . . . People don't understand Madonna. Before we walked out onto Arsenio, I looked at her, and she was shaking. And I go, 'Why are you nervous? These people slept on the concrete outside to see you.' But you know what? This wasn't her venue. If I had to go out and sing, 'Don't Cry for Me Argentina,' I'd be shaking, too. . . . After the [Late Show with David] Letterman thing [a few years after the Hall fiasco], when she said 'f—' a thousand times, she stopped acting like that. And I say to her all the time, 'It's so nice to not have to apologize for being your friend any-more,' because she's been letting her real self be seen. She's really a wonderful person, and I have a tremendous amount of respect for her."

Before *A League of Their Own* was released, knowing Madonna was a great (if unexpected and unplanned) career boost for Rosie. Once the film debuted and became a major hit, Rosie's career really took off. It then became not so much a matter of "Who's that with Madonna" but increasingly, "Oh look. There's Rosie again with the Material Girl." Despite her own growing prestige, O'Donnell remained her friend's most vocal goodwill ambassador. Rosie would insist to Larry King when the talk show host interviewed Rosie in July 1993 that Madonna was a victim of her misconstrued image. "She's not callous at all. She's an incredible businesswoman, and we're very good friends. She's very sensitive and loving, and what she portrays to the public is not really very similar to who she is in real life."

As a part of this mutual admiration society, Madonna would sometimes theorize aloud to the media about her closeness to Rosie, "We have a collective longing for strong female role models. We like to be the center of attention and make people laugh—obviously her jokes are more mainstream than mine. We both like to sing—obviously my voice is more mainstream than hers. Our personal lives are usually a mess. We both love candy." A few years later, she was even to be more perceptive about their kinship, "Rosie and I speak the language of hurt people. She is very protective, loyal and maternal with me."

As more time passed, Rosie and Madonna would remain great friends, but their careers and personal lives took them in different directions. Nevertheless, they would continue to help one another out or ask the other for advice. Since Madonna had bought oceanfront property in Miami Beach, Rosie would follow suit and buy a condo in a high-rise in the South Beach section of Miami. When Rosie wanted to purchase a home outside of New York in 1996, it was Madonna who suggested she look at the former Helen Hayes estate in Nyack, New York. And when Madonna was planning ahead for stocking a well-equipped nursery for her baby girl, Lourdes Maria Ciccone Leon, born on October 14, 1996, she turned for advice to Rosie who had adopted a baby boy in May 1995.

This was long-term friendship.

· 12 ·

I think an actor *can step into a role in a sitcom and people can know they're acting. But a comic—people think that's them. Because when you do stand-up you give them you, and they're used to getting you.*

Rosie O'Donnell, June 1994

*A*fter Rosie O'Donnell completed *A League of Their Own* in late October, there was an eight-month window before the movie would be released in the summer of 1992. During this period, *League* was in post-production and the industry was buzzing whether or not it would succeed at the box-office. Perhaps the finished results would be that successful blend of *Bull Durham* (1988) and *Thelma & Louise* (1991) that the studio predicted. On the other hand, although baseball was America's favorite (sports) pastime, sports stories were notoriously chancy financial propositions with the fickle movie going public.

If *League* proved to be a smash hit, Rosie could promote "her" success into other big screen options. If, however, the movie only did mediocre business or, worse, was a flop, then the blame would be placed on O'Donnell and the other *League* participants. With her future in movies on such tenterhooks, it was reasoned that it was better to seek and accept new work now. With the mishmash *Car 54, Where Are You?* still shelved, at least Rosie's representatives could point to her having just completed a feature role in a really major motion picture. That big screen credential along with her continued success and visibility on VH-1's *Stand-Up Spotlight*, brought in some professional offers.

Carol Burnett had long been one of Rosie's idols, almost in the same pantheon with her cherished Barbra Streisand and Bette Midler. Lo and behold, Burnett summoned a very nervous O'Donnell to a meeting. Carol was about to start a new comedy variety hour on CBS-TV, that would use a repertory of mostly young talent. There was a possibility that O'Donnell could join the troupe (which eventually encompassed Chris Barnes, Meagan Fay, Roger Kabler, Richard Kind and Jessica Lundy). This potential offer did not work out and it was just as well, as Burnett's latest effort to recapture the huge TV success she'd enjoyed in the 1960s and 1970s fizzled. Her new offering, *The Carol Burnett Show*, had only a brief run (November 1, 1991—December 27, 1991) before it was canceled.

Thankfully, another viable option appeared on the horizon for Rosie. Fox TV—the fourth national network which was struggling to catch up with its well-established rivals (ABC, CBS, NBC)—was looking for new programming to flesh out its schedule. Its target audience was still geared to both teens and twentysomethings and its flagship shows remained the sitcom *Married . . . With Children*, the sketch comedy series, *In Living Color*, and the teen-oriented drama, *Beverly Hills 90210*. For the 1991-1992 season, Fox was counting on several new sitcoms: Charles S. Dutton in *Roc*, William Ragsdale in *Herman's Head*, as well as *The Sunday Comics* (which had premiered in April 1991) and *The Best of the Worst*. The former featured a mix of stand-up comedy and variety entertainment. The latter was hosted by Greg Kinnear and was, if you will, a celebration of the inane, the stupid and the really dumb things in life.

It was not exactly a stellar show lineup! However, Fox Entertainment Group President Peter Chernin was determined that, in the near future, his network would be able to supply its TV station affiliates around the country with both year-round programming and prime time entries seven-days-a-week. It was an ambitious goal in an era in which not only did a newcomer have to compete with the big three broadcast networks, but also with the increasingly popular cable networks.

As backup for the fall 1991 season, Fox had already committed to *Charlie Hoover*, a new sitcom featuring outrageous Sam Kinison. This wild man stand-up comic would play the 12" high alter ego/conscience of a 40-year-old accountant (Tim Matheson) who was suffering through a mid-life crisis. Additionally, Fox intended to air an Americanized version of a hit British TV series, *Birds of a Feather*, a dark comedy which had appeared on the BBC network. (Initially, back in March 1991, the U.S. version of *Birds of a Feather* had been a CBS-TV project but had been dropped by that network and later was acquired by Fox.) Fox reasoned that this new sitcom about blue collar workers might have some of the appeal of the hugely successful *Roseanne*, another sitcom about similar lower-income types.

Fox followed the TV industry trend in casting *Stand by Your Man* by planning to hire a stand-up comic in a focal, recurring role. Using a popular or up-and-coming comedian rather than "just" an actor made a lot of sense. It was a hip thing to do, especially for a network devoted to attracting young viewers. Besides, hopefully, the comic would have a built-in following from his club and TV/cable stand-up comedy appearances. Then too, often it was cheaper to contract a club comedian than an "established" film name. It was reasoned that, since this was supposed to be a funny show, who better to deliver the comic lines than a stand-up comic.

Rosie was uncertain whether to accept the Fox series offer. The very unpleasant and frustrating *Gimme a Break* experience of five years ago still stuck in her memory. Then she had been merely a featured player, but now she would be a co-star. That in itself presented several new complications. For one thing, the weight of the program succeeding or failing would be far more on her shoulders this time around than with *Gimme a Break*. Moreover, as she would analyze, "Unless you can have a lot of input and a lot of control, it's very hard. . . . It's not like in a movie, where somebody knows you're playing another character. When you see a sitcom, America thinks, 'Well, that's them.' . . . [On a sitcom] you really have to fight very hard if you already have a persona or an attitude."

Fox persisted in wooing Rosie and she finally agreed to their offer. Part of her acceptance was based on the fact that Leila Kenzle was to play her sister, Cindy, on the program. She was to be "the skinny, pretty version of me" said O'Donnell. The talented dark-haired Kenzle had just come off *Princesses*, a CBS-TV comedy that had fallen victim to poor ratings and the sudden departure of co-star Julie Haggerty only a month after its September 1991 launch. One of the other *Princesses* had been Rosie's acquaintance from *Car 54* days, Fran Drescher, who told Rosie of Kenzle's fine abilities and her capacity as a team player.

Pre-production got under way, with tapings set for ABC-TV City in Hollywood. Suddenly, it was decided that Kenzle's New York-like accent, delivery and overall presence—albeit far softer than

O'Donnell's rat-a-tat-tat performance rhythm—was too similar to Rosie's presentation. The producers also felt that the show needed a bigger "name" to help attract a larger viewing audience. Thus Kenzle was out after the unaired pilot was completed. (The next season, she would become Helen Hunt's best friend and business partner, Fran Devanow, on Paul Resier's hit sitcom, *Mad About You.*) As Leila's replacement, those in charge picked Melissa Gilbert. Rosie recalls, "When they told me Melissa was going to play my sister, I said, 'Yeah, of course, when you think comedy, you think Melissa Gilbert, *Little House on the Prairie.*' But she was great."

What was Melissa Gilbert, best known as a "serious" actor, doing on an assembly-line sitcom? She had spent nine seasons on Michael Landon's well-regarded *Little House on the Prairie* (1974-1983) playing Laura Ingalls Wilder. Later, she had co-starred in such TV movies as *Blood Vows: The Story of a Mafia Wife* (1987). The Los Angeles-born actress came from a noteworthy show business family. Her grandfather, Robert Crane, was the creator of Jackie Gleason's classic TV series, *The Honeymooners.* Her dad, Paul Gilbert, was an actor, and her mother, Barbara Crane, was a dancer and actor. Her younger brother, Jonathan, had played Willie Oleson on *Little House,* while younger sister, Sara, was a cast regular on the highly popular sitcom, *Roseanne.*

The truth was, by late 1991, Melissa was in need of a new project. At 27 (she was 25½ months younger than Rosie), she was at a professional crossroads. Having ended a six-year romance with actor Rob Lowe in the mid-1980s, she had since married actor/writer Paul Brinkman and they were now the parents of a three-year-old, Dakota. (She now used the professional name of Melissa Gilbert-Brinkman.) Melissa had taken time off from her career during her son's early years. Now she sought employment, but wished to avoid going on location for (TV) movies. As such, she hoped for an ongoing project that would permit her to live at home and to have greater career continuity.

It was not only Rosie who questioned Melissa's rightness for this upcoming comedy series which was to be titled *Stand by Your Man.* The veteran actress had to audition for fifteen Fox executives before she was considered acceptable. ("They laughed out loud," said Melissa. "Then I knew I was good and . . . that nobody could play the part but me." As for adopting the proper cadence and idiosyncratic movements of an unsophisticated New Jerseyite, she explained, "The minute I put on the clothes, all the mannerisms came out and just fell into place.")

The 1991-1992 TV season got under way in late August of that year.

By early 1992, at the annual Los Angeles winter gathering of TV critics from around the nation, Fox hyped its four new shows that were due to premiere that spring. There was *Stand by Your Man*, *Stray Cats* (about two good-looking men who are college roommates), *Down the Shore* (three men and three women sharing a summer beach house in New Jersey) and *Bill & Ted's Excellent Adventure* (based on the popular feature film of 1989).

By late January 1992, Fox's *Best of the Worst* had been canceled and the hour-long *The Sunday Comics* died as of March 22, 1992. The latter's demise left a chunk of empty programming time, and *Stand by Your Man* was pulled out of the bull pen to fill the Sunday night 10 to 10:30 p.m. time slot.

Taped in front of a live TV audience, *Stand by Your Man* showcased a very stocky Rosie as Lorraine Marie Dunphy Popowski who lives with her shiftless husband, Artie (Rick Hall), in a bedraggled unit at the Camelot Court Trailer Park in New Jersey. To make matters worse, worthless Artie is always carrying on with one woman or another, leaving Lorraine high and dry in all aspects of her married life. In contrast, her sister, Rochelle (Melissa Gilbert-Brinkman), is doing far better. She resides with her slick spouse, Roger (Sam McMurray), in a fashionable home at 866 Fairlawn Avenue in Paramus, New Jersey. Subservient Rochelle is very proud of Roger who owns the Prestige Patio Company and who has been selected "Builder of the Year" by *Porch and Patio News*. Whenever he can be bothered to make the effort, Lorraine's husband, Artie, does occasional odd jobs for Roger at his business.

Unbeknownst to the two sisters, Prestige Patio is an illegal business operation which launders money that Roger and Artie have been robbing from local banks. When they are caught the duo are sentenced to eight years of incarceration at the New Jersey State Penitentiary. Thereafter, distraught but bubbly Rochelle invites cynical Lorraine to live with her.

Rochelle is sweet and sexy but very naive and inept. She can't believe that her wonderful husband could have been convicted by that nasty judge and jury. In contrast, hard-as-nails Lorraine has been working since she was sixteen (just like Rosie O'Donnell in real life) and is now a stockroom clerk at Bargain Circus, a discount store. She has no illusions about life or her good-for-nothing husband. In fact, his being stuck in prison is a welcome relief for her, as, at least, she knows where he is every day.

Once moved into suburbia, blue-collar, no-frills Lorraine quickly discovers it is a big pain to abide by Rochelle's stringent house rules: wipe your shoes before entering the house, do not slam doors, put your food dishes and drink glasses in the sink, etc. What is even more annoying is that Rochelle has absolutely no understanding of finances or how to reduce her weekly expenses which are quickly depleting what little money is left in her bank account.

During the course of the weekly installments, dedicated Rochelle drags disinterested Lorraine to the prison for weekly visits with their husbands. As such, there are stale, predictable jokes about what can happen to a man locked behind bars with sex-starved inmates, the joys of abandoning adult responsibilities while a guest of the state, etc. On the home front, for "comic relief" there is snooty, horny Adrienne Stone (Miriam Flynn), Rochelle's next-door neighbor. She thrives on observing the girls' plight and crude lifestyle—it makes her feel so much better about her own ritzy, if boring existence.

Obstacles to be overcome on the weekly episodes included retrieving what's left of their husbands' stashed loot so they can pay the mounting bills; Lorraine coping with sexual harassment at Bargain Circus from her weasel of a boss; hard-nosed Lorraine pushing the insecure, work-inexperienced Rochelle to find employment; Rochelle coincidentally being hired to manage Bargain Circus which, in turn, makes her Lorraine's boss (!); Lorraine's very inelegant pals, including motorcycle slob Scab (Don Gibb), becoming undesirable habitués at Rochelle's fancy home, and so forth.

All in all, there wasn't much pay dirt to mine in these segments written by executive producers Neil Thompson and Nancy Steen and directed at a snail's pace by John Sgueglia. Matters were not improved by Melissa pushing too hard at portraying her caricature of an upscale bimbo role. The result was that Rosie, as the lowbrow blue collar woman, was left to shoulder the burden of injecting snap and believability into the ragamuffin proceedings.

Stand by Your Man debuted on Sunday, April 5, 1992. Being a Fox show, there wasn't the needed budget for a huge promotional campaign to plug the premiere. Nevertheless, with a 6.2 rating, it received the highest viewership ever for Fox in its time period. However, that still wasn't saying too much for the Sunday night 10 p.m. time slot. Fox had always run a poor fourth to the established networks and their Sunday night movies, not to mention the competition from the many cable networks and pay movie channels.

The critics roasted the meandering new half-hour show. David Bianculli (*New York Post*) rated the show a paltry ½ stars. He reasoned, "*Stand by Your Man* does not deserve much space to criticize; comedies, for one thing, should be funny." *People* magazine was equally unkind, giving the show a "D+".

On the other hand, in the midst of the round of pans there were plaudits for Rosie's efforts in bringing fun, energy and credibility to the lackluster offering. Tony Scott (*Daily Variety*) underlined, "O'Donnell plays rough well; Gilbert-Brinkman wrestles with the comic spirit but takes a fall. . . . [N]ew comedy needs lots of settling in before it draws adherents. Writers Nancy Steen, Neil Thompson play to the obvious without suggesting real mirth, while director John Sgueglia is uninspired." Howard Rosenberg (*Los Angeles Times*) was no fan of the new series. He headlined his thumbs-down review, "*Stand by Your Man* does not inspire much loyalty. In fact, it's fall-down unfunny." However, he further detailed, "Although the wee-voiced Gilbert-Brinkman . . . puts a little too much Joisey into her Jersey, this is an able cast, with stand-up comic O'Donnell and McMurray especially adroit. Unfortunately, the mostly flat script doesn't give them many opportunities to exercise their talent."

And the bible of the television industry, *TV Guide*, which rated *Stand by Your Man* a 7 out of a possible 10 rating, informed its huge readership: "It's a perfecting opportunity for some of that refreshing Fox . . . uh . . . frankness—for instance, O'Donnell would 'choose a pap smear' over a visit with her husband. Melissa tries so hard to be funny, but can't help looking as if she landed on a show called *Big House on the Prairie*. This is Rosie's show, and she's the reason to watch."

Despite the round of praise for Rosie's scene-stealing talents, *Stand by Your Man* was too leaden a proposition to survive long in the 1990s television marketplace where a show had to be an instant hit to stay alive. *Stand by Your Man* was canceled after only seven of its episodes aired, leaving four segments on the shelf.

By now, having grown far more philosophical about the ups-and-downs of show business, Rosie took the demise of *Stand by Your Man* with fairly good grace. She was buoyed by the applause of critics for her latest TV series effort. So she was able to joke of the fiasco, "It got canceled, because the Richard Simmons Deal-a-Meal program got higher ratings."

With her TV vehicle grounded, Rosie resumed her fall-back positions: accepting stand-up comedy engagements, doing charity fund-raisers, preparing for the next round of *Stand-Up Spotlight*, etc. Actually the axing of *Stand by Your Man* couldn't have happened at a better time. It left her free to promote more fully the forthcoming release of *A League of Their Own* and she quickly proved to be a movie producer's dream representative. Whether on *CBS This Morning*, *NBC Today* or *The Late Show with Jay Leno*, she demonstrated a relaxed, enthusiastic on camera presence. The result was a series of joyful on-the-air interviews which showcased exuberant Rosie to millions of TV viewers as the sharp, observant comic that she had become.

· 13 ·

... I learned from League of Their Own. *... When we were filming that, I'd watch Geena Davis and think to myself, 'She's not acting enough. She really needs to act more. She's hardly doing anything.' I didn't tell her that, because she had an Academy Award,
but in my own head, I was thinking that. Then I saw* League *and
I saw what she did, and I saw how my character was so big and so
loud. But it worked in an ensemble. ... Well, in a two-or four-char-
acter movie, it's smaller and I tried to remember Geena and how
she brought everything down and internalized everything. That's
really what I tried to do in this film [*Sleepless in Seattle*], *because
there was no room for that sort of bigness.*

Rosie O'Donnell, June 1993

B oth before and after her short-lived TV series, *Stand by Your
Man*, Rosie O'Donnell pushed hard to keep her career
momentum going. A tremendous support for her was her
fast-acting talent agent, Risa Shapiro. Not only was Shapiro responsive to O'Donnell's several career goals but she was aggressive in making them happen. Shapiro was well-positioned to accomplish this,
being part of International Creative Management (ICM), a powerful
multimedia talent agency headquartered in Los Angeles.

Since she was a little girl, Rosie had always loved to sing. She had
the type of memory which easily stored lyrics, whether they be from
beloved Broadway shows, theme songs and commercials from TV or
rock/pop words from contemporary music. She sang both loud and
enthusiastically, but was always the first to say that she didn't always
do it very well. In fact, she has said, ". . . the person I sound like when
I sing is Roseanne Arnold. But I guess the person I would like to
sound like is Wynonna Judd."

Having very eclectic music tastes, O'Donnell had long been a fan of
country singer Wynonna Judd. One evening in 1992, when Rosie was
a guest once again on Arsenio Hall's TV talk show, O'Donnell wore an
especially bouffant hairdo. When she came onstage to chat with Hall,

he commented, "Boy, you're wearing some big hair tonight." To which Rosie replied, "Yes, this is my Wynonna Judd hair." She then launched into an explanation about how big a fan she was of the Nashville star.

Within days, Wynonna's manager was in touch with Rosie's people and asked if O'Donnell would be the opening act for the singer in an upcoming Las Vegas engagement. (Judd had heard about Rosie's hairdo comment and thought it quite funny.) By now Rosie was at, or nearly at, the stage where she could be a major club headliner herself. However, she accepted the job offer because "I like the way she moves—when she sings she growls like a tiger. Of all the people out there, I really think she's the next Elvis." So O'Donnell did her stand-up shtick at Caesars Palace each night before Wynonna took over the stage. On a few occasions, Rosie also got to provide a bit of backup harmonizing for the show.

If Rosie's enthusiasm for favorite celebrities often (accidentally) guided the path of her entertainment career, her verve was often put to good use in other arenas. She was proving to be a crackerjack asset at charity fund-raisers. For example, in June 1992, she participated in the annual event on behalf of the Scleroderma Foundation held in Los Angeles. Between comedy sets (including that of Bob Saget), Rosie was in charge of the auction. When the bidding for a particular item didn't seem high enough or move fast enough, O'Donnell would jovially call on members of the audience—many of them celebrities—and badger them good-naturedly until they relented and made the desired bid. By the end of that night, she'd raised $50,000 for the charity.

When Rosie wasn't working, she took occasion to learn to play the piano, having recently bought one for her two-bedroom house in Studio City. She also loved to go online with her computer modem, chatting away on America Online under a variety of handles which she'd have to change once word got out whom she was. She also went back East, visiting friends in Commack and stopping by her former home on Rhonda Lane, now owned by another family. Seeing the same basketball hoop still nailed up over the garage door and kids playing in the street brought back memories—some of them good. While on her old home turf, she had occasion to reflect on the state of her growing celebrityhood. "People from high school would come up and say, 'Do you remember me?' And I'm like, 'Do you think I've been in a coma? That I've forgotten the first 20 years of my life'!"

In her bid for fame, Rosie also hadn't sacrificed her love of spontaneity. Years before, as a lark, she'd had her ears double-pierced, following the example of actress Nancy Addison, a regular on Rosie's beloved daytime TV soap opera, *Ryan's Hope*. Now, O'Donnell was impulsive once again. According to Rosie, ". . . my sister was in a period in her life where she wanted to do something different. I said, 'I'll go with you.'" They went to a tattoo shop where they each had one of their ankles tattooed. During the procedure, Rosie was holding Maureen's younger child, while her sister held the older girl. O'Donnell remembers, "All these big biker men were flinching, but we just sat and talked. . . ." Rosie's tattoo was of a small cross and a garland of roses that encircled her right ankle. A few years later, she proudly displayed this tattoo to Cher on O'Donnell's daytime TV talk show.

• • •

In the months before *A League of Their Own* was released, Rosie continued to audition for upcoming movies. One of these readings she was sent on was for a project by Nora Ephron. Ephron had authored such Oscar-nominated screenplays as *Silkwood* (1983) and *When Harry Met Sally . . .* (1989). For *This Is My Life* (1992), about a stand-up comic (Julie Kavner) who finds it difficult to combine motherhood with her demanding career, Nora had also directed the picture. Now she had written (with her sister Delia) a new movie about romance, based on an original story/screenplay by Jeff Arch which had been revised later by David S. Ward. One of the story's major premises was that fated mutual attraction *did* exist even in the cynical 1990s. As Ephron explained, "I think that the belief that there is some special human being out there for a person is a very strong, almost atavistic, fantasy for many people, and that fantasy has great emotional power."

Ephron also insisted that her upcoming film ". . . isn't just a movie about love. It is also about love in the movies. For so many of us who grew up on the movies, a great deal of what we feel about love is shaped by the movies we saw as kids and the movie stars we idealized." As a metaphor for this new celluloid love story, Ephron intended to interweave clips from the Cary Grant-Deborah Kerr tearjerker, *An Affair to Remember* (1957), itself a remake of *Love Affair* (1939) with Charles Boyer and Irene Dunne. Nora chose *Affair* not only because it was so well-remembered, but because of its special ties to her teenage years: ". . . my mother took me to a screening in '56, and by the end—I was about fourteen or fifteen—I was this pathetic sight, tears rolling down my face. I was convulsed in sobs. . . ."

Before too long, Tristar Pictures became committed to making Nora's project, entitled *Sleepless in Seattle* (1993). Several actors were immediately considered for a lead role. One of them was Julia Roberts. If she accepted, the studio wanted as the director either Ron Howard or Garry Marshall (who had guided Roberts through the 1990 smash hit, *Pretty Woman*). It was Roberts, however, who announced she wanted Ephron to direct the vehicle. After director Nick Castle came and went on the project, Nora was substituted to helm the project. However, by then, Julia had bowed out of the production. Another actress who coveted the female lead was Demi Moore: "Someone got me a copy of the script and I loved it. Whatever part of my fucked-up psychology it has to do with, I don't like to put myself out there like this, but I called the head of Tristar and said, 'I want to do this!' I don't like feeling that vulnerable. . . . Anyway, on *Sleepless in Seattle*, they were very nice, respectful, pleasant, all that kind of stuff they all do, but obviously, I got rejected. They wanted Meg Ryan."

Meg Ryan was a favored choice for both Tri-Star and Ephron because the actress had starred in Nora's *When Harry Met Sally . . .* Ryan let it be known that she would like her real-life husband, actor Dennis Quaid, to be her co-star. But, the studio had other thoughts. They wanted Tom Hanks who had previously co-starred with Ryan in the fantasy romance *Joe Versus the Volcano* (1990). Although that movie had misfired, the duo had displayed solid screen chemistry. More recently, they had been slated to appear opposite one another in Lawrence Kasdan's *Inns of New England*. When that project fell apart, Hanks and Ryan were brought into *Sleepless in Seattle* as a team. By now, Gary Foster was involved as the film's producer. His mother, Jackie, and Nora had been school classmates years before.

Meanwhile, even before Hanks had been committed to *Sleepless*, his actress wife, Rita Wilson, had obtained a copy of the script. The same night she read it, she and Hanks happened to attend the American Comedy Awards with Penny Marshall [who had directed Hanks in *A League of Their Own*]. After the presentations, Penny took the Hanks to a party at the home of Linda Obst, who was to be executive producer on *Sleepless*. Nora Ephron was also at the get-together. Per Wilson: "I told her that this was one of the most amazing scripts I had ever read and if she wasn't going to cast Carrie Fisher [who had played the second female lead in *When Harry Met Sally . . .*], I wanted to audition." What Wilson didn't know at the time was that Rosie O'Donnell had been signed for the role in question. (Eventually, Rita would be given a small part in *Sleepless* as Suzy, a friend of the Hanks' character, who gives an amazing recitation of why *An Affair to Remember* has such a powerful hold on women.)

However, Rosie almost did NOT win the *Sleepless* role of skeptical Becky, the Baltimore newspaper editor who is both Ryan's boss and best friend. When O'Donnell first auditioned for Nora Ephron, Rosie assumed that the screenwriter/director knew her professional credentials. However, that was not the case, for *A League of Their Own* had yet to be released and Ephron was not familiar with O'Donnell's work on TV or in the clubs. Originally, according to Ephron, O'Donnell ". . . was supposed to stay for 10 minutes, and almost an hour later we were still there." One of the chief reasons was that Rosie made it a point to explain to Ephron that, from childhood experiences, she related very much to *Sleepless'* plotline in which widower Hanks copes with bringing up a young son.

A very honest Rosie also informed her potential employer that the screenplay was ". . . a real movie-fantasy version of what happens when a mother dies and leaves young children behind: that the father is together and talks about the feelings of it. . . ." She explained how the plot differed from her father's reaction to the death of her mother. The mixture of Rosie's empathy for the story and her candor about the narrative's credibility convinced Nora to further audition this forthright candidate. According to Ephron, "The script was in the process of becoming, and after she finished reading what was there . . . I went and printed out more that was still in the computer. . . ."

By the end of the interview, Ephron was not certain what to do. Much as she had liked Rosie's reading and tart comic timing, she was still not convinced that she should hire this "unknown" for the key supporting role. "So that night at dinner," Ephron recalls, "I said to my kids, 'Oh, I saw this woman, I don't know if you've heard of her, she's on VH-1.' And they looked at me like, 'You're even older and more washed up than we've dreamed,' and that was it." So, thanks to Ephron's offsprings Rosie won the role in *Sleepless in Seattle*. It would be her second movie in a row with Tom Hanks. Meanwhile, in another instance of recrossing paths, Rob Reiner, who had directed *When Harry Met Sally . . .* agreed to play the role of Hanks' good friend in Ephron's new project.

Not long after Rosie grabbed this prime acting assignment, *A League of Their Own* was finally about to be released. While making the rounds of TV talk shows to promote the picture, O'Donnell appeared again on Arsenio Hall's talk program. In her chat session with Hall, she offered a comical impersonation—complete with nasal mumble, unique mannerisms, etc.—to illustrate Penny Marshall's quirky directing style on the set. (Never very overly reverential, except regarding her special idols—Barbra Streisand, Bette Midler, *et al*—Rosie could never resist satirizing her industry co-workers, especially those whom she really liked.) The next day Penny Marshall phoned her pal: "Ro-sie you wuh fu-nny. But you looked so fat. You gotta lose weight befoh you do No-ra's mo-vie."

That was just the start of Rosie's preparation for *Sleepless in Seattle*. On one of the first days on the project, Ephron sat down with her four leading players (Hanks, Ryan, Rosie and Bill Pullman who was cast as Ryan's soon-to-be-jilted fiancé). Nora asked the cast whether they believed in destiny. Ryan said yes, and Rosie agreed, to a point.

However, on the subject of the virtues of *An Affair to Remember*, Rosie was not as enamored of the movie "classic" as was Nora Ephron. Later, once the movie was completed, O'Donnell would publicly elaborate—to good comic effect—on the romantic excesses and lack of plotline logic in Nora's beloved *An Affair*: "First of all, she gets hit by a cab, she should've been in the emergency room and said, 'Send someone to the Empire State Building, tell him I got hit and to come over to the hospital right now.' You know, he comes in at the end of the movie and she's not even like 'Ah, you know what happened. I can't get up off the couch. I'm crippled!' If I had seen it when I was younger and more impressionable and not quite so cynical, I probably would have been moved. But being 30 when I saw it, it didn't get me."

Since Rosie's seemingly tough but really soft-hearted character would have an extended scene with Ryan in *Sleepless* in which, with tears in their eyes, they watched *An Affair to Remember* on the VCR, it required "real" acting on O'Donnell's part to convey the proper mood. About that important emotional scene, Rosie would remember, "Hysterical laughing, out-of-control laughing." Ryan would recall, "We completely just lost it, laughing, crying. It was actually part of the scene because they were like, 'Here we are crying again, we're so queer.'"

Once filming actually began in mid-July 1992, Rosie discovered how different Ephron's directing style was from Penny Marshall's. O'Donnell would later spell out the chief distinction to Bob Strauss (*Los Angeles Daily News*): "Nora was insistent that we do it exactly as written. Verbatim. Which was very difficult for me because the film I had done before was totally ad-libbed. Penny Marshall would say,

'Rosie, get anywhere close.' . . . And Nora would say, 'You said "the" instead of "a." And I'd go, 'Oh my God, I'm sunk.' I ended up writing some of the lines on pieces of paper and taping them to the grip stand—y'know, cheating. . . .It was really nice, it was really being directed and molded. It was difficult for me in a good way, in a challenging way. There was no room to be lazy."

In fact, Ephron was quite strict about all aspects of Rosie's performance on camera, from what the character wore, to the way she walked and even as to how she talked. O'Donnell recalls, "During filming, I'd sometimes fall back into my normal speaking voice which is very New York City street-sounding. Nora would get up and say, 'Cut, Rosie, it's mother—with an R.'" On other occasions, Ephron would have to remind the actor of her character's background: "You graduated with a master's from the Columbia School of Journalism, you don't speak like you're from the street."

In retrospect. O'Donnell admits, "She really helped me . . . Because I noticed in my stand-up act, or when I do *Arsenio*, my accent is much thicker. It's not on purpose, it's out of nerves. When I get nervous and I push, it becomes much more streety, much more Fonzie and Sylvester Stallone-ish. She wouldn't let that happen for which I'm glad."

Sleepless in Seattle was filmed between July 13, 1992 and September 25, 1992 with the renowned Sven Nykvist in charge of cinematography. Nine of those production weeks were spent on location in Washington shooting at such Seattle sites as Queen Anne Hills, a houseboat on Lake Union and Pike's Market. Even the key New York City Empire State Building sequences were filmed in the Seattle area. The Building's famed observation platform was recreated in an airplane hangar at Seattle's soon-to-be-defunct Sand Point Naval Base. However, none of the Washington locale work included O'Donnell's character.

In actuality, all of Rosie's scenes were shot in Hollywood, with the exception of brief establishment shots showing O'Donnell and Meg Ryan entering and leaving the *Baltimore Sun*'s office building in Maryland. As has always been true in filmmaking, not every scene an actor films ends up in the final cut used for theatrical release. One such instance was a sequence involving Rosie's and Meg's characters dealing with a Christmas tree in the bathroom of her place. Rosie found this cut to be ironic. It was the ". . . scene I couldn't remember because it was a whole page long, and I ended up, like, writing it and taping it to a guy's leg. This poor guy was trying to stand there . . . I sexually harassed him the entire time . . . In a loving, non-offensive way."

As in *League*'s filming, Rosie's presence on the set had residual benefits. During downtime between scenes, she would amuse co-workers with comedy routines, spontaneous jokes about the day's events or engage others in games of trivia—especially dealing with television subjects. As Meg Ryan would attest of the *Sleepless* shoot, "Whenever I saw I was working with her that day, I knew I would be having a blast and my stomach would cramp because I was laughing so hard. She is so amazingly quick. . . ."

In a different vein, Rosie proved to be an iconoclast on the movie lot. As much as it meant to her to be making grade A movies, she had an inner compulsion that demanded she be her irrepressible self. This was especially true when it came to speaking her mind. Such an attitude from a relative industry newcomer impressed her co-stars. Meg Ryan cites, "When we were filming *Sleepless*, there were about eight of us gathered around a table for lunch. A big studio executive was telling us how he was going to release Woody Allen's *Husbands and Wives* early to capitalize on the pubic scandal that had engulfed Allen and Mia Farrow. Rosie told him she thought it was a really slimy thing to do. She was funny about it, but she didn't back from telling him just how offensive she found it."

By the time *Sleepless in Seattle* was released on June 24, 1993 (almost exactly a year after Rosie's and Tom's *A League of Their Own* had bowed), the movie had been much hyped and its romantic plotline had become familiar to one degree or another to a great many potential filmgoers.

Sleepless in Seattle revolves around recently widowed architect Sam Baldwin (Tom Hanks). Deeply grieving over his wife's death, he and his young son, Jonah (Ross Maliger), relocate to Seattle where they live on a plush houseboat. Time passes, but Sam cannot put the tragedy behind him. On Christmas Eve, the son happens to tune in to a radio call-in program, *You and Your Emotions*. He is inspired to phone into the show to get advice about his dad's morose behavior. The talk show psychologist (Linda Wallem) convinces Jonah to put Sam on the line. As Baldwin relates his sad story to a nationwide radio audience, it becomes clear how sensitive and caring this pained man is. Soon thereafter, the talk show is besieged by letters and calls from female listeners who want to get in touch with this appealing single parent who was nicknamed on the air as "Sleepless in Seattle."

One of those who hears the broadcast is Annie Reed (Meg Ryan), a

Baltimore newspaper reporter who is engaged to marry Walter Jackson (Bill Pullman), a nice but too predictable man. Annie confides her romantic fantasy about "Sleepless in Seattle" to her good friend, Becky (Rosie O'Donnell) who is also her editor at the newspaper. Annie impulsively writes a letter to the anonymous phone caller in which she pours forth her inner feelings on life and suggests that they meet at the top of the Empire State Building on St. Valentine's Day. Later, in a more rational mood, she throws the letter away. Unbeknownst to her, Becky mails the letter which is among the huge stack that reaches Sam. Anxious for his father to find new happiness, Jonah encourages his dad—as does Sam's friends—into meeting a few of the letter-writers who live in the area. In the meantime, Jonah, who has taken a liking to Annie through her sincere yet romantic letter, replies to her in his father's name.

Tired of being so logical, Annie gives in to her inner romantic self and flies to Seattle on a whim. She tracks down Sam and Jonah whom she sees briefly from across the street. However, she doesn't introduce herself and quickly leaves. Back on the East Coast, she is now determined to be rational and go through with her marriage to the very patient Walter.

Later, Jonah, who has a strong desire to meet Annie, flies to Manhattan on his own. When Sam discovers his son's whereabouts, he takes the next plane to New York City where he is reunited with his "runaway" boy. Explaining the truth to his dad, Jonah urges him to keep the Empire State Building rendezvous. Sam reluctantly agrees. Meanwhile, Annie comes to New York City on St. Valentine's Day with her fiancé. At dinner she breaks off the engagement, and rushes to the Empire State Building, hoping against hope that Sam will have kept their "appointment." Sam, Jonah and Annie have an emotional meeting, full of bright promise for their futures together.

As was traditional with big movie releases, *Sleepless in Seattle* had dual premieres, one in New York City and another in Los Angeles, with the after-screening festivities geared as charity fund-raisers. Rosie was on hand for both events. On the East Coast she attended the screening and the post-showing party at the Plaza Hotel, where the celebrity guests included Madonna. The Los Angeles premiere was held at a Century City movie theatre with the post-screening party at the Los Angeles Ballroom of the nearby Century Plaza Hotel. The occasion raised a whopping $2.5 million for the Motion Picture and TV Fund Foundation. At the gala, when Rosie was questioned by the media—yet again—what she thought of the movie's romantic theme, she agreed that thanks to destiny there is someone for everyone. She then quipped, ". . . and whoever it is, I hope they send me an application soon, because the space has been vacant for an awfully long time."

A great many mainstream critics found the PG-13-rated *Sleepless in Seattle* too prefabricated and coy, even in its nostalgic soundtrack score which included old recordings of pop standards sung by Jimmy Durante. Owen Gleiberman (*Entertainment Weekly*) graded it a "C". He reasoned, ". . . don't get me wrong: I have no objection to shamelessly corny love stories that make you well up with tearful joy. I just don't like when the movie does the welling up for you." An equally uncharmed Joanne Kaufman (*People*) complained, ". . . the movie's problems go deeper than the dialogue; it's whole premise is flawed. Hanks is never made to seem sufficiently winning, nor Pullman sufficiently outclassed (in fact, he's a sweetheart) to make Ryan's obsession comprehensible."

Less critical was Roger Ebert (*Chicago Sun-Times*) who judged, "*Sleepless in Seattle* is as ephemeral as a talk show, as contrived as the late show and yet so warm and gentle I smiled the whole way through." Even more positive was Michael Wilmington (*Los Angeles Times*): ". . . a real charmer, [it] is a romantic comedy about an ultimate long-distance relationship. Emphasize 'romantic.' Emphasize 'comedy.' It delivers both."

Long Island's *Newsday* newspaper found merit to the picture ("Ephron is a very funny writer, and we're never far from a good laugh") and took occasion to praise its hometown-girl-made-good: "Comedian Rosie O'Donnell, playing Annie's pep-talking co-worker, has the bulk of the best one-liners and her performance is a joy." The *Los Angeles Village View* lauded, "With terrific supporting performances, Rob Reiner, Rosie O'Donnell, Bill Pullman, and Rita Wilson, the film frequently lampoons its own melodramatic ancestry." Andy Klein (*Los Angeles Reader*) endorsed, "The supporting cast includes very funny turns by Rosie O'Donnell, Amanda Maher, Rob Reiner, and even Calvin Trilin [who played Meg Ryan's grandfather]. . . ."

Contrary to the cynical critics, *Sleepless in Seattle* proved to be perfect summer fare for many moviegoers. By mid-August 1993, the weepy movie which cost about $23.3 million to make, had grossed over $100 million at the box-office. Its success proved anew that Nora Ephron knew what the public wanted. (On the other hand, Warren Beatty's very costly, laboriously produced remake of *An Affair to*

Remember, entitled *Love Affair*, released in 1994, was both a critical and financial disappointment, despite a cast that included Annette Bening, Garry Shandling and Katharine Hepburn.)

For her performance as the abrasive but sweetly supportive foil for Meg Ryan, Rosie received an American Comedy Award nomination, but lost the prize to Lily Tomlin of *Short Cuts*. Of greater importance to O'Donnell's future in films was the effect that *Sleepless* helped to keep her from being typecast in tomboy roles similar to her part in *A League of Their Own*. Michael P. Scasserra (*Theater Week*) would be among those show business watchers who saw a trend developing in Rosie's latest movie releases: "The effectiveness of these [screen] roles is the result of an easy-going, trustworthy quality O'Donnell herself has dubbed 'best friendish.' Without planning, she has become a kind of a contemporary version of Eve Arden [the talented, acerbic second banana in countless movies of the 1930-1950s as well as the star of radio/TV/movies' *Our Miss Brooks*]. She's the girl-next-door—the one you have a blast with at the prom after the homecoming queen turns you down or, perhaps, the sister who teases you at home and then defends you when the big kids get on your case."

Rosie was now an established movie name.

· 14 ·

It feels good to know what my limits are and my boundaries and what I will do and won't do, you know.

Rosie O'Donnell, July 1993

*B*y mid-summer 1992, Rosie O'Donnell was on a roll! Her *A League of Their Own* was a smash hit, and she was already at work on her showy if smaller role in the prestige production, *Sleepless in Seattle*. However, that was just the beginning of her professional whirlwind that year.

On national TV she seemed to be "everywhere." She was a guest on the premiere episode of *Women Aloud* (July 13, 1992) on the Comedy Central Cable Network. She was a presenter on the 44th annual Prime Time Emmy Awards (August 30, 1992) where she wore a most off-beat Todd Oldham-designed leopard-and-velvet outfit and delivered a quasi TV-bashing monologue. Later, she was one of the celebrity participants on CBS-TV's *Back to School '92* special (September 8, 1992) and performed via a brief taped segment on Showtime Cable's *Hurricane Relief* special (October 16, 1992) that singer Gloria Estefan put together on behalf of the disaster victims in Florida. Rosie even showed up on a segment (November 4, 1992) of Fox Network's Generation X soap opera, *Beverly Hills 90210*. In this episode, Brandon (Jason Priestley), Donna (Tori Spelling) and David (Brian Austin Green) are among those attending an AIDS charity fund-raiser. Hosting the televised event is none other than boisterous Ms.

131

O'Donnell exuding her patented snappy joviality. (What typecasting!) In the course of the plot, she chit-chats with the studio audience and offers demure, blushing Donna dating advice regarding her boyfriend, David: "Don't let him pressure you," she advises. "There's nothing wrong with being a virgin."

Of this rash of TV appearances, the most fun for Rosie was her *Jeopardy* stint. For the week of October 26-30, 1992, the game show devoted itself to rounds of *Celebrity Jeopardy* using such personalities as Regis Philbin, Carol Burnett, Cheech Marin, Donna Mills, Luke Perry, Beau Bridges, Andrew Shue and Rosie as special contestants. All their winnings were earmarked for charity. No slouch when it came to trivia, Rosie beat such fellow rivals as Ed Begley Jr. and Robert Guillaume in their *Jeopardy* rounds.

Once she completed *Sleepless in Seattle*, Rosie accepted roles in several additional films—some good projects, some not. To her way of thinking, moviemaking was a more effective (and of course more lucrative) alternative to pursuing the comedy club circuit, and it proved to be a wise decision. The 1980s' stand-up comedy boom which had generated such a tremendous expansion in the number of clubs around the country had reached a saturation point. As Rick Vanderkynff cited in a January 1993 *Los Angeles Times* article, "The business of being funny has finally met the realities of the more austere '90s." Vanderkynff explained, "Nationally, club attendance has fallen sharply at even the prestige venues, a situation blamed not only on a delayed reaction to the nation's economic woes, but also on everything from too much stand-up on cable TV to too many mediocre sound-alike comics." In addition, comic Barry Weintraub, the publisher of the *Comedy USA* industry trade directory, pointed out to Vanderkynff: "What the clubs get [today] are bodies to buy drinks. It's no longer people who love comedy as much as people who are looking for something to do." According to Weintraub, many clubs had or were switching to more variety-type entertainment—to break up the steady stream of straight monologists.

When an established film actor accepts a movie cameo, it's usually for one of two reasons beyond receiving a hefty paycheck for little effort. Typically, the performer is either on the way up or the way down on the Hollywood ladder and wants big-screen exposure. There was no doubt that Rosie was in the former category.

James L. Brooks had won three Oscars (writer/director/producer) for *Terms of Endearment* (1983) and his follow-up film, *Broadcast News*

(1987), had been equally well received. More importantly to a TV maven such as Rosie O'Donnell, Brooks had spent 25 years in TV creating such landmark programming as *The Mary Tyler Moore Show*, *Rhoda*, *Taxi*, *Lou Grant* and *The Simpsons*. Now Brooks was preparing a new film, one that would explore his personal observations of the movie industry. Nick Nolte and Albert Brooks (no relation to the filmmaker), Julie Kavner and Joely Richardson would star. However, director Brooks announced that the story would unfold as a musical, a bad choice of genre in the 1990s! Nevertheless, when Rosie was offered a cameo in *I'll Do Anything* she accepted, thrilled to work with "the legendary Jim Brooks."

Brooks was well aware that such recent Hollywood musicals as Bette Midler's *For the Boys* (1991) and Disney's *Newsies* (1992) had floundered at the box-office. Nevertheless, the filmmaker was insistent on having song and dance in his production because, as he later analyzed, "I thought the musical form would get me to more of the truth. . . . I thought music would articulate that which you couldn't legitimately articulate in dialogue like a child talking about her loneliness, something you don't express at that age." Since this was Brooks' first movie since *Broadcast News*, Columbia Pictures acceded to his many wishes. Meanwhile, everyone puzzled how the director would make on camera singers of such non-singers as gravel-voiced Nolte, Albert Brooks and nasal-twanging Julie Kavner.

The storyline of *I'll Do Anything* deals with Matt Hobbs (Nick Nolte), a talented, middle-aged New York actor who hopes to find that big break in the Hollywood moviemaking scene. While doing the required casting rounds he meets beautiful Cathy Breslow (Joely Richardson), an ambitious and rising studio project development executive. She introduces him to her powerful industry boss, Burke Adler (Albert Brooks), the head of Popcorn Pictures. The latter is a crass purveyor of schlock action pictures and a growling man too blinded by his own ego to appreciate his proficient audience research analyst, Nan Mulhanney (Julie Kavner), who just happens to love him.

Later, Adler offers Matt a humiliating job as his chauffeur/gofer, one which the actor accepts because he desperately needs money. Hobbs' ex-wife (Tracey Ullman) has just been jailed for criminal activity and now Matt must raise their six-year-old daughter (Whittni Wright) whom he's not seen in years. As the earnest father and once-bratty daughter begin to bond, she ironically lands the lead in a TV series. Meanwhile Matt is further disillusioned by the film business when his girlfriend, Cathy, sacrifices him to better her career.

To provide a sense of tinseltown reality to his film, Brooks hired several well-known personalities for small cameo assignments. For example, there were Woody Harrelson and Patrick Cassidy as performers in *Ground Zero*, the action film within the film. In the proceedings, Sir Ian McKellen and Joely Fisher have brief appearances. Then, partway into the movie, Rosie pops up on camera. She is the chatty makeup artist at *The Rainbow House* TV show where the hero is making an on camera test. Dressed in a smock, she gossips nonstop as she dabbles makeup onto Matt Hobbs' face. Then she disappears completely from the storyline, i.e., at least in the movie's final cut. Originally Rosie and Woody Harrelson were to have shared a rap song number.

I'll Do Anything finished its filming in late January 1993, with its twelve musical numbers (which included songs by Sinead O'Connor, Carole King and The Artist Formerly Known as Prince) intact. Twyla Tharp had provided the choreography for the full-scale production numbers. At this point, the movie was still within its $39.5 million budget. Everything went downhill thereafter when the results were viewed by displeased studio executives. Brooks spent months tinkering with the film. Then, after unfavorable test screenings in August 1993, Brooks went through an elongated additional period of severe reediting. He cut the bulk of the musical numbers, then put them back in, then deleted them again. Most of the recorded songs ended as background music in the final release print. Meanwhile, he had to shoot new connective scenes to replace the plot points when he sliced out the key songs. At the end of the lengthy and expensive post-production, a weary Brooks sighed, "I lost sight of my goals, and then I got them back, for which I'm really grateful. I feel like I made three movies. The first was a musical, the second was the compromise, and the third is what you see now."

When the emasculated movie finally opened in early 1994 it was given respectful attention because of James L. Brooks' industry standing. However, as Brian Lowry (*Daily Variety*) reported, it was "Destined to be known forever in industry circles as the musical that wasn't . . . [it] suffers from a choppiness that betrays its history." Ralph Novak (*People*) noted, "Even that veteran schmaltzmeister, writer-director James L. Brooks, can't wring much charm out of the story, allowing everyone to overact egregiously. He also recycles the standard Hollywood clichés, from car phones to power dinners, without scoring any satirical points."

After only three weeks in national release, *I'll Do Anything* dropped off the film money earning charts, having taken in only $10.16 million at the box-office. Thankfully, O'Donnell's participation in the disastrous venture had been minimal and did no damage to her burgeoning career.

• • •

Carl Reiner, a veteran actor, director, producer and writer from TV's golden age had in more recent years turned to directing feature films: *Enter Laughing* (1967), *Oh, God!* (1977), *Summer School* (1987), etc. He was also the father of actor/director Rob Reiner and the ex-father-in-law of Penny Marshall who had once been married to Rob. So it was not surprising that when he was casting his new movie, Carl Reiner should think of Rosie for a part. After all, she'd worked for Penny in *A League of Their Own* and with Rob in *Sleepless in Seattle*. As such, he offered her a fun cameo in his new feature, first titled *Triple Indemnity* and then released as *Fatal Instinct* (1993).

The project was one of the many screen spoofs that owed their supposed box-office viability to the long-ago but still trend-setting film comedy, *Airplane!* (1980). Reiner's entry was a satirical send-up of such steamy, dark studies of compulsive behavior as *Fatal Attraction* (1987), *Basic Instinct* (1992), *Sleeping with the Enemy* (1991), *A Kiss Before Dying* (1991) and *Double Indemnity* (1944). Its premise revolves around an amazingly obtuse individual (Armand Assante) who works as a lawyer by day and a cop at night. His sexually insatiable wife (Kate Nelligan) is having a torrid affair with a bumbling auto mechanic (Christopher McDonald). She schemes to murder her husband to gain her freedom and his life insurance. Tied into the helter-skelter caper is the hero's vengeful ex-client (James Remar), a panty-free sexpot (Sean Young), and the lawyer's sadomasochistic girl Friday (Sherilyn Fenn). In a non-essential sequence within this soggy parody, O'Donnell appears as a tough-looking bird shop owner. In her brief moments on camera with the hero, she screeches louder than her feathered merchandise.

When *Fatal Instinct* bowed in late October 1993, Chris Williams (*Los Angeles Times*) warned of this PG-13 rated entry: "If you somehow managed to miss any of the erotic murder thrillers of the last five years or so, *Fatal Instinct* offers a quick—though not painless—primer in virtually every psychosexual one of them." Owen Gleiberman

(*Entertainment Weekly*) cautioned, ". . . we know this school of parody almost too well by now; even its surprises don't surprise us." On the plus side, he indicated that the movie boasted ". . . a group of actors who inhabit their roles with glee." *Fatal Instinct* made little impact with moviegoers. It grossed only $7.63 million in its first three weeks of domestic release. And of course Rosie's participation was so minimal that some viewers were sure that it had been Kathy Bates as the eccentric bird keeper.

Far more central to O'Donnell's expanding movie career was her participation in *Another Stakeout* (1993). This film would provide her with her largest, if not most fully developed, movie role to date. It also proved to be her most creatively satisfying assignment thus far. The picture was to be directed by John Badham, who had made his mark with such earlier features as *Saturday Night Fever* (1977), *Dracula* (1979) and *Blue Thunder* (1983). After completing her assignment in *Another Stakeout*, Rosie would say of Badham, "He knew exactly what he wanted. He knew what shots to do. He let the actors improvise."

Actually, there were several reasons why she coveted the *Another Stakeout* part. For one thing, it would satisfy one more of her moviemaking ambitions. According to Rosie, ". . . I've been a huge Richard Dreyfuss fan since *The Goodbye Girl* (1977). After *A League of Their Own*, whenever I would get a script, I'd say to my agent, 'Is Richard Dreyfuss getting this script, too, because I think me and Richard Dreyfuss would be cute. . . .'" For another, "After *A League of Their Own* I got all the tough girl roles [submitted to me]. So I've tried to stay away from that. *Sleepless in Seattle* was very different. I try to do different things within the parameters of what I feel I'm capable of doing."

Back in 1987, John Badham had directed Richard Dreyfuss and Emilio Estevez in *Stakeout*, a surprise box-office hit about two undercover cops on a dangerous surveillance assignment. This audience-pleaser blended comedy with action in a pleasing concoction that grossed $56 million in ticket sales for Touchstone, a film company that is part of Disney Pictures. Quite naturally, since then, Badham and Touchstone had been toying with a potential sequel. Finally, in the fall of 1992, the pieces fell into place with Dreyfuss and Estevez signed to repeat their roles. Another returning player would be the unbilled Madeleine Stowe who would again be Dreyfuss' girlfriend onscreen, a fiery woman frustrated by the toll his career has taken on their seesawing relationship.

O'Donnell's name had first come up for consideration at a planning session for *Another Stakeout*. It was then that studio head, Jeffrey Katzenberg, had blurted out Rosie's name as an interesting possibility for the lead female role. That notion had never occurred to director Badham. However, he respected the suggestion because Katzenberg's "instincts are million-dollar instincts." Once the director met Rosie and she auditioned with Dreyfuss, Badham was convinced that O'Donnell was right for the part. "There were instant sparks with Dreyfuss," he would explain.

At a later point in the casting process, O'Donnell was asked if she could drive a stunt car. It was a talent deemed necessary for the film's proposed action scenes. Always game and particularly eager for this job, Rosie said "yes." Actually, at the time, she couldn't even drive a stick shift vehicle.

Before O'Donnell had been brought into the mix, the character of uptight assistant district attorney Gina Garrett was planned to be a far more straight-laced role. However, said Emilio Estevez, "When we brought her [Rosie] aboard, the dynamics changed." What had happened was that the filmmakers had decided to take a leaf out of a competing and very successful cop movie series, *Lethal Weapon (1987)*. That Mel Gibson-Danny Glover franchise had relied on the comic presence of Joe Pesci in its two follow-ups (1989, 1992) to keep the series premise from going entirely flat. It was anticipated that Rosie could do the same for *Another Stakeout*.

In comparing the composition of *Stakeout* to its sequel, Dreyfuss would later assess, "The first film is a tripod. It's a comedy, thriller, romance. And the comedy doesn't stand out overwhelmingly above the other elements." As to the follow-up venture, he analyzed, "This film is 80 percent comedy, 20 percent thriller, and no romance."

Production got under way in late January 1993. After location work in Las Vegas for the opening sequence (which included a huge explosion), the production moved to British Columbia. Although the film was set in Seattle, Washington, shooting in Vancouver was more convenient and economical. Much of the moviemaking was accomplished at the Bridge Studios in Burnaby, as well as the False Creek marina area. Once again, rather than going to Bainbridge Island (near Seattle), the filmmakers substituted Bowen Island (which is 20 minutes by boat from Vancouver) as the site for much of the plot activity. The exteriors of two houses on Bowen Island were duplicated on the Vancouver sound stages.

Right from the start of filming, Rosie recalls, "Nearly every scene had some form of improvisation." In fact, Badham encouraged the cast to be involved and provide suggestions. Of the trio, Dreyfuss took the most opportunities to add a lot of his ideas to the project. As Estevez details, "Richard is a wonderful comedian. Often time he would goose Rosie and me to make it bigger, broader. The two of us would look at each other and say, 'It's too big.' These scenes ended up in the movie with all of Richard's ideas and there really was no ceiling too high. They're in the movie, they're funny and he was right."

Meanwhile, back in Burbank, California, the extensive improvisational process on *Another Stakeout* greatly concerned Touchstone and Disney executives. As Dreyfuss explains, "On this film we worried because we were going down a particular path wearing a certain set of clown hats and big, funny red noses. And every once in a while the studio would call and say, 'Take off those noses! Take off those clown hats! Make this movie like adults!' And we'd say, 'Well, we think we're going down the right path.' We didn't really know until we put the film together and showed it in previews that the stuff we had gone down that road for . . . stood up."

On the whole, Rosie has fond memories of making *Another Stakeout*: "It was such a wonderful working environment. It was so much improvisation—you know, give and take. And we laughed all day on the set . . . It reminded me of when I would watch outtakes as a kid of Burt Reynolds-Dom DeLuise movies. . . ."

If working with Oscar-winner Dreyfuss met her expectations, she was pleasantly surprised by her other co-star, Emilio Estevez. To her astonishment, this refugee from the 1980s Hollywood Brat Pack proved to be ". . . the most gorgeous and the nicest man that I have ever met. Bar none." Then too there was singer Paula Abdul, who, at the time, was married to Estevez. O'Donnell describes, "Paula would come up to visit. We went roller skating and all these children would see Paula and start to cry. Not scream. She went over and lifted them up and talked to them. It was the most beautiful thing that I have ever seen . . . Angelic. I thought I had to put this in a film. So I wrote a film, a musical with her videos. Where she would do the soundtrack. A movie with children." (The project never came to be.) Even after the wrap-up of *Another Stakeout*, Rosie kept in touch with both Estevez and Dreyfuss ". . . in a way that I haven't with other people in films that I've done."

On the other hand, there was one cast member of *Another Stakeout* who tremendously annoyed Rosie. It was the canine who played her pet dog, Archie, within the film. "Stupidest dog on the planet. It's the dumbest dog in America. You'd be doing a simple scene, it would take off the other way. And . . . the dog trainer of no personality, would say things like, 'Well, you know, Ryder's keying on somebody in the other house. They must be opening a candy bar somewhere. And I don't think that, you know, people are distracting. There must be a baby around the block or something, that's why Ryder keeps getting a little spooked by that.' Ryder is a stupid dog. That's the bottom line. It's the dumbest dog I ever met in my life, and I hope I never see it again. And when I—we wrapped I gave her an ID bracelet, the dog trainer, that said 'Kill the dog.' Can't stand it. Now Betty White's going to hate me forever." As a postscript, O'Donnell adds, ". . . . Hey, I love dogs. It's that specific dog that I'm not crazy about. I would never harm the dog. No animals were hurt making this film."

In actuality, *Another Stakeout* had a rather flat premise. A major witness, Lu Delano (Cathy Moriarity), for an upcoming big organized crime trial is on the lam after her Las Vegas safe house has been blown up by the mob. The law anticipates that she will eventually resurface at the Bainbridge Island summer home of her friends, Brian and Pam O'Hara (Dennis Farina, Marcia Strassman). As such, veteran Seattle police detective Chris Lecce (Richard Dreyfuss) and Bill Reimers (Emilio Estevez) are temporarily reassigned to help the DA's office locate Lu.

To the cops' chagrin, they must work as a closely-knit team with bossy, worrywart Gina Garrett (Rosie O'Donnell), a loud-speaking, plain-appearing lawyer. Under her browbeating command, the trio rent the home next to the O'Haras. She creates their cover: Chris is to pretend to be her husband, while Bill is his son by a prior marriage. As the stakeout proceeds, Lu appears on the island, but so do hitman Tony Castellano (Miguel Ferrer) and a crooked federal agent (John Rubinstein). Before the finale, there is the requisite shoot-out/showdown. In the process, Gina has become a more carefree person, the happily married Bill has matured and the highly neurotic Chris has gained a more useful perspective on romantic relationships and work.

The chief virtues of *Another Stakeout* are the antic banter between the cop partners, and, more importantly, the give and take between O'Donnell's and Dreyfuss' characters as they constantly attempt to outsmart one another. Actually, their scenes together are immediately amusing because of their obvious physical disparity: i.e., taller and big-boned Rosie towers over Richard's aberrant cop. Sadly, the plotline does not allow for romantic overtones between the two characters.

In her best footage, Rosie's Gina displays an amusing amount of self-control as she pretends to be blissfully serene and passive while the O'Haras are their dinner guests. Then the next moment, when the O'Haras are out of range, she is sniping at her pretend-mate. At other instances, workaholic Gina who has always been a straight arrow on the job now turns weepy when under pressure. She also proves to be a bit nutty in the kitchen. She is the one with a penchant for such bizarre culinary concoctions as boiled eggs dressed up like penguins, a meat loaf shaped like an armadillo, etc.

Interestingly, it would prove to be actor Dennis Farina, as the next-door neighbor, who grabbed the limelight in *Another Stakeout*. In actuality, he was a veteran of 18 years with the Chicago police force and had begun his screen career with a small role in *Thief* (1981). Once he had turned full-time professional performer, he'd gone on to such projects as playing Windy City cop Mike Torello on TV's *Crime Story* (1986-1988) and being featured in such movies as Robert De Niro's *Midnight Run* (1988). In *Another Stakeout*, Farina has a memorable sequence in which his Brian O'Hara, along with his on camera wife, are reluctant dinner guests at their neighbors. In short order, he makes all kinds of wrong assumptions about his hosts and gobbles down his meal hoping to put a quick end to the bewildering evening.

By the time *Another Stakeout* was released in July 1993, studio executives had edited out much of the on-screen violence and had eliminated most of the foul language so that the film would receive at least a PG-13 rating rather than R rating its predecessor had earned. Vincent Canby (*New York Times*) spoke for the majority when he summarized, "It's thin material, but what appears to have been a fortune was spent to make it look heftier than it is. . . . *Another Stakeout* defies criticism. Everyone who goes to see it will probably know what to expect. There's no need to say more."

Rosie received mixed film notices. Leah Rozen (*People*) decided, "Only O'Donnell, all brass leavened with sudden comic weeping spells, adds life to the proceedings." Abbie Bernstein (*Drama-Logue*) concurred. He labeled her ". . . the formidable Rosie O'Donnell, who is a force to be reckoned with as Gina. Almost absurdly emotional yet wonderfully sharp and bulldog-stubborn, Gina as played by O'Donnell is a splendidly comic figure who remains in the memory after the film concludes." Roger Ebert (*Chicago Sun-Times*) endorsed, "O'Donnell is good at standing her ground and speaking her mind. . . ."

In contrast, Bob Strauss (*Los Angeles Daily News*) reported, ". . . the saddest casualty of this indifferent sale item is O'Donnell. Because she was such a wisecracking firecracker . . . [in past films] you're really pulling for her to sparkle in a more sensitive, less cartoonish role. But this isn't it; Gina is so drab, you just wish Rosie would have gone all out for the gags. . . ."

A sympathetic John Anderson (*Newsday*) felt that Rosie had gotten shortchanged: "The one peculiar thing in *Another Stakeout* is that the talented O'Donnell, currently appearing in *Sleepless in Seattle* and in the part-time role of 'Madonna's best friend,' would be given a role that relies so exclusively on the kind of clichéd female characterizations that went out with June Cleaver."

Then, there was Sean O'Neill (*Los Angeles Village View*) who used his reviewer's post to make a prediction about Rosie's movie career: "O'Donnell is betrayed by her inexperience at times, surrounded as she is by veterans, but her comic timing, perfected by years of stand-up, finally gets her through. (With any luck and a good agent, she will be the female equivalent of a John Goodman/George Wendt type—the hefty, goodhearted second banana who makes the star look glamorous—and she'll have a film career for years.)"

In its first eight weeks of domestic distribution, *Another Stakeout* grossed only $19.06 million at the box-office. As such, in ratio to its heavy production cost, it was both a critical and financial disappointment. A few years later, when a major newspaper critic mentioned to Rosie that he'd missed seeing *Another Stakeout*, she shrugged and said, "A lot of people did. It just screams 'video.'"

· 15 ·

*I hate to say this because I think real actors are going to be miffed,
but I don't really prepare [for screen roles]. I read the script and
think who the character is to me. . . . I haven't done any roles like*
Sophie's Choice *or* The French Lieutenant's Woman *or* Norma
Rae, *where I really had to work on the character. My movies have
been funny and light, with well-written and well-defined characters. I haven't had to delve into who I think the person really is.*

Rosie O'Donnell, September 1993

*I*n the spring of 1993, Rosie O'Donnell was settling into a comfortable routine of making one movie after another. She was still
involved with VH-1's *Stand-Up Spotlight*, but it was becoming a
less important facet of her blossoming career. She also did stand-up,
but now on an infrequent basis. As she explained, "I do gigs if somebody I like is working in Vegas and they want me to open for them. I
love working in Vegas; a lot of comics hate it. I love it. And I do it all
the time for benefits. But I'm doing jokes that I've been doing for 15
years, and the audience can mouth them along with me. Well, it's time
to get a new act, and if I don't have the time to work on it, it's really
unfair of me to go tour around the country and do the same old jokes
that I've been doing forever."

When asked if she didn't think it was now beneath her to be a club's
opening act, she responded, "No, I love to open. See, a lot of comics
don't like to open . . . I love it. You only have 20 minutes, you go on
first, you're like the appetizer, you don't have to have new material, and
then you get to see a great show."

By now O'Donnell was an increasingly recognized personality
everywhere she went and she feared that fame could easily go to her
head. "It's strange, celebritydom: it's like a tidal wave. You try to keep

your head above water until it rushes over and you can get your feet back on the ground. It'd be easy to be a complete asshole: everyone defers to you. Everyone thinks you're of more value. And you lose your humanity in many ways. The real goal is to accept yourself, and then it's not as difficult. You're not as pliable to other people's image or demands or accusations. You have a firm grasp of who you are and what you're about and on you go."

She also admitted that being a laugh-maker had its downsides: "Some people expect a comedian to be funny all the time. When I'm doing an interview on TV . . . I'm performing. Off stage when I'm just myself—being normal—people ask me 'What's wrong? Is everything OK? Are you upset?' Reporters are surprised during an interview that I'm not witty."

Despite being a rising celebrity, Rosie was living a middle-class existence. Never an ostentatious type of person, she drove an electric blue Miata car. She was content with her Studio City home ("My neighborhood is like the street I grew up on. Kids on Big Wheels and dogs barking at all hours") and, at the moment, had no plans to trade upward in her real estate. (Later in the year she would briefly consider taking a house with a view at the top of Mulholland Drive off of Laurel Canyon in the Hollywood Hills, but her plans never materialized.) O'Donnell's conservatism in material things was based on the realization, "You start to make more money and it's like, 'You need bigger and better.' And you get in over your head."

Although she'd been featured in two mega hit movies (*League*, *Sleepless*), Rosie still had no true sense of the degree of her growing fame with the public. People would pass her on the street or at the mall and nod hello. However, she was still convinced that, mostly, the onlooker was confusing her with either comedian Roseanne or dramatic actress Kathy Bates. (In a quasi self-effacing moment Rosie noted, "When Kathy Bates showed up at the Oscars having lost weight, I thought, 'I hope she didn't lose weight because I kept saying everyone thought I was her.' I actually felt guilty.") On other occasions, the still-modest celebrity would insist, "It's not until I talk that people go, 'You *are* her!'"

Thanks to her blue collar upbringing on Long Island, Rosie couldn't bring herself to become part of the fashionable Hollywood social set. Pretensions were too alien to her meat-and-potatoes outlook on life. While she might want to mingle with celebrities—even when it was not a charity event or a career-necessitated appearance—too often the occasion left her feeling empty. For example, at agent Swifty Lazar's Oscar party in March 1993, Rosie found herself seated between Walter Cronkite and Dennis Hopper: "Faye Dunaway walked by and Walter Cronkite started talking about Bonnie and Clyde and how he'd known the real Clyde. On the other side, Dennis Hopper was telling me about his wild days and who he'd been with. It was like being in two worlds—yes, Mr. Cronkite, yes, Dennis. . . . After that party I went home and felt sort of depressed. I didn't know why."

Another of Rosie's concerns was her insecurity about her film acting abilities. In more introspective moments, she still questioned whether she was professionally adequate in the eyes of her peers. There were even public occasions when these uncertainties poked through her protective shell and flip talk. For example, she confided to Nancy Griffin (*Premiere* magazine) about *Sleepless in Seattle*: "When they did the screening here [Los Angeles] I called [director] Nora and Nick [Pileggi—Nora Ephron's husband] answered the phone. I go, 'It's Rosie, can I go to the screening tonight?' And Nick's like, 'Oh, yeah. I'll have Nora call you back.' She never called me back. About a month later, I called Nora—I was in New York—and Nora says, 'Well, I guess you don't want to see the movie.' I say, 'Go ask your husband.' I was waiting by the phone feeling . . . 'Oh my God, they don't want me to see it. Maybe I'm not in it!'"

And she was not above performing her own audience research to test moviegoers' reactions to her big screen performances. For example, one day in July 1993 she drove to a multiplex theater in Los Angeles. As she recalls, "I paid to get in. I went to see *Free Willy*—which was cute—and then I went and looked in *Another Stakeout*, and then I closed that door and went and looked in *Sleepless in Seattle*." The fact that she was in two major movies simultaneously playing the theater circuits should have convinced even her that she was doing better than just okay. If Rosie couldn't see it, others could. For instance, Larry King alerted TV viewers when O'Donnell was interviewed on his talk show in mid-1993: "Except for maybe the Boston Red Sox, who is having as big a July as Rosie O'Donnell? . . . This season, O'Donnell dominates multiplexes everywhere. . . . She's getting great reviews; has two more movies coming out before 1993 is over. . . ."

There were other areas of her life that bothered Rosie. As she had confided to the media, "I'd like to be in a committed lifelong relationship that involves children and a family. . . . It gets to me on Christmas that I go to my sister's family. That is a little bit painful." And there was always the ongoing problem of her weight which fluctuated between 140-170 or even higher when she was in a "dumpy" mode. As before, she would start and then stop dieting and fitness programs. She appreciated that her excess poundage was a result of rebelling against authority and wanting not to live by other people's standards of what is a normal weight. Yet, part of her wished to fulfill a particular goal: "I want to be healthy so I can run for a mile and not die because I'm out of breath. I don't want to have a body like Madonna. I'm just trying to get to a place where self-loathing is no longer paramount."

At other times, when she was more svelte, Rosie still had doubts as to whether her dieting did or would enhance her on-screen image. She expressed this ambivalence to TV chat host Larry King: "I think I still look like somebody's buddy, but maybe I don't. . . ." She also admitted to another rationale for her indecision about getting and staying thinner. "When I was doing stand-up comedy, some producers or directors would say, 'If you lose weight and look different than you do, you won't be as funny . . . " When King asked if she really believed that concept, her response was not that convincing, "Not really. But they'd cite examples, like Rhoda—Valerie Harper. They'd say, 'She was much funnier when she was chubbier than when she was thinner. . . .'"

• • •

At first blush, it seemed as if Rosie never said no to a firm film offer in Hollywood. Such was not the case. She had rejected co-starring with Bette Midler and Sarah Jessica Parker in Walt Disney Pictures' *Hocus Pocus* (1993). Kathy Najimy (*Sister Act*) had been substituted for her on that project. O'Donnell refused to do the Disney movie because ". . . I didn't want to kill any kids, which is what they had one of the witches do. To me, it wasn't funny. That's my own line. Everyone has their own line that they won't cross."

Later, Rosie amplified further on her reasoning about *Hocus Pocus*: "Now this may seem absurd to you for me, a woman who did *Another Stakeout*, a movie where there was violence and people were shot, but I would not do a movie where I was the one who wanted to kill any children. I won't do anything that could hurt a child, but I'm not against shooting a bad guy if I'm the cop." It also proved, in retrospect, to be a good career move, because *Hocus Pocus* was not well received.

Unlike some other movie newcomers who'd enjoyed a healthy streak of box-office luck, Rosie remained levelheaded about her film career:

"I don't have any aspirations to carry a film. Not a big goal of mine. I like to work and I know what my strengths are and what they are not. If there was a part specifically for my strength that was a leading role, I would want to do it, but I don't have any desire to be above the title."

Meanwhile, in the spring of 1993 Rosie's agent called with very interesting news. Director Steven Spielberg's Amblin Entertainment company was interested in O'Donnell for a forthcoming film to be released by Universal Pictures. Would she consider coming by for a reading? When her representative told her it was for *The Flintstones* (1994) and for the role of Betty Rubble, ". . . I laughed so hard. I thought, are you kidding me? She is this tiny little petite thing, and I'm not exactly similar to the cartoon rendering in my own physicality. I didn't see it at first. Then when I went in and read it and everyone laughed, I thought, OK. But I didn't lust after it my whole life, no. I never thought there'd be a *Flintstones* film, to tell you the truth. I was interested in playing Scooby Doo at one point. . . ."

When Rosie auditioned for *The Flintstones*, she claims that what most impressed the casting people was her conspiratorial laugh which she interjected repeatedly into her reading. "These guys asked what this giggle was from. I said, 'Betty does that after every line, watch the show.' . . . I also held my wrists backwards. Did you ever notice that Betty always stands like that?"

Brian Levant, who was to direct *The Flintstones*, remembers his first meeting with Rosie. "I was embarrassed. She even knew the words to 'The Twitch,' the song from the 1963 series opener—which, incidentally, is also in the movie." When he was later asked why he was considering someone of Rosie's physical stature to play a character noted for her tiny figure, he answered, "We only wanted the funniest person for the role, not necessarily someone who physically resembled the cartoon character."

Unbeknownst to Rosie, she already had an edge in grabbing the coveted role of Betty Rubble from her chief competitors: British-born comedian Tracey Ullman and Janine Turner (of TV's *Northern Exposure*). It so happened that director Brian Levant's wife, Alison, had sometime before seen O'Donnell on VH-1 cable. Mrs. Levant had been so impressed with Rosie's stand-up comedy technique that she'd suggested to her husband that Rosie should be considered for Betty Rubble.

Before long, the final decision was made. Rosie was to play Betty Rubble in the upcoming *The Flintstones*. O'Donnell's first thought was

"Oh my God! Betty is so *thin*. I'll have to lose weight." Since this was to be such a tremendously high-profile project, Rosie's casting in the picture received far more coverage than for any of her past screen work. When the media inquired as to her reaction in being cast as yet another best friend in her new movie, O'Donnell assessed: "I'll be the best friend forever. It's fine with me. I mean, in my first [sic] movie I'm best friends with Madonna, my second movie, I'm best friends with Meg Ryan. That's not a bad career right there. . . ."

Originally, *The Flintstones* had been an animated TV series. When it debuted on ABC-TV on September 30, 1960, it was the first prime-time cartoon program made especially for television. It had been geared as a not very subtle parody of modern day suburbia. The show had a dual purpose of sporting adult satire wedded to kiddie fun. The program was conceived by William Hanna and Joe Barbera, the creative duo responsible for such beloved cartoon characters as Huckleberry Hound and Quick Draw McGraw. Hanna-Barbera unashamedly based their new concept on Jackie Gleason's classic TV sitcom, *The Honeymooners*.

It was only after much experimentation that Hanna-Barbera settled on the Stone Age as the proper backdrop for their new show. According to Barbera, one of their staff". . . came up with a little rough sketch of the characters in the Stone-Age skins and a bird with a long beak playing a phonograph record. As soon as you saw the bird with the long beak, a flood of gags came out like the elephant with the trunk for taking a shower or watering the lawn or washing the dishes or washing the car. Everything else is foot-powered—a bus moving with twenty feet, that kind of thing. It just opened a world of gags which I think gave it universal appeal. . . ." In actuality, the pilot for the show was called *The Flagstones*, but there was already a comic strip character with that surname.

During the course of the TV series' 166 episodes, the action focused largely on caveman Fred Flintstone, his wife Wilma, their daughter Pebbles and the Flintstones' best friends, Barney and Betty Rubble and their adopted child, Bamm Bamm. Each segment was filled with a steady stream of inventive rock puns and rather ingenious prehistoric gizmos for making life more sophisticated. There were also special appearances by such contemporary figures as Stony Curtis, Cary Granite and Ann Margrock. The show featured the voices of Alan Reed as Fred, Jean Vander Pyl as Wilma and Pebbles, with Mel Blanc as both Barney and Dino the Pet Dinosaur. First Bea Benaderet then

Gerry Johnson was heard as Betty. Don Messick was the voice of Bamm Bamm. For the record, it was actor Alan Reed who came up with the television program's definitive trademark of "Yabba Dabba Doo." Originally, he was to merely say, "Yahoo."

The Flintstones ended its initial prime-time run in 1966 but returned with new episodes in 1972 and again in 1981. It led to such spin-off series as *Pebbles and Bamm Bamm* (1971-1976) as well as *The Flintstone Kids* (1986-1988) and some TV specials. Meanwhile, the original series had remained in syndication and continues to be aired to this day.

For years, Hollywood talked of adapting *The Flintstones* to the big screen. However, nothing materialized until 1986 when film producer Joel Silver (later known for his super action movies like *Die Hard*) and his associates hired Steve E. de Souza (*48 Hrs.*) to write a script. Meanwhile, James Belushi and Rick Moranis were targeted to play, respectively, Fred and Barney. By the time de Souza had completed his draft in 1987, the project had fallen apart only to be revived later at Universal Pictures by Steven Spielberg's Amblin Pictures. It was Spielberg's idea to cast bulky actor John Goodman instead of Belushi as Fred Flintstone. For a time, Danny DeVito was considered for Barney but then the consensus opinion returned to employing Rick Moranis as Barney.

After other false starts, *The Flintstones* was given to Brian Levant (*Problem Child II, Beethoven*) to direct. Before the "final" script was approved in 1993, some 32 (!) writers had been involved in bringing the essentially simple cartoon series to the screen. Before settling on Elizabeth Perkins as Wilma, Geena Davis, Catherine O'Hara and Faith Ford (TV's *Murphy Brown* show) were in the running for the female lead. For the role of Fred's conniving secretary at Slate & Company, Halle Berry was selected as a replacement for the originally-wanted Sharon Stone.

Among the offbeat casting for *The Flintstones* was the hiring of TV talk show host Jay Leno for a cameo as a prehistoric version of his professional self. Comedian Harvey Korman was asked to provide the voice of the Dictabird down at Fred's office. Jean Vander Pyl, the voice of Wilma from the original TV series, was given a tiny role as Mrs. Feldspar. Bill Hanna and Joe Barbera, the co-creators of *The Flintstones*, would appear in the 1994 release, respectively, as a boardroom executive and a man in a "Mersandes" car.

The most publicized casting coup of the venture was wooing Elizabeth Taylor back to the big screen for her first theatrical feature in many years. Brian Levant chose her to play Fred's shrill mother-in-law over such other contenders as Elizabeth Montgomery and Audrey Meadows because ". . . I thought if we got Liz, it would be special. It might even get people to see the movie who wouldn't normally have come." Taylor finally agreed to the project for a healthy salary and a promise that the movie's New York City gala would be earmarked as a charity fund-raiser for the Elizabeth Taylor AIDS Foundation. During the course of production, producer Spielberg (billed on the film's credits as Steven Spielrock) would shower La Taylor with some $10,000 in gifts including a Cartier clock, an elegant sugar bowl, a classic picture frame and a hand-carved Stone Age-style bottle of her perfume, *Passion*. The investment would be well worth it, for the former Mrs. Richard Burton generated a tremendous amount of publicity for *The Flintstones*.

By the time *The Flintstones* began shooting on May 17, 1993, Rosie had been issued her special Betty Rubble outfit: a blue suede dress, blue hair bow and bone earrings. To hide the tattoo on her ankle, the costume department provided her with a blue band to wear over the ankle. Although she made a concerted effort to diet down to a slimmer size, realistic Rosie, nevertheless, had costumes made in bigger and smaller sizes to accommodate her fluctuating waistline. After completing the movie, Rosie would acknowledge, "I kind of don't have a waistline. I sort of go straight down. So they had this really tight corset to schmoosh my waist. It made it uncomfortable for me to sit. . . ."

Much of the outdoor filming was accomplished at Vasquez Rocks in Santa Clarita Valley which is about forty miles northeast of Los Angeles. Rosie enthused: "The sets are unbelievable. Visually it is so startling to see out at Vasquez Rocks, where they created the whole exterior of Bedrock. There are all of these natural rock formations and they put these pastel colored stone houses and trees and cars [in the midst of them]. It is so hysterical visually." The funky rock houses were actually made of a very lightweight sculpted foam and special construction was utilized for fabricating the terrain which included bubbling volcanoes in a still-unsettled earth. The big brontosaurus bones flanking the doorway to the Flintstones' home on the cul-de-sac were of plaster of Paris. Jim Henson's studio and Industrial Light & Magic designed such specialty items as the computer-generated Dino the pet dinosaur, while the special effects department supervised the making of the hidden mechanisms to move the foot-powered cars and other rock-wheeled vehicles.

Filming at the outdoor sets was definitely no piece of cake. For one thing, it was extremely hot—well over 100°—and there was no real shade to protect the cast and crew. For another, because Vasquez Rocks is part of a county park, it is open to the public. As such, during production some 100,000 tourists found their way to the site where they gawked at the proceedings. Because of the noise from these tourists, most of the dialogue tracks had to be redubbed back at the studio.

During downtime in shooting, Rosie would entertain on the set with her own version of *Jeopardy*. She had 200 trivia questions from her favorite TV series (*The Mary Tyler Moore Show*) neatly typed on 3" x 5" cards. Of her fellow cast members, Rosie was most amused by John Goodman because ". . . he loves to laugh. He's not a guy who makes a lot of jokes himself, but when somebody makes a joke on the set he has this huge big belly laugh. So I would always play to him and try to get him to crack up." As for Elizabeth Perkins, O'Donnell couldn't always appreciate her serious attempts to find motivation for her one-dimensional role. One day, a bemused Rosie snapped at her teammate, "For heaven's sakes, you're a cartoon character!"

Just as on *Another Stakeout* where Rosie had no empathy for the canine cast member, so she had her particular source of frustration on *The Flintstones*. It revolved around her on camera interaction with Hlynur and Marino Sigurdsson, the four-year-old identical twins from Iceland who had been cast to play her adopted son, Bamm Bamm. As Rosie would say at the time, "They don't speak English very well, and neither do their parents. They are the nicest boys. They are gentle. They read books, they don't watch TV. They're cute and adorable. But they cannot do this movie to save their life."

She further detailed, "They cannot do things like run at you with a club. Now, you tell any American kid in the world that's 4 years old, 'Chase me and hit me with a club.' They watch the [*Ninja*] *Turtles* all day; you're dead meat. This boy Hlynur goes, 'I don't vand to hurd you, Rodie. I von't hit you vid da club.' . . . I said to the director 'This is gonna be the hugest error of your life.' He said to me, 'They look beautiful on camera.' And they are the most beautiful children I've ever seen in my life. They have fine blond hair, huge eyes and these great smiles. They look like Bamm Bamm exactly. But, but . . . I said to Brian [Levant], 'They're gonna look like Bamm Bamm when we're still shooting in December, 'cause they've made us run over schedule." However, O'Donnell could never be hard-nosed for too long when it came to children. Finally, she relented and admitted, "I adore them. I absolutely love them. I bring them presents every day. . . ."

Eventually, it came time in the shooting schedule for Elizabeth Taylor to commence work on *The Flintstones*. (Her five days of actual shooting were to be spread over a few weeks because of her recent bouts of ill health.) Days before her much-anticipated arrival, Taylor began dispatching bouquets of flowers to the set from her European headquarters. It was her regal way of both announcing her pending arrival and a way to let everyone know that she was glad to be part of the project.

When Taylor showed up at the studio, she found that her dressing room and the steps leading up to it had been painted her favorite color—violet. To accommodate her wishes, famed couturier Oscar de la Renta had designed to specifications her low-cut Jurassic fake animal skin threads and bone jewelry. On the first day of her shoot, Spielberg presented her with a bowling ball with her character's name engraved on it.

When the screen legend actually walked onto the sound stage for her first scenes, there was a noticeable quiet—both cast and crew were awed by their celebrity co-worker. This was not Rosie's style. Figuring that someone should do something, she walked over to Liz and blurted out, "I really love your perfume." That broke the ice. The next day, when Rosie came to the studio, she found that a sizable carton had been placed in her trailer. Upon opening it she discovered it was a case of assorted perfumes—courtesy of Taylor. Thereafter, Rosie would refer to Liz as "such a sweet woman."

As Pearl Slaghoople, Taylor was the one who berates her daughter, Wilma, for having married Fred, when she could have wed Eliot Firestone "who invented the wheel." It was also Liz's Pearl, dressed in a fake red leather gown with fake ermine cuffs and fake jewelry, who leads a conga line at one point within the storyline. During her workdays on the set, Taylor was visited by another royal personage, Michael Jackson, the self-proclaimed "King of Pop." But Liz also demonstrated that she could be a regular person. Once at lunch time she joined the midday masses on the Universal Studio tour. On her final day of filming, Spielberg presented her with a faux stone plaque which read "Having you visit us in Bedrock was a thrill we'll never forget. Here is a little something to remember your 'time' with us." Inside the Stone Age sundial watch was another box, it contained an expensive Cartier timepiece.

By August 20, 1993, *The Flintstones* had completed its expensive shooting schedule. By the time it was ready for release in May 1994, it had cost some $45 million to tell a rather primitive story. In prehistoric Bedrock, good-natured Fred Flintstone donates the family savings to his next cave neighbor, Barney Rubble, so that Barney and his wife, Betty, can adopt a child. Pearl is aghast at her son-in-law's extravagance, but Fred's wife, Wilma, applauds the kind deed. Later, at the local quarry where Fred and Barney work, foreman Cliff Vandercave (Kyle McLachlan) announces that the winner of a new aptitude test will be given a company promotion. To repay Fred's favor, Barney substitutes his exam for Flintstone's and thus the latter is made company vice president. As it develops, Vandecave and his devious cohort, Miss Stone (Halle Berry), are embezzling funds from the company and need a fall guy. Dimwitted Fred is the perfect foil.

Meanwhile, with his salary raise, Fred and Wilma lead the good life, while workers such as Barney are laid off, leaving the Rubbles in a financial predicament. Eventually, Wilma turns against the apparently mercenary Fred and when the police and townsfolk come after him, Flintstone goes into hiding. Later, Wilma arrives in the nick of time with the office Dictabird who recites the actual facts of Fred being duped. Now redeemed, Flintstone rushes to rescue the kidnapped Pebbles and Bamm Bamm from the villainous Vandecave. In the process, Fred accidentally invents concrete. As a reward, the company president offers him another executive position. He declines it, asking, instead, that he and his pals be reinstated in their old jobs.

If any ingredient makes the laid-back *The Flintstones* palatable, especially to adults, it is the abundance of visual jokes within the elaborate production. There are the Stone-Age foot-powered autos, the Stone-Age bowling alleys, Stone-Age office toys and Stone-Age shopping malls. Not to be overlooked is the settlement's Cavern on the Green, or the local drive-in where the film *Tar Wars* is playing. Then, of course, there is the rash of rock puns ranging from the local newspaper with its motto "all the news that's fit to chip" to such products as Chevrok to power one's vehicle.

Garbed in his spotted orange caveman suit, Goodman had the swaggering gait of dimwitted Fred down perfectly, while Rick Moranis' good-natured Barney was appropriately blubbery. Sadly, Elizabeth Perkins' Wilma and Rosie's Betty—a prehistoric version of TV's Lucille Ball and Vivian Vance—really had little to do in the film, beyond mincing around, laughing their shrill laughs and watching their spouses bungle their every activity. As restructured for the movie adaptation, Perkins' Mrs. Flintstone was a watered-down sharp-tongued wife, while O'Donnell's Mrs. Rubble was hardly the pliant sexpot of the original cartoon episodes.

By the time *The Flintstones* opened nationwide, the country had been saturated with a full line of promotional merchandising, all part of a $100 million campaign. Among the myriad of items were the McDonald's Happy Meals figures (including one of Rosie's Betty Rubble—complete with blue ankle band) and a new line of *Flintstones* vitamins (with a Betty Rubble vitamin pill now added to the mix).

It was almost inevitable, given the heavy dose of visual and verbal puns within the picture that the critics would have a field day incorporating puns into their critiques of *The Flintstones*. Not that many reviewers were thrilled by the thrust of the very glitzy-on-the-surface, but hollow-beneath-the-surface movie. Expensive trappings and clever special effects could not disguise the extremely unimaginative plotline and paper-thin characterizations. Jack Kroll headlined his *Newsweek* review with "Hollywood Hits Rock Bottom" and ended his commentary with "*The Flintstones* is a lot of Yabba-Dabba-Doo-Doo." The *New York Daily News* labeled it a "Yabba Dabba Dud" while *USA Today* called it "Yabba Dabba Don't." Caryn James (*New York Times*) complained, "The greatest lost opportunity in *The Flintstones* is that its writers (more than 30) are so faithful to the '60's television series that they failed to add enough updated pop-culture references. The few included are among the film's best jokes."

Owen Gleiberman (*Entertainment Weekly*) wondered, "Does it say something about the infantilization of American cinema that an absurdly literal-minded big-budget version of a goofy cartoon series is now our idea of a major motion-picture event? You bet it does." Giving the movie a "B" rating (largely due to the "amazingly elaborate sets" and "its acid-trip vision of a prehistoric suburbia") he pointed out, "And if Rosie O'Donnell is hardly a double for the svelte Betty, that's forgotten the moment she duplicates Betty's delighted rapid-fire giggle."

Joe Levy (*Village Voice*) decided that the acting was no more than "stilted clowning." However, he made haste to mention ". . . Rosie O'Donnell's triumph cannot be overstated (she *sound*s like Betty Rubble, she *actually sounds* like Betty Rubble, though there's nothing she can do about having eyelashes even when she's not blinking). . . ."

If the initial and nearly universal critical drubbing of *The Flintstones* was any indicator, the expensively mounted movie should have been a flop. But this prediction did not take into account its potential attraction as a family picture, one that had nostalgia value for adults and juvenile appeal to youngsters. Within three days of its opening, *The Flintstones* was well on its way to becoming a major hit with a opening weekend gross of $37.2 million in the United States. By the middle of August 1994, the movie had a domestic gross of $125.6 million and its international release has pulled in over $100 million—and the picture was still going strong. When questioned how she felt about the negative critical reaction to the movie as a whole, Rosie reasoned to TV's *CBS This Morning*, "You don't go to *The Flintstones* expecting anything but a cartoon, you know. You go to McDonald's, you get a Big Mac. . . . You go see *The Flintstones*, you get the Flintstones."

With its great global financial success, it was, of course, touted that there would be a *Flintstones* sequel with much of the cast repeating their screen assignments. At one point it was to have been filmed in the summer of 1995 when John Goodman would be on vacation from his TV sitcom, *Roseanne*. When asked how she felt about doing a follow-up to *The Flintstones*, O'Donnell enthused that it would mean ". . . some Yabba Dabba dough for me." (As provided by her original contract for *The Flintstones*, Rosie would receive an estimated $3 million if she appeared as Betty Rubble in the sequel.) However, the much-promoted sequel has yet to materialize. More recently O'Donnell took occasion to make public her current evaluation of *The Flintstones*. While she thought the film had been okay, ". . . I wished it had been funnier."

Personally, *The Flintstones* had several aftereffects for Rosie. Before she had made this feature she was fairly well known to adult moviegoers because of her film and club work. The teenage and twentysomething crowd knew her from TV, especially her *Stand-Up Spotlight* chores. Because *The Flintstones* had been such a tremendously promoted and merchandised feature film, and because it was such a huge mainstream success, it now gave O'Donnell a far-higher recognition level with the public at large and with pre-teens in particular. In addition, it forever equated her in many people's minds with the cartoony Betty Rubble character. And, just as comedian Carol Burnett is permanently associated with her amazing Tarzan yell, so O'Donnell has become indelibly tied to her Betty Rubble laugh/cackle. It seems most people can't hear it often enough and she is constantly being asked to do it "just one more time."

Despite some critical opinion among the press and her peers, Rosie had her share of *The Flintstones* admirers. Although she didn't receive an American Comedy Awards nomination for *The Flintstones*, she did win in May 1995 the annual Kids Choice Award. It was a prize voted on by 26 million Nickelodeon cable TV viewers. For O'Donnell, it was an important acknowledgment. "Of all the awards that I've ever been nominated for or received, the one that's most important is that one. It's the only one I kept. All the other awards I sign and give to charities and they auction them off. The Nickelodeon blimp I kept because that's a great one. I can't really explain the appeal I have to children, but I know that I adore them and it's a mutual admiration club."

· 16 ·

If it wasn't Garry Marshall, the man who took Pretty Woman
[1990—with Julia Roberts and Richard Gere], which had been a
story about a prostitute who winds up dead in Hollywood and
turned it into Cinderella for the Eighties I don't think I would have
*done it [*Exit to Eden*].*

Rosie O'Donnell, May 1994

*I*n the latter part of 1993 Rosie O'Donnell had three movies in
release (*Sleepless in Seattle, Another Stakeout, Fatal Instinct*). She
had just finished the big-budgeted *The Flintstones* and had two
other completed features sitting on the shelf *(Car 54, Where Are You?*
and *I'll Do Anything*). She was about to start yet another motion picture. Meanwhile she continued to participate in a slew of charity fund-
raisers, including a 30-hour Laugh-athon benefit held at the LA
Improv on August 13-14, 1993. It was a money-raiser for Midwestern
flood victims. A few days later, on August 26, 1993, O'Donnell co-
emceed with Gloria Steinem *Voices for Choice.* This was a benefit at the
Santa Monica (California) Civil Auditorium on behalf of the
Washington, D.C.-based Voters for Choice organization.

By now, Rosie had finally relinquished her on camera hosting chores
on *Stand-Up Spotlight*, although she remained as executive producer of
this VH-1 show. She helped to choose 38-year-old stand-up comedian Bobby Collins, another fellow Long Islander, as her successor to
emcee the half-hour weekly cable show. He'd been on the comedy club
circuit for years. At the bigger nightclubs he had been the opening act
for the likes of Cher and Frank Sinatra and, more recently, Julio
Iglesias. He had appeared in small roles in such feature films as *Hero*

(1992) and *Indecent Proposal* (1993) and was recognized for his series of Certs Mints TV commercials. O'Donnell had known Bobby for years; in fact, they had both acted in *Car 54* together.

Regarding her years on *Stand-Up Spotlight*, Rosie explained, "It's really been a great experience for me. It got me behind the scenes, which is something that I'd like to go into more in my career. . . . I'm still going to cast—book the shows, so I'll still have control over who goes on. And that's one of the most enjoyable parts . . . finding young talent who haven't done TV."

O'Donnell was still making noises about getting herself a life: "I'd like to have a family, you know. But then again, that's that whole wax-on-wax-off balance thing. I mean, I would love to have, really—put as much effort into my private life as I seem to put into my career, but I think that's to come." O'Donnell was also getting restless living in California. As she explained to Madonna, "I miss New York City. I miss the whole feeling of New York City, but I don't miss Long Island, nor would I ever want to raise children there." Regarding her career, Rosie said, "I think I'd be good at [film] directing because of being a control freak and meticulous. There's no control as an actor because all you are is a color of paint. The director gets to be the artist."

• • •

When describing her role in her next movie which was to start filming in mid-September 1993, Rosie confided, "Well, I'm an undercover cop, and I play a stripper in the opening scene. . . . The hair removal, alone, for this role is going to take me an extra two weeks." That was not the half of it! During the course of the movie, O'Donnell would parade about in a very revealing studded, leather bustier. In addition, the picture would contain nude scenes (not of her), several sado-masochism sequences (not with her) and lots of talk about sexual fantasies (some with her). In short, Rosie had been signed to appear in *Exit to Eden* (1994), based on the erotic novel (1985) written by Anne "Interview with the Vampire" Rice.

Originally, when Garry Marshall agreed to direct this controversial screen vehicle, his casting wish list had included Bridget Fonda or Nicole Kidman for the lead female role. Other possibilities for the key part had been Theresa Russell or Susan Sarandan. However, it was Dana Delany, formerly of TV's *China Beach*, who accepted the assignment. For the male lead, Spanish-born Antonio Banderas had been sought. Instead, it was Australia's Paul Mercurio, the former ballet-star-turned-actor (*Strictly Ballroom*, 1992) who came aboard the project to play opposite Delany. And for the role of the female law enforcer, who goes to any length to do the job, Sharon Stone had been Marshall's first consideration. When Stone rejected the offer at the last minute, he turned to Rosie.

As Rosie recalls, ". . . Garry Marshall is a wonderful man, and he called me and told me that Sharon Stone was offered the part and she said no. And . . . he wanted me to be the second person offered the role, and I was hysterical laughing on the phone. And I couldn't imagine that meeting where they say, you know, 'Can't get Mel Gibson, let's get Danny DeVito.' You know, it didn't make sense to me that they would go from Sharon Stone to me. So I took the gig just on that premise alone."

There were other reasons that propelled Rosie to accept this way-out-there role. For one, Marshall had mentioned when he called about *Exit to Eden*: "Rosie, you worked with my sister [Penny Marshall], and I want you to do this for me—I won't embarrass you. . . ." (Similarly, when Garry Marshall was wooing Dana Delany to do the film which would require her to do nude scenes, he had said, "Remember I'm the man who brought you [the TV sitcom] *Happy Days*" and he snared her when he promised, "I want you to look really beautiful [on screen].") For another reason, it would be a liberating experience for O'Donnell. As she explained to Janis Paige *(Los Angeles Times)*, "I'm nearly nude. Nude enough to scare people. . . . I'm in S&M sort of clothing, and it's really not that much different from wearing a one-piece bathing suit, but I have enough problems wearing a one-piece bathing suit at family parties never mind in front of all America in a film. So I took it in a way to get over my own problems about my body image and to try to face the things that I fear." And, yet another factor, certainly not to be overlooked, was that accepting the role would provide Rosie with three weeks of filming in the Hawaiian sun.

With O'Donnell aboard, the other cast members were announced. These included Dan Aykroyd, the veteran comedian of TV (*Saturday Night Live*) and movies (*Ghostbusters, The Blues Brothers, Trading Places*, etc.) as Rosie's straight-laced police partner. Iman, an African-American super model who had appeared in such movies as *Out of Africa, House Party II* and *Star Trek VI*, was to play the exotic villain of the piece. Her partner in crime would be portrayed by British-born Stuart Wilson, who had been on screen in *Lethal Weapon II, Wethersby*, etc. (Iman had wanted her real-life husband David Bowie to take that assignment, but the singer/actor declined.) Hector Elizondo, who had appeared in all of Garry Marshall's movies—and was now considered a good-luck charm—was hired to play the psychiatrist who had founded Club Eden, the island of uninhibited pleasure.

New Orleans-born Anne Rice is best known for her series of Vampire books *(Interview with the Vampire, The Vampire Lestat,* etc.), as well as her several tomes on ancient Egypt *(The Mummy or Ramses the Damned,* etc.) and fiction on witches *(The Witching Hour,* etc.). She has also authored heavily erotic novels: *Exit to Eden, Belinda,* etc., using the pseudonym of Anne Rampling. When asked in early 1994 why she'd written *Exit to Eden,* the very prolific and unique Rice explained, "I wanted to really take it [the topic of sadomasochism] to the max. I wanted to take that fantasy and put it in a playful setting where somebody could enjoy all of that and get away from the gruesome headlines and reality." As to why she had labeled her book hard-core pornography, Rice offered: ". . . by hard-core, I mean it is absolutely uncompromising. It contains the most detailed sex scenes that I knew how to write. I would imagine that soft porn means kind of blurring of the genitalia and stuff, and my stuff doesn't do that."

Film producer Alexandra Rose had read *Exit to Eden* in the early 1990s and thought it could, despite its erotic excesses, be brought to the screen as a mainstream picture. She reasoned, "At its heart, *Exit to Eden* is a contemporary love story" and, as such, could somehow be translated into an acceptable Hollywood release. Because of Garry Marshall's success with turning a tawdry tale of a Hollywood hooker into a highly romantic, sanitized box-office smash, he was an immediate choice to direct the vehicle for the relatively newly formed Savoy Pictures. (On that same topic, Dana Delany had her own take on why Marshall was drawn to *Edit to Eden,* "He's a very sexy man. He has a hell of a curiosity about these matters, and I think he wanted to see if it could be made mainstream. People who know him are not surprised by his doing this movie.")

As *Exit to Eden* moved into production, the process of how Rice's explicit sex tale would be transformed into a censor-approved mainstream movie became apparent. As Marshall voiced, "The book was a very sensitive, in-depth probing of the sexualities of our society. We're handling it with humor and hope Anne Rice fans will accept it, not as a true adaptation, but as an interpretation of the book." Marshall believed *Eden* could provide a cogent analysis of the changing state of the battle of the sexes: "In the '70s we asked ourselves whether a man should open a car door for a woman, or if she should open it herself. In the '90s, we're well beyond car doors. Now we're discussing who should be on top."

Asked if the film adaptation of Rice's steamy book would replicate the erotic sequences of the original book, Marshall conceded, "We weren't going for the soft porn. Although it was still a stretch for me." He hastened to add, ". . . you will see scenes that audiences have never seen before—plus the kind of erotic subject matter that has always been done dark and terrible and sick."

Later, the director would concede the inevitable dilution of Rice's sexually fervent and highly titillating text. "We've put another story on top to make it more entertaining. We have two undercover cops—Dan Aykroyd and Rosie O'Donnell—coming to the island, and what we have, we hope, is something very funny. That's how I deliver my messages—with comedy." And comedy it would be, for one of *Eden*'s two acknowledged scripters was Bob Brunner who had written for Marshall's *Happy Days* teleseries. Deborah Amelon, the other—and original—script writer on *Eden* would later brag of the feature, "It's humor that never demeans what people into S&M are about."

When Marshall was questioned later on why he had fastened on Rosie for *Exit to Eden*, he cited, in retrospect, her ability at "mixing the comic with the erotic. We were trying something very new, and we needed someone with whom the audience could identify to ease them into this slightly kinky, slightly threatening, world. Rosie's innocent, but hers is a hip innocence. It helps take the edge off the sex in the movie. Yet she's still sexy and, for the first time in her career, she even has a romantic thing going. She's also very brave. She was taken aback by having to wear some of the skimpy costumes, but she did. She doesn't worry about how she looks all the time. That can be very refreshing in Hollywood."

While Rosie was in the throes of completing *The Flintstones* before exchanging her blue suede outfit of that movie for the black leather of *Exit to Eden*, other *Eden* cast members were researching their *Eden* movie roles. (They were assisted by the film's technical advisor, Race Bannon, author of *Learning the Ropes*.) Most verbal about exploring her film part was Dana Delany, the former soap opera performer (*Love of Life, As the World Turns*) who had been Emmy-awarded for playing nurse Colleen McMurphy on TV's *China Beach*. More recently, Delany had been seen to little advantage in such theatrical releases as

Housesitter (1992) and *Tombstone* (1994). So, not only did she hope that *Exit to Eden* would allow her to explore her sexuality on camera, but that it would push her movie career into higher gear. She was the cast member who informed filmmaker Marshall about her pending nude scenes, "I can tell you what I like and what I don't like about my body or you can discover it for yourself."

Part of Delany's *Eden* preparation was to visit with an honest-to-goodness dominatrix in Los Angeles. "I went to a dinner party at her house and I met a lot of people who are into the S&M scene. We had a round-table discussion, with a slave who served us. . . . Then afterward we went up to her bedroom and a couple of the men stripped down to their underwear and demonstrated whipping to me. They showed me the techniques. It's all in the wrist. She gave me a whip to take home so that I could practice."

Not to be outdone, Rosie got into the act with her own investigations into the world of S&M. She would describe in mock seriousness: "It was a great excuse to get to go to all the sexual-paraphernalia stores" where she could decide, "Oh, I need to get this. It's for research. I'll have one of those in every color." On a more serious note, she claimed the "seamy" shopping "made me not as puritanical. I don't have the angst I used to." She also forced herself to diet, getting herself down to 150 pounds, which for her was incredibly skinny.

As for well-developed co-star Paul Mercurio, who was making his American movie debut herein, he had agreed to performing nude scenes in *Exit to Eden*. When asked if exposing himself on camera was a problem, he replied, "I don't find nudity a big deal at all." That was true, because he had once danced naked on the New York stage in a ballet version of *Death in Venice*.

Exit to Eden got under way in mid-September 1993. Location work involved treks to New Orleans, different areas of Los Angeles and, best of all, twenty-one days in Hawaii. The latter scenes were shot on the island of Lanai at the exclusive Manele Bay Hotel Resort. This entertainment oasis boasts six different gardens on the premises with their own fountains, waterfalls and ponds. The complex provided a great deal of variety for shooting the outdoor scenes supposedly taking place at the pleasure isle. The hotel itself is unusual in that its exotic architecture has an Eastern flavor that is not typically Hawaiian.

In the context of the storyline, Rosie's first appearance on camera finds her and her undercover cop partner (Dan Aykroyd) on stakeout in a Los Angeles strip club. O'Donnell saunters into view as a zaftig stripper who wiggles and waggles as she cases the seedy joint. It is a marvelous entrance for game O'Donnell who displays a sense of rhythm, a playful coyness and plenty of the real Rosie in the flesh. She would later describe filming this scene: ". . . he [Garry Marshall] creates a real environment of family on his films. Like I was acting with this guy in a scene where I'm humping a pole and being an undercover cop, and this guy is looking at me lecherously and he's pretty good, and I said, 'Who is that guy?' And they said, 'It's Garry's dentist.' That's the people he casts in the film! His hairdresser, his mother's friend from Brooklyn, whatever."

As the filming proceeded, it came time for O'Donnell's highly touted sequences wearing her black leather bustier and fishnet stockings. She looks back on the process of becoming comfortable with her "boudoir" look as positive, although she claims her efforts to be a sexy object on camera were akin to shock therapy. "The first day I was very embarrassed. But then the camera crew started making wisecracks, like, 'Wow, you look really hot!' and I'd say, 'I do?' After a while I started strutting around, going, 'Yeah, I'm pretty in this, aren't' I?' I mean, there are some gorgeous people around who aren't ninety pounds right?" In fact, it got to the point where she reveled in wearing the revealing outfit on the set even on days when it was not a required script prop.

In his autobiography, *Wake Me When It's Funny* (1996), Garry Marshall recalls:

"Once we started filming *Exit to Eden*, Rosie O'Donnell's character proved to be so popular in dailies that we gave her a love interest. It wasn't something we had originally planned, and it didn't really affect the plot, but it gave another dimension to her character that we simply couldn't pass up." Her beau in the picture was Tommy (Sean O'Bryan), a clean-cut sex slave who wants to belong to Rosie's character—now and forever, no matter what. They even share a kissing scene oncamera.

Beyond having a revealing wardrobe, wisecracks and double entendres in this project, Rosie undertook a very athletic fight scene with Iman. In the tradition of the classic brawl between Marlene Dietrich and Una Merkel in *Destry Rides Again* (1939), the two women—one tall and lithe, the other shorter and much stockier—battle it out on the island retreat. In actuality, O'Donnell found her on screen opponent gave as good as she took, especially with Iman's flailing legs and pointy shoes. It was Rosie who ended with bruises, cuts (which required two stitches to her head) and a sore ego. (When O'Donnell began her TV talk show in mid-1996, Iman would be a recurring guest and/or consultant on the program, often giving mock-serious on camera lifestyle tips to perplexed show guests.)

The movie's climactic shoot-out occurs in New Orleans. While on-location in Louisiana, the principal cast had the opportunity to meet a famous local resident—Anne Rice. As Dana Delany describes, "I don't even know if she [Anne Rice] knew who I was. I met her in New Orleans and she didn't say anything to me. But when she met Paul [Mercurio], she said, 'Oh, what a hunk.'"

When the movie finished shooting in December 1993, there was the usual cast party for which Garry Marshall created his traditional gag reel of outtakes from the movie. The footage featured bloopers, deleted and/or fun moments with several of the cast and crew, etc. Rosie assumed that the festivities marked the end of her *Exit to Eden* work. In this, she was mistaken.

As Marshall and his staff assembled the *Eden* footage into a work print, it became apparent that the results were not what had been anticipated. It became obvious at test screenings that viewers were not comfortable with the film's blatant erotic elements. As the movie was further edited, it was decided to use more of O'Donnell's comedic moments than planned, to bolster the rest of the proceedings. As Rosie explains, ". . . it wasn't originally supposed to be a heavy comedy. It was originally supposed to be a sort of, you know, erotic film with a little comedy in it. And then as we got going, the comedy got a little bit more, and so it's become a comedy with some erotica in it, and . . . Oh, it would have been more erotic if somebody else was cast aside from me."

To make room for additional lighter moments, other already-filmed material was discarded. Relegated to the cutting room floor were some of the sadomasochism footage, snippets of the sexual/romantic scenes between the Delany and Mercurio characters, and all but subtext references to the lesbian sexual relationship between the dominatrix and her personal slave (Stephanie Niznik).

In the course of the drastic reediting, vital continuity was lost and some of the existing comedy scenes weren't playing well in the remix. The only salvation, Marshall decided, would be to bring O'Donnell back for both off-screen bridging narration and for additional oncamera comedy scenes. To carry through this plan required working around Rosie's work commitments and flying her back to the sound stage. The problem was, O'Donnell's weight had mushroomed after her work in *Eden* had ended.

When asked about these add-on scenes with the inflated Rosie, she would admit, "Yeah. It's true. In fact, you can tell when you're watching the movie, because there's my character, Sheila Kingston, in her size 12 little jeans, and then there's Sheila Kingston in the grip's size 36 jeans, because—true story—we reshot a scene and I'm—they give me the jeans, and there was no way they were buttoning. And it was a Sunday and I had to fly back to do *Grease!* So I got on the walkie talkie, I'm like, 'If there is any grip within the sound of my voice wearing a size 34 [sic] Levi's, please report to my trailer immediately.' So I'm actually wearing Vinny the grip's Levi's in half of the film."

Finally, after months and months of previewing and tinkering with the reassembled movie, *Exit to Eden* was scheduled for release in October 1994. It was no easy task to define a proper promotional build-up for *Eden*. As Kevin Goldman would report in the *Wall Street Journal*, "Though there's plenty of slapstick in this movie, there's also plenty of slapping—and therein lies a big marketing challenge for what may be the steamiest movie ever to garner an 'R' rating." Savoy Pictures spent an estimated $10-12 million in marketing this controversial feature. It was forced to walk a tight wire because none of the explicit footage (frontal male and female nudity) could be used in TV ads, and what could be shown from the film in TV promotions could only barely hint at the film's focus on sadomasochistic sex practices. As a result, the movie was sold as a new-style cop buddy picture, which proved to be an error in judgment.

When it came time to send the stars on promotional tours, director Garry Marshall understood that O'Donnell and Dan Aykroyd would be key elements in selling the picture. This was particularly true now that their once near-cameo characters had been so expanded in the final print. Thus, in wooing the media, he relied heavily on Rosie and Dan because they ". . . enjoy doing publicity and can sometimes drive people into theatres just by a single appearance."

O'Donnell has always been in her element in promoting herself or a creative project in which she was a part. *Exit to Eden* was a wonderful opportunity for her to shine. There were so many slants to exploit: going from the super wholesome *The Flintstones* to the super kinky *Exit to Eden*; the new film's salacious subject matter, her daring costumes, her love scene, her character's sexual fantasies, etc.

As usual, she was her forthright self, calling the shots as they were. When asked about her rather glamorous publicity photos for the movie, she replied, "One word comes to mind: airbrush. Everyone says to me, 'You look so great in those photos.' Yeah, go see the film. . . . They can't, like, remove a chin, take away underarm flaps." As to whether she, like Dana Delany had actual nude scenes in the film, she retorted with tongue-somewhat-in-cheek: "No, and sadly Garry Marshall's been promoting the movie using that fact. I saw him on [*The Late Show with David*] *Letterman* saying, 'Yeah, you know, it's an erotic comedy. We've got Rosie O'Donnell, but she doesn't take her clothes off.' As if, you know, this would keep people away, which it may. But you know."

Based extremely loosely on the Anne Rice novel, the revamped *Exit to Eden* finds Los Angeles undercover cop Sheila Kingston (Rosie O'Donnell) and her partner, Fred Lavery (Dan Aykroyd), on the trail of two international diamond smugglers/murderers, Omar (Stuart Wilson) and Nina (Iman). The police's best chance of pinning a recent murder on the duo is to obtain the snapshots that professional photographer Elliot Slater (Paul Mercurio) had accidentally taken at the airport crime scene. However, he's left town for the lush and plush Club Eden. This is the tropical resort where the affluent visiting patrons can explore their sexuality, inhibitions and fantasies in an ambiance of liberating nudity.

Once at Club Eden, Slater becomes enamored of the beautiful resort leader, Mistress Lisa (Dana Delany). This basically sweet dominatrix makes Elliot her personal slave and, in the process, falls in love with him. Meanwhile, Sheila and Fred arrive on the island. She poses as a curious client, he in the guise of a Club worker. Before long, Omar and Nina make their appearance, bent on getting the incriminating evidence from Elliot's camera case and eliminating him as well.

As the caper progresses, the opposing forces descend on New Orleans. By the time the lawbreakers are finally subdued, Lisa and Elliot have resolved their love interest, while Sheila and Fred are each far less repressed than before their special assignment. And, as a bonus, Sheila has captured the devoted attention of an island love slave (Sean O'Bryan).

The film's erotica and kindness to one side, *Eden*'s few highlights include two amusing sound bytes by O'Donnell. As she and her police partner attempt to subdue the lethal Nina, they discover that they've left their police tools back on the mainland. This leads Rosie's character to snap, "Are we the only ones on this island who don't have a pair of handcuffs?" At another juncture, Nina is confronted by a scantily-clad young man who's been assigned to please her every whim.

Bursting with expectation, he asks, "How can I fulfill your fantasy?" She zings back, "Go paint my house." (For any who find these jokes lame, they play much better than they read. And they are definitely better than the anemic double entendres which pepper the storyline. For example there is the groaner when an announcement is made over the Club's loudspeaker system: "Citizen Julie, report to the sticky buns booth.")

On October 11, 1994, *Exit to Eden* opened in 1800 U.S. and Canadian theatres. It was slaughtered by the critics. Peter Rainer (*Los Angeles Times*) asked, "Did the filmmakers really think they could get away with making a wholesome movie about the S&M scene?" He added, "there's so little erotic heat in this movie that it gives sex a bad name. . . . Now *that*'s an achievement." David Denby (*New York* magazine) panned: "Garry Marshall titillates us and then ridicules what turns him on: he's a dirty old man with a guilty conscience—not the best state in which to direct a comedy." Janet Maslin (*New York Times*) berated, ". . . *Exit to Eden* is an incredible mess, a movie that changes gears so often and so nonsensically it seems to have been edited in a blender." Jon Silberg (*Boxoffice* magazine) complained, "Watching Garry Marshall's take on the sadomasochistic novel by Anne Rice is like sitting through a Vegas lounge act based on *The Story of O*."

In reviewing Rosie's performance, Maslin of the *New York Times* insisted, "Miss O'Donnell's performance deserves a Purple Heart. Bravely storming her way through a queasy, unfunny story, she delivers enough wisecracks and voice-over witticisms to paper over the movie's worst embarrassments." The reporter also cited, "And Ms. O'Donnell, a walking sight gag in black leather regalia, is good sport enough to make the best of Sheila's down-to-earth attitude." David Hunter (*Hollywood Reporter*) observed, "That leaves O'Donnell and Aykroyd to flop around in pursuit of a plot going nowhere, trying on leather outfits and standing in for repressed Joe and Jane America. The former hits another homer while the latter could have stayed home and no one would have noticed."

One of the many critics who disliked the film but one of the few who dismissed Rosie's performance was Roger Ebert (*Chicago Sun-Times*). Having assessed the cast as a whole ("The actors look so uncomfortable they could be experiencing alarming intestinal symptoms") he continued, "I'm sorry, but I just don't get Rosie O'Donnell. I've seen her in three or four movies now, and she has generally had the same effect on me as fingernails on a blackboard She's harsh and abrupt and staccato and doesn't seem to be having any fun. She looks mean."

During its opening weekend, *Exit to Eden* took in a paltry $3 million at the box-office and within a few weeks had disappeared from theatres everywhere. In Saskatchewan, Canada, it never even played. The local Film Classification Board banned it because it violated a section of its regulations barring the depiction on screen of ". . . physical abuse or humiliation of human beings as a means of sexual gratification or as pleasing to the victim." The last such movie to be so censored in that province was Brooke Shield's *Pretty Baby* (1978). In 1995, Rosie would receive the Golden Raspberry Award in the Supporting Actress category in reaction to her trio of 1994 releases: *Exit to Eden*, *The Flintstones* and *Car 54, Where Are You?* (Ironically, that year, O.J. Simpson, who was an ongoing target of Rosie's sardonic humor and disgust in her comedy act, won a Golden Raspberry in the Supporting Actors Category for *Naked Gun 33 1/3: The Final Insult*.)

In the aftermath of this big screen fiasco, Anne Rice would say, "Well! First of all, I want to say that I love Garry Marshall, and everybody involved with *Eden* has been very sweet to me. After I saw the final script, which they were kind enough to show me, I basically disconnected myself from that film. I mean, it was impossible. They were obviously afraid of the material or didn't understand it. Although my emotional attachment to *Exit to Eden* wasn't nearly as strong as to [the movie version of *Interview with the*] *Vampire* [released in later 1994]— it was another lesson learned. I won't ever give up my power to OK a script of my work again!"

Marshall would admit of his misfire: ". . . the box-office numbers were bad and the reviews were even worse. I was the first director to bring S&M to a mainstream audience and the critics spanked me for it."

As for Rosie, she would reveal on a computer online forum in 1996: "I actually wouldn't let anyone go see *Exit to Eden*. I'd like to refund your money if you did see it. *Exit to Eden* was actually an idea of Garry Marshall, who is probably my favorite human being and should he call me tomorrow saying we're doing *Exit to Eden II*, I would have to admit, I would do it because I adore him. It was the most fun I ever had and by far the worst film I've ever made and probably one of the worst I've ever seen. It's not something I want my child to see, although I do have it on laser disc. Whenever I feel depressed about my life I put it on and show it."

Exit to Eden would fade quickly into film history as would the touted reteaming of Rosie and Aykroyd—whom she enjoyed working with—as cop partners in an entirely new project. However, *Eden* added more lore surrounding Rosie's ever-burgeoning career. Now, whenever a devout fan would encounter her face-to-face, he or she would ask two things: "Would you do the Betty Rubble laugh?" and "Did you get to keep the leather outfit from *Exit to Eden*?" (Her answer to the latter is "No . . . What was I gonna do with it?")

· 17 ·

. . . when you do a movie, when you mess up, they go, you know, "Cut, let's do it again." When you mess up here [on Broadway], everybody looks at you and goes, "You messed up." And, you know, you have to do your part, because there are other people there who are relying on you to get through. So it's a whole different experience for me. It's very challenging.

Rosie O'Donnell, December 1993

*B*etween the end of filming *The Flintstones* in late August 1993 and the start of making *Exit to Eden,* Rosie O'Donnell had only a two-week breather. Professionally, she was whirling along at such a productive clip that she neither had the luxury of time, nor allowed herself a pause, to appreciate what she had been accomplishing in her career. As she would tell *Theater Week* reporter Michael P. Scasserra in May 1994, "There were only two times during the last couple of years that it actually hit me that I had made it. One was while I was doing some campaigning for Bill Clinton. I was at an event, waiting in the green room [with a pal], and Bette Midler walked by and casually said, 'Hi, Rosie.' I looked at my friend and said, 'Check, please. That's it. I've done everything I need to do.' The other time was when I was on [Mr. Blackwell's] worst dressed list. That's when it hit me, 'God, I'm famous.'"

Caught in her own momentum of moviemaking, TV, club dates, charity benefits, etc., events began to blur together. As she admitted, ". . . the last two years have been a kick, but it's still like I don't feel the things I've done. I'll be watching *Saturday Night Live* and think, 'Gee, I wish I could host that show,' then I'd realize, 'Oh yeah, I did!'"

It was on the November 13, 1993 edition of *Saturday Night Live* that

169

Rosie was the host. Emceeing and doing sketches on this long-running program was the realization of yet another of her childhood dreams. However, by this time she had maneuvered an even bigger coup. It was one that would have made her late mother very proud. It was one that would fulfill her long-cherished goal to star in a Broadway musical. She had contracted to co-star in a full-scale revival of *Grease!*

It had been during the making of *The Flintstones* that Rosie learned that dancer, choreographer and director Tommy Tune planned to bring *Grease!* back to Broadway in 1994. His approach was to add Nineties' sensibilities to the revival of the famed Seventies' show which pays tribute to the Fifties. Although she'd never seen *Grease!* during its $7\frac{1}{2}$ year-run on Broadway in the 1970s, Rosie fondly remembered the 1978 movie version. John Travolta and Olivia Newton-John may have been the film's stars, but it'd been Stockard Channing who made the biggest impression on O'Donnell. In that movie musical, Channing inherited Adrienne Barbeau's stage part of Betty Rizzo, the Rydell High student who was the toughest of the tough members of the Pink Ladies. Rosie reasoned, ". . . now that's a role I could do—and hopefully soon because at 31 and with gray hair, I'm getting a little too old to play a high school student." In fact. Rosie had already played the leather-jacketed Rizzo role—in her backyard as a youngster with her sister Maureen in the Olivia Newton-John heroine part.

When O'Donnell informed her representatives that she wanted to take on Rizzo in *Grease!,* their initial reaction was "Are you crazy? You just did five movies in a row. You don't want to do Broadway now!" But she did! In a practical vein, she knew that with several films completed or about to open, there would be no lack of O'Donnell product in movie theatres while she did the show. As such, the industry would not likely forget her during her sabbatical from Hollywood. Besides, if she did do the musical for a limited period, it would give her a chance to stand back and determine where she actually stood in the film business. Depending how everything was shaping up, she would be in a better situation to reposition herself, if need be.

Thus, a determined Rosie called Tommy Tune's office in New York City in the summer of 1993 to offer her services. She received a very weak reception. She was told, "We don't know who you are. You have to audition." It was definitely not the response she had expected or hoped for from Tune. Later, she would come to realize from firsthand experience, ". . . theater people live very insulated, isolated lives—I mean, eight performances a week. They are working during prime time and during moviegoing time. What do they know?"

By June of 1993, O'Donnell had completed *Another Stakeout* and was making *The Flintstones*. During a scheduled filming break in the latter, she flew back East to promote the release of *Sleepless in Seattle*. On Monday, June 21, she appeared on ABC-TV's *Good Morning America* where she was interviewed by Charles Gibson. Having plugged *Sleepless*, Rosie, who generally took charge of her on-air interviews, casually mentioned that, later in the day, she was auditioning for *Grease!* A rather surprised Gibson inquired if she could really sing. To which Rosie said, "Well, we'll find out at one o'clock today when I sing for Tommy and the [other] producers. I mean, I can sing as well as . . . Tyne Daly, perhaps, or Stockard Channing. I'm no Patti LuPone."

That said, O'Donnell chose to prove her point to both Gibson and the millions of TV viewers throughout the country. With the same chutzpah that had served her so well all these years, she spontaneously launched into the song "Happy Talk." It was from *South Pacific*, one of her all-time favorite shows. In the midst of her a cappela rendition, a bemused Gibson interrupted with "You're booked, you got the part!" Not to be put off, O'Donnell said "Thank you" and immediately returned to her impromptu performance of the Rodgers and Hammerstein number. As she did, she explained to the nonplused *Good Morning America* co-host, "I've got to do the whole song, Charlie." And she did just that!

As arranged, Rosie was at Tommy Tune's production office by 1 p.m. that day. By the time she'd arrived the producers had already received many calls concerning O'Donnell's earlier *Good Morning America* appearance and the possibility that she'd be in *Grease!* Even some of Tune's staff had seen her "Happy Talk" performance that day. Therefore, Rosie came into the meeting with an aura of someone whom the public cared about. It boosted her confidence and her stock with the decision-makers.

After polite chit-chat she auditioned by singing two song numbers for Tommy Tune and his protégé, Jeff Calhoun. The latter was to direct and choreograph the revival while simultaneously doing a similar chore for Tune's other upcoming show, *The Best Little Whorehouse in Texas Goes Public*. The songs out of the way, the next obvious question was "You can dance, right?" She responded, "Oh, yeah, I can dance." (A year later she would admit in a *Vogue* magazine interview, "Sure. The big dancer. I lied.")

A veteran of auditions, Rosie knew that she had not yet won over the Tune team. Scrambling for an advantage point, the inwardly nervous Rosie launched into a detailed discussion of how she had been featured in last year's huge movie hit, *A League of Their Own*, and that her new picture, *Sleepless in Seattle*, was projected to do as well. Besides, as she reminded her examiners, she had just finished another very high-profile movie, *The Flintstones*, which would be released about the time *Grease!* was scheduled to make its Broadway bow. As she rattled onward, she successfully made her point that her name would definitely sell tickets. Before she left, Tune agreed to look at her movie work.

Eventually, Rosie was approved for the part of Betty Rizzo. The show's director, Jeff Calhoun, would say that one of the reasons O'Donnell was hired was that she ". . . made us laugh. There was just this quality she had." She signed a ten-month contract, during which period the show would rehearse, try out around the country and return for its May 1994 Broadway premiere. Meanwhile, when O'Donnell returned to *Good Morning America* in late 1993, interviewer Morton Dean queried Rosie on just how much her June appearance on the morning TV show had influenced the *Grease!* casting decision. O'Donnell answered, "I think definitely it played a part. . . . It didn't 'hoit.'"

Having made up her mind to go Broadway, she would not budge from her decision to abandon Hollywood—albeit temporarily. She reckoned, "As a performer and an artist, I want to stretch myself to do things that I thought I couldn't or that other people didn't expect me to do. I've always dreamed of being on Broadway. The film career is always going to be there. Some people don't understand why I'd do this now, but everyone makes their own choices. There's not one road map to follow that automatically lands you at success. You have to cut your own way through the jungle." Besides, Rosie reasoned, accepting the stage offer would bring her back to New York, the hub of excitement that she had so sorely missed during her Los Angeles years.

As 1993 wound down, Rosie completed her *Exit to Eden* sound stage chores. Thereafter, she jetted to New York City to begin rehearsing *Grease!* Her show co-workers included former soap opera star Ricky Paull Goldin (Danny Zuko), Susan Wood (Sandy Dumbrowski), Sam Harris (Doody), Marcia Lewis (Miss Lynch) and Billy Porter (Teen Angel). Much was made of the fact that Rosie the comedian and Sam Harris the singer had each been on TV's *Star Search* during its early years. (Harris had gone on to win the $100,000 prize in the vocalist category.) On the marquees and playbills, Rosie received special billing in oversized letters which read "and Rosie O'Donnell."

For Rosie, who professed that she did very little prep work for her screen roles, the regimen of preparing for a demanding stage musical was a big rush of reality. As she allowed, "I'm out of shape. I'm not a fit, young woman. I sweat my ass off. It's hard, but I thought that this kind of discipline would be good for me at this point. As a stand-up comic, you only have yourself to answer to. You don't have 23 other members of the cast to think about."

Rosie would be the first to admit that she was ". . . never really a singer, except for maybe in the shower. . . ." To limber up her voice for the challenge, she worked with a private coach. The stress in their sessions was on characterization and "acting interpretation" for the song numbers. As she would concede over the weeks to come, "I have a loud voice, but being blaring and obnoxious was not the right choice. I've worked a lot on acting interpretation for the songs because that's my strength."

She found the pre-tour work schedule hectic compared to the relative slow pace of filmmaking: "There's a five-minute break every hour, and that's it. And if you're not singing or dancing, you're learning your lines upstairs or going over your vocal part with the musical director. It's very grueling, although it's very fun." But, as she kept reminding herself, "The reason to do Broadway, for me, is because of my love for theater and how much it influenced my life and changed my career and goals, and just—it really enriched me as a child, and I hope to pass that on to other children who come to see this show. And it's really a family fun show and so the reason to do it is not the money."

At rehearsals, O'Donnell was definitely the new kid on the block. Therefore, the first cast work-out session was a mini-nightmare for her. When associate choreographer Jerry Mitchell called the cast to order, he announced, "We're going to step-touch, step-touch, hip, hip together, back, and up. And two and three and go." Everyone understood the directions and executed the proper movements—that is everyone but Rosie. She was as lost as a deer at a shopping mall. A befuddled Rosie piped up, "Excuse me, what was the first part? The step what? *Hello?*" She admits, "And they practically had to tutor me. . . . I've been nurtured and really held together by this wonderful cast."

As the pre-tour sessions wore on, rehearsals progressed to the dialogue scenes. Director Jeff Calhoun kept urging Rosie to play the part

with "less Stockard Channing." And she'd reply, "I'm trying, I'm trying." However, she had been so mesmerized by Channing's screen
interpretation that she found it very hard to shake the mimicry.
Meanwhile, Calhoun was having his own self-doubts. This was his first
directing job and he found himself ". . . walking on eggshells around
Rosie. I knew she was nervous, and I was intimidated." It was not a
productive situation.

Finally, one evening the two went out alone for several pitchers of
beer. Between brews, he eventually convinced Rosie that "this isn't
Hamlet we're doing" and, once this sunk in, "Rosie basically gave me
permission to do my job." As such, Calhoun relaxed and so did Rosie.
One morning, thereafter, she brought a yo-yo to rehearsal. Inwardly,
the director breathed a sigh of relief because "I never in a million years
would have thought of the yo-yo. From that moment, I knew that we
were okay."

During the course of the musical, Rosie's Rizzo has two major vocal
numbers: Act One's "Look at Me, I'm Sandra Dee" and Act Two's
"There Are Worse Things I Could Do." Calhoun and the others
revised the arrangements of the songs so that each ended with other
singers onstage joining in for the final bars of music. Calhoun realized
that although "Rosie could be a very good singer with the proper training" he had to deal with the here and now. As such he ". . . wanted to
protect her, so she never has to end a song [by herself] to applause."

Fortunately, Rosie endeared herself to much of the cast, in particular, the chorus members. One step in accomplishing that was not to act
like Big Miss Hollywood star. Rosie, actually, was just the reverse, as
she was in awe of their professionalism and the high caliber of their
talent. They, in turn, showed their appreciation by frequently helping
her out. O'Donnell explained, "So when I'm singing something and,
like, I hit the wrong note, there's a 20-year-old girl in the ensemble
named Katy [Grenfell], and she'll turn and sing louder and then look
at me and . . . try to get me towards the right note." As to the dance
parts of the show, O'Donnell had another life saver: "Sandra Purpuro,
who plays Cha-Cha, who's a great dancer [and also the understudy for
the Rizzo role] helped me a lot—and still does—through the dance
numbers. She'd go, 'left . . . and turn . . . and three and . . .' every night
until I got it ingrained in my muscles and I remembered what to do."

At last, in February 1994, the *Grease!* company embarked on a
twelve-week, multi-city tour (including Wilmington, DE, Seattle,
WA, Costa Mesa, CA, Detroit, MI, Minneapolis, MN, Washington

DC and Boston, MA). By now, Rosie had gained perspective about her performance: "You're not going to say ouch when I sing, but you're not going to be wowed the way you are with Sam Harris and Billy Porter." She also was thriving on the camaraderie of being part of a generally tight-knit stage cast. She enthused, "This is like high school to me. You get to have friends and buddies and go out after the show for a drink, and it's very nice." Of course, there were downsides to so much togetherness, "When one person gets a cold, we all get colds." And she did just that in California. By now her best friend in the cast was slim blonde Michelle Blakely who played Patty Simcox and who sang the "Rydell Fight Song."

Once O'Donnell was performing in front of appreciative theatergoers on the road, her confidence level rose and she felt empowered: "The audiences have been great. Nobody is really expecting me to get up there and be Whitney Houston. They know who I am and what I do, and I think they do expect me to be funny, and hopefully I am funny. Then the rest . . . they think, 'You know, she is all right.' Even the critics have said, 'She's all right; she's not the best singer.' Which is fine. I can take that. It's the truth."

Rosie, being Rosie, always spoke her mind. When the media inquired once too often what it was like working with Tommy Tune (since the show was billed as a Tommy Tune production) she replied, "I haven't worked with Tommy Tune, he was there only three days." When her representatives chastised her about such lack of diplomacy, she shot back, "Well, it's the truth. What do you expect me to say? 'It's great to work with Tommy! The thing about Tommy is . . .' You know, because I don't know!"

On Tuesday, March 29, 1994, *Grease!* was scheduled to open at the Orange County Performing Arts Center in Costa Mesa, California. Eight days before, on her 32nd birthday, Rosie was part of the globally televised 66th Annual Academy Awards as a presenter. As to her performance in the pre-Broadway musical revival, Don Shirley *(Los Angeles Times)* reported, "Forget the ads, you might surmise that Rosie O'Donnell is the star. Think again . . . the stars are offstage. We're talking John Amone on sets and Howell Binkley on lights." (The multilevel sets were eye-catchers using day-glo colors, spinning tires, Hula Hoops, giving it a *Happy Days* look.) As to the quality of Rosie's performance, Shirley registered, "O'Donnell's shtick is on target, though her singing voice doesn't sustain extended notes well."

Critics in other cities had much the same response to Rosie's interpretation of Betty Rizzo. Kevin Kelly (*Boston Globe*): "She has the brazen delivery of Ethel Merman. She snaps one-liners like gum, she burps, she boogies. She has two songs . . . which she sings in an even tone but, often, with the wrong emphasis." In D.C., Pamela Sommers (*Washington Post*) judged, "The part of Rizzo . . . is no stretch for the pasty-faced, tough-talking O'Donnell, but the less said about her off-key, blaring singing, the better." Nevertheless, thanks to *Grease!*'s built-in audience appeal, an intensive promotional campaign and Rosie's drawing power, *Grease!* did well financially on its road trek.

While on the road Rosie remained a favorite of interviewers because she was so down-home simple and refused to put on affectations. For example, she met with writer Patrick Pacheco at the Ritz-Carlton Hotel in Washington, D.C. while *Grease!* was playing in the nation's capital. He was researching a *Cosmopolitan* magazine profile on her and he suggested they dine at the hotel's posh Jockey Club. Rosie arrived wearing faded jeans and a sweatshirt. Noting that he had observed that she didn't fit in with the plush crowd, she launched into her philosophy of being herself: "Most people who don't want to be seen not looking their best go out in full makeup. But I always want to be myself. I'm out and look like this and the paparazzi are there. I say, 'Go right ahead.' I don't run and hide. I'm just trying to be the same person I was in the beginning."

As the 1994 version of *Grease!* headed toward its New York City debut, Rosie constantly (re)told the media that she was thrilled to be finally doing a Broadway show. She said "I always get goose bumps" when "the lights go down and you have the orchestra in front of you." For O'Donnell, "It's the reason I went into show business in the first place." Now, a veteran of a stage tour, she could assess, "Part of the reason I took this gig was for stability—six months in New York—but I never thought three months on the road would be that hard."

Finally, on Wednesday, May 11, 1994, the show opened at Broadway's Eugene O'Neill Theatre. It marked the return of the fifth longest-running show in Broadway's history, and it was one of seven Broadway music revivals that season. To get the audience in the proper mood for the show, the theatre had been redone in shades of hot pink with a matching awning outside the building. Before each performance, a cast "radio announcer" worked the audience with his patter and music, bringing selected audience members up on the stage to dance. It was much like a warm-up comic's routine before a TV sitcom taping.

In the course of *Grease!*, Rosie—wearing a pink-and-black baseball jacket, chomping on bubble gum and fiddling with a yo-yo—parades through the time-worn tale of young love between opposite types at Rydell High School. She is the tough card with the heart-of-gold who fears that her promiscuity has led her to an unwanted pregnancy. Her character is supposed to smoke cigarettes, but O'Donnell refused to light up during the show, reasoning, "I've never tried a cigarette. I'm repulsed by it."

After the opening night performance the *Grease!*, producers hosted festivities at Roseland. Liz Smith, a veteran show business reporter, was among the many on hand at Roseland to report on Rosie's entrance. Per Smith, the star arrived, ". . . in the blinding glare of TV cameras and flashbulbs. She was pawed, handled and screamed at affectionately. . . . Rosie seemed a bit shell-shocked and overwhelmed by it all, but she plunged right in and gave the press and her fans what they wanted. She posed, she mugged, she joked, she spoke. . . . She also seemed pleased with herself and she had a right to be. As *Grease*'s tough-talking Pink Lady, Rizzo, she is terrific!"

Throughout the night and during the next days, the reviewers provided their judgments about Broadway's latest arrival. Many were underwhelmed by the production. Linda Winer (*New York Newsday*) concluded, ". . . everything is busy and boring and overblown and, perhaps most damaging of all, seriously confused about its target audience . . . . Then there is O'Donnell, who seems to be a good sport, in what cannot be considered a great career move. . . . She seems way too smart for the juvenilia onstage." Clive Barnes (*New York Post*) chided the show's "dusty road company look to it" and that it "appears low-tech in everything except amplification." As to its box-office attraction he viewed, "The nominal star is Rosie O'Donnell, who looks like a cadet version of Roseanne Arnold in the secondary role of tough-baby Rizzo."

John Simon (*New York*) decided, "My only problem is with Rosie O'Donnell: She delivers her lines with the proper deadpan hauteur, but a fat Rizzo?" For Frank Scheck (*Christian Science Monitor*), "Rosie O'Donnell, playing Rizzo, barely makes an impression, which is surprising considering her exuberantly comic persona."

More sympathetic to the Hollywood expatriate was Nancy Franklin (*The New Yorker*). She thought Rosie is ". . . so game and seems so happy to be part of this enterprise that even though she doesn't project very well and doesn't have much of a singing voice, you're on her side."

Barbara and Scott Siegel (*Drama-Logue*) were more enthusiastic: "Her sardonic humor suits the role and she, more than any other actor, gives her character a little extra dimension. . . . By virtue of her strong personality, she puts over her numbers despite the fact that she has the weakest voice in the cast."

One aisle-sitter, Jeremy Gerard (*Daily Variety*), used the opening of *Grease!* as a springboard to editorialize and slam at the same time: "The draw . . . is Rosie O'Donnell, and perhaps it's fitting that an actress about to open on the big screen as Betty Rubble in *The Flintstones* proves to be something of a Neanderthal on stage as well. It seems odd to cast as the lead in a musical someone who, based on this performance, can't sing or dance—unless, of course, singing and dancing are beside the point. The point is money, and this touring production lands at the beautifully restored O'Neill having already made plenty of it, so O'Donnell must be doing something right, even if it's not singing or dancing."

Just as on the road, *Grease!* survived the critical beating and thrived on the New York stage. A new original cast album was issued, starring Rosie and the others. Thus, Rosie O'Donnell of the close-cropped hair and booming voice was now a Broadway star.

Before Rosie had signed to do *Grease!,* her former movie co-star, Tom Hanks, had warned her of a stage play, "You'll get so bored you're going to want to kill yourself after two weeks." It took a little longer, but O'Donnell soon discovered that doing the same show eight times a week, without the distraction of being on the road, was tedious. Occasionally to maintain her interest level she'd ad-lib which upset the company stage manager. Her rationale was, "I am very in tune with the audience. Being a stand-up comic you need to be. Because you have to get what's coming back so that you know what to put out. So I look at the audience. And I hear what they're saying, while I'm doing my lines. I see little girls going, 'Look Mommy, there she is, there she is!' So during 'Summer Lovin' I'll go 'had me a blast' [with a downstage wink]. And the stage manager goes, 'Why are you winking?' I'm like, 'Because they're seven, and it's a big thrill for them.'"

Sometimes, a spontaneous situation would originate with a playgoer. There was the evening where a man seated down front in the orchestra had his cellular phone ringing in the midst of the performance. Instead of turning it off, he answered the call! Later, Rosie worked that situation into a routine for her stand-up comedy act. In the riff, the man answers the phone and says, "Yeah I'm at *Grease!* You know, the show starring that chubby girl, Madonna's friend. She can't sing for x%*# . . ."

In contrast, there were occasionally obnoxious playgoers. One time there were four unruly characters out front who started punching the two elderly couples seated in front of them because these senior citizens had dared to ask them to be quiet. For the remainder of the show the quartet kept badgering their victims, mocking them with "Are we too loud now?" By the end of the performance, Rosie was fed up. After going through the daily ritual of bringing a young theatergoer up on stage to receive a show T-shirt, Rosie lashed out at the four offenders. "You four people are pieces of shit. You're scum—and you should never walk into a theater again. Who do you think you are to punch somebody in the head? If it was up to me I would've thrown your sorry asses out into the street." The audience cheered. However, three days later, Rosie opened the gossip page of a New York paper and read an item that not only was she shouting these days at the producers, but she was yelling at the audience. It was hard to win.

Ultimately, for Rosie, the joy of being in the theatre were the youngsters who waited by the stage door after the show—just as she had done years ago with her mother. It always recharged her to see them ". . . with that shiny *Playbill* in their hands and their eyes all wide and full of wonder. *That's* why you do it!"

During the *Grease!* run, Rosie shared an Upper West Side Manhattan apartment with cast-mate, Michelle Blakely. Despite playing on the Broadway bowling league (Rosie bowled a 168) and softball teams, O'Donnell found herself packing on the pounds. She noticeably weighed a lot during this period, which led to a few tart exchanges with the media. For example, she advised one interviewer, "I'm not staying at a hundred-seventy pounds because I want to." As she lost the battle with her diet, it got harder and harder to get into her *Grease!* costumes. She claimed that her dresser, Carol, needed her mother's help to zip up O'Donnell's corset which she required to create a Fifties' sort of hourglass figure.

As time wore on, the monotony of her work routine got to Rosie. It didn't help matters that, by now, she really abhorred the show's basic message: "if you're a good girl, you should become a slutty girl to fit in, and then everyone will like you." She even had her least favored scene in *Grease!*, one she couldn't wait to get through each performance. Per Rosie, it occurs in the show when Rizzo thinks she's pregnant. ". . . and she's so upset and she cries, and then she does this song ["There Are

Worse Things I Could Do"] with her friends. And then five seconds later she goes, 'Good thing, I got my friends, phew!' Like the whole thing is resolved because she's not pregnant. . . . Every night that I go out and I have to do that I think, 'Oh, God!' I hate what I have to say."

Finally, Rosie's *Grease!* contract expired and she left the production in the fall of 1994. (By this point O'Donnell had nodes on her vocal chords from the strain of her weekly onstage singing.) The musical continued its Broadway run, first with Maureen McCormick (Marcia of TV's *The Brady Bunch*) as Rizzo and then, as of November 22, 1994, Brooke Shields assuming O'Donnell's former assignment. Shields admitted that she'd seen Rosie in the role a few times ". . . just to get a sense of the production as a whole. And although the dialogue is seemingly the same, I didn't really take any tips from her. They've added a great deal of dancing to my part."

Later, when someone asked Rosie if she'd ever do another Broadway musical, she said, "Buy the [*Grease!*] CD, my days as a singer are over. Did they ever begin?"

· 18 ·

Well, I have a lot of friends and I go out socially, but I haven't had the time to really focus on a relationship.

Rosie O'Donnell, July 1993

*B*eing a successful stand-up comic on the club circuit brings with it a degree of public visibility, but nothing compared to being the host of a hip, long-running cable program (*Stand-Up Spotlight*). And that, in turn, pales next to being the star of highly promoted motion pictures (*A League of Their Own, Sleepless in Seattle, The Flintstones, Exit to Eden*). Add into the mix touring and starring on Broadway in a popular musical (*Grease!*) and being the veteran of two TV sitcoms (*Gimme a Break, Stand by Your Man*). Taking all these achievements into account, as well as charity fund-raising activities and guest appearances on assorted TV talk shows, and you have the very well-known Rosie O'Donnell as of late 1994.

It was only natural, as Rosie became increasingly prominent in show business, that the media would more frequently seek her out as a subject to profile. At first, it had been enough to cite and discuss her many accomplishments in her increasingly remarkable career. However, it was inevitable that "just" reciting the latest facts in her rise up the show business ladder would not satisfy the media's thirst for hard copy and the public's curiosity about this laugh-maker.

While Rosie has long been forthright about many subjects dealing with her life and work, her private social life has remained, thus far, mostly just that. For example, there was the following exchange on national television. It was July 26, 1993 and Rosie was being interviewed on *Larry King Live*, the CNN-Cable talk show.

ROSIE O'DONNELL: I didn't date at all. I started doing stand-up when I was 16, and I'm 31 years old and I have yet to really date—seriously.
LARRY KING: You don't see a boy?
ROSIE O'DONNELL: Well, really, I mean, I have sort of this myopic focus on my career, and I'm trying right now to have more balance in my life. . . .

Not taking the apparent cue from his guest in the "hot seat" to drop the current topic, King, the persistent journalist, continued to probe in a most friendly way:

LARRY KING: So you, then, have not been in love with anyone?
ROSIE O'DONNELL: Not really in a way that I think—more than sort of initial infatuation. I don't know, I mean, I've been in love but not in that—.
LARRY KING: Deep sense.
ROSIE O'DONNELL: . . . you know, not in that 'forever' kind of way.

This line of pointed interrogation was nothing new for the show business veteran. As a stand-up comic turned TV, film and stage actor, she had been subjected to journalists' scrutiny over two decades. By now, this energetic public figure had become expert at giving obscure responses whenever she was so inclined or, better yet, to divert the interrogator into more neutral territory—i.e., her career, her political beliefs, etc. Intriguingly, reflecting on and/or discussing her unhappy childhood, as well as her limited interaction with her dad over the past several years, were not in the "No-No" territory when Rosie was undergoing a hard-core question-and-answer session with the media.

It was not that sophisticated investigative journalists were misled by Rosie's diversionary tactics on topics they thought would interest the public. For example, a few years later, in May 1996, when Gail Shister of the Knight-Ridder Newspapers Syndicate interviewed Rosie for a forthcoming article, Shister would observe, "O'Donnell is communicative about everything except her private life. Her mantra is that she's single and doesn't have time to date." And O'Donnell knew exactly what she was doing in her ongoing cat-and-mouse game when news gatherers got too personal in their lines of questioning. As O'Donnell admitted in Shister's newspaper piece, "I'm as vague as I need to be or want to be, for the time being."

On another occasion when a journalist was politely pushing O'Donnell to the wall to say something more precise and quotable than "I'm much too busy" regarding her romantic life, Rosie snapped back, "it's the answer I give." Then in a complete about-face, that smacks of the lady-doth-protest-too-much syndrome, O'Donnell answered, "Not that I'm bothered by the questions."

Rosie has not always dished out serious or raw-nerve responses when the subject of dating came up in the conversation. Sometimes, she has relied on her comedic stock-in-trade abilities to answer deftly but really not answer, the targeted query. For example, when she was a guest on Sally Jessy Raphael's syndicated TV talk show in July 1990, Raphael observed that none of the panel of five women comics (Rosie, Susie Essman, Pudgy, Carol Siskind and Carrie Snow) was married at the time. It led Sally to wondering, "Why are none of you married? This is very scary. Is there something that says the minute you get married you're not funny anymore?"

Rosie's on-the-spot response to Raphael was to quip, ". . . Sally, you ever notice the word 'engaged' has the word 'gag' in the middle of it? Just something to think about, ladies. Something to think about." When that didn't end the matter, O'Donnell parried another joke: "It's hard to meet people. I'm dating a guy now, he's on TV. You might know him. He's on *America's Most Wanted*. . . . Sally, he looks a lot better than that sketch. He really does. I'm telling you right now. Whenever he gets out of line—You know, whenever he gets out of line, I go, 'Hey I've got that 1-800 number, buddy.' You know, and it keeps him right. . . ."

O'Donnell has also employed the bashful tactic as when, for example, the subject of romance came up with Marjorie Rosen for a July 1992 *People* magazine profile. Rosie's demure response was that she was "single, dating and available." Or, on occasion, Rosie has utilized the semi-disclosure gambit that leaves the reader wondering what of the statement is real and what it is really saying: "I'm a workaholic who isn't happy without a 24-hour day, I can't give up the comedy gig, either . . . . [There's] no one special, but, believe me, I'm looking. Actually I lied, I'm in love."

Yet another of Rosie's public postures has been to both avoid naming the subject(s) of her romantic attention (one could label that being discreet), but also to NOT refer to the object(s) of her amorous attention by gender. One case in point occurred when *People* magazine in mid-1993 asked the comic what made her sleepless. O'Donnell answered: "Heartache. When I'm in a turbulent relationship. I'm usually sleepless, tossing and turning and trying to find a remedy. I get up and play Nintendo: Super Mario Bros.3." Or: "Once I fell madly in love and was going to Paris and as was this person the same day which was nicely surprising. I thought it somehow fated." Additionally, in a recent question-and-answer session with the press, Rosie would insist regarding marriage: "No, I never give up on it. I think you should never give up. No matter what your quest is."

Sometimes, even, Rosie would seemingly obscure the status and direction of her romantic life by remarks of indirection which could mean a number of things depending on how much one really knew about the subject's private life. For example, when explaining one of the reasons she chose to adopt a child as a single parent in mid-1995, she would say, "If I was with a man I wanted to have a child with, I would have gotten pregnant. But that was not the case."

• • •

How long Rosie will maintain her "for the time being" non-disclosure rule about her private social life is anyone's guess. Nevertheless, and meanwhile, there is much to be learned from what Rosie has said and not said about her personal social life and from what others have reported on the same subject.

As her mother had died when she was ten, Rosie lived, for the next several years, in a single-parent household in which her father was an "absentee" dad, too involved in providing for his family and dealing with his grief in his own way, to pay much attention to his kids. This turn of events most probably squelched any real potential of his being a male role model for his older daughter as she matured. In fact, years later, in an article entitled "Why Rosie O'Donnell Doesn't Have a Guy," *Globe* reporter Joe Mullins cites an unspecified pal on the subject of how Mr. O'Donnell's emotional withdrawal affected Rosie: "That's seared into her mind. Rosie decided men could never meet her emotional needs."

And Rosie couldn't look to her two older brothers—only a few years her senior—as replacement male role models. When Mrs. O'Donnell died in 1973, all five children had, by necessity, bonded into a team unit with each member often sharing equal responsibilities for their joint emotional survival and doing chores around the house. Thus, Rosie, so it seems, was on a par with her older siblings and couldn't be expected to look to them for guidance. This situation did not change with time. She increasingly took on more responsibility for running the household and she became, to a degree, a replacement mother figure for her brothers (two older, one younger) and sister (younger).

In such an emotionally confused environment, Rosie found an early refuge in heavy-duty TV watching (as did her brothers and sister). Rosie relied on the tube for much of her role modeling during her crucial pre-teen years. (She would tell *TV Guide* in August 1993, "My mother died when I was little, so I liked all the shows with single parents—*Nanny and the Professor, Eight Is Enough, The Courtship of Eddie's Father*. They represented what I was living.") This intensive TV viewing was, at best, a weak substitute for real life. In many ways, most likely, the young O'Donnell was learning to sublimate important one-on-one actual relationships with vicarious experiences.

When O'Donnell was not absorbed in the world of TV, she found diversion at the movies and in theater-going. Like TV, these were not only a welcome means of entertainment and escape, but they were teaching her about her chosen profession—being an entertainer. In addition, her ardent, almost obsessive, hopes of becoming a performer were another way not to deal with personal relationships because she could tell herself that she was too busy with her career plans for such mundane things as interpersonal relationships on any kind of level.

Meanwhile, like so many pre-teen and adolescent girls, Rosie was a tomboy, excelling in sports at school and in the neighborhood. A high achiever on the playing field as in her other pursuits, she again broke with tradition. She was excelling in sports, an area that was considered—especially in the past—the domain of males. Thus, she was again breaking with the then-accepted gender balance of the dominant male and the more passive female. Just as at home she was considered an equal with the other males of the family, so was she in the domain of athletic competition. It was a situation almost certain to dissuade boys her age from wanting to date her. This lack of males interested in dating her certainly would have been upsetting to her feminine self-esteem, already shaky due to being big-boned and at times hefty.

Rosie's long-cherished dream was to be a Broadway star like her idols Barbra Streisand and Bette Midler. Instead, she drifted into the world of stand-up comedy partly by accident and partly from her growing awareness that she could make others laugh. Years earlier she'd learned, as did the rest of her siblings, that it was far easier to express their emotions to their widowed father through a joke or wisecrack than by saying exactly how they felt. It became a way of life to be funny even about serious matters.

At the age of sixteen Rosie first dabbled in the world of stand-up comedy. Even with her faltering initial efforts, it reinforced her childhood habit of gaining attention and approval by being funny. Making jokes in a comedy club or in the high school corridor may have been good for honing her craft, but it was strengthening her habit of communicating *at* people rather than *with* people. It would create an odd disparity in her high school years and thereafter. On one hand she was outgoing, supportive and fun when she was one of the gang with girls or one of the guys when she was kidding with the boys. However, it certainly did not require her to be emotionally open on any great level with her schoolmates of either sex.

While other high-schoolers her age were date-happy, Rosie, at least so far as she has revealed, was not. Over the years, she would frequently repeat the statement, "Because I started doing stand-up comedy when I was 16, I rarely dated." On another occasion she would say about her apparently workaholic life, ". . . I took all that energy and gut instinct and channeled it into my career. I had tunnel vision from sixteen to thirty. . . ."

Thus, apparently, during these years she remained engrossed in her world of education, school extracurricular activities, part-time work, household-running, career-learning, TV watching, theater-going, etc. Such a conclusion is reinforced by a mid-1996 tabloid article which quoted one of Rosie's Commack South High School classmates as saying, "I don't remember her ever having a boyfriend, even though she was very popular with the boys."

At first blush, it would seem likely that Rosie's pattern of total career-focus remained the same during her brief college tenure, first at Dickinson in Carlyle, Pennsylvania and then at Boston University in Massachusetts. However, years later she would remark, out of the blue, "If I were a gay man, I'd probably be dead by now. . . . When I was in college and sexually active, no one was that careful."

When Rosie entered the professional world of stand-up comedy, she found that traveling on the road for such playdates was traumatic on several levels. It's tough enough for any beginner to make headway in any profession. However, the world of comedy is a particularly tough battleground in that it requires great dedication and stamina to keep afloat in the field. What made it even harder for O'Donnell was that, at the time, there were very few female comics in the stand-up business. If it took a lot of nerve for a young male comic to survive the course to make a name for himself, it was that much more difficult for a woman in the 1980s to do the same. O'Donnell had to be even more aggressive, determined and thick-skinned than her male peers. It meant that she had to build an emotional shield against hurt and disappointment, diverting such wounds through a stubborn, tunnel-vision focus on succeeding in the joke business.

That Rosie had created such an ingrained pattern of emotional self-protection is substantiated by entertainment industry co-workers. Gary Foster who produced *Sleepless in Seattle* (1992) would observe of featured player, Rosie, "She's always deflecting things toward everyone else so nobody can get that close." John Badham, who directed O'Donnell in *Another Stakeout* would note of her outer toughness quality, "That's a defense mechanism." Even O'Donnell would acknowledge in 1994, "I think I need to figure out why it is I distract myself from having a real private life by working constantly. And when I've figured that out, I think then it'll be time to find someone."

There was another aspect to O'Donnell's embarking on stand-up comedy, a field dominated by men. Once again, she was breaking "accepted" social tradition. As when she was a child/adult homemaker and also when she played sports, she was knocking through the walls of a male-controlled business. In doing so, she was once more proving that she was as good as most, and better than many, men in the business. It certainly would not have scored her dating points with male co-workers who would have easily been intimidated and/or put off by her success. And if they weren't going to make the first move—which was then and still is considered the right thing to do by many people— it is easy to see why a still inwardly shy Rosie would ignore or repress the matter of dating at this stage in her life.

In addition, there were Rosie's bad experiences in her early adult life when she was doing comedy on the road. On such out-of-town engagements, she frequently had to share apartments temporarily with older, more seasoned male comedians who'd pick up a girl here or there and bring them back to the club condo for a quick bout of noisy sex, unmindful of the effect it would and did have on Rosie. Such experiences certainly would have done nothing to make dating or quick sex with men seem appealing to the impressionable Rosie.

As the years passed, Rosie moved from small stand-up comedy gigs to more important ones and then on to TV assignments and major motion pictures. While making *A League of Their Own*, O'Donnell met and became the new best friend of that most emancipated of women, Madonna. With this superstar, Rosie began circulating in an A-list crowd in New York and Los Angeles and observing firsthand a far more sophisticated, plush lifestyle. As time went on, other show business friends in O'Donnell's widening circle of celebrity pals would include Ellen DeGeneres, Demi Moore, Melanie Griffith and Rita Wilson (the actress wife of Tom Hanks).

In the early to mid-1990s, a new image emerged of Rosie O'Donnell as a very together person who was in full command of her life in front of or out of the spotlight. However, that was not the actual case. As she would reveal in a 1996 TV interview, "I always need to be kinda in control and I have this kind of omnipotence of force in my career and nearly impotence in my private life because as much as I am powerful and I know what movie I want to do and . . . I'm going to direct this, and I'm going to go here . . . . I have that not knowing in my private life. I don't know which apartment I should buy, who I should get involved with, if I should be committed, if I should be monogamous. I'm in a constant state of confusion."

And when she was on this inconclusive dating search, how was she going about it? From the scant information she fed the media in the early 1990s, Rosie the successful businessperson gave the impression of a somewhat shy individual pushing tentatively into the world of typical dating. To Nancy Griffin (*Premiere* magazine) she confided in mid-1993 about her experience with the world of high technology and the options it opened: "I have this computer service, America Online, where you talk to other people in the country. You can type to people in Texas, New York—you all have aliases. And it's men as much as women, looking for romance and love. I think that men just don't discuss it as much as women do." (At one time, O'Donnell's handle on America Online was "Rosie Oh O;" at another point it was "squiggly butt.")

She was also, so it seemed, extremely fanciful about love beneath her tough outer shell. When asked what was her favorite romantic movie, she answered, "You're not going to believe this: *The Sound of Music*, I'm not kidding! That was, like, the ultimate love story. There was the baroness, and she won even though she was plain and humble and beautiful and wholesome. And the sexy, voluptuous, mean woman lost. That was really a romantic ideal for me."

As more time passed and Rosie became even more successful, she enunciated to the press that she was blossoming into a date-oriented woman of the '90s. In discussing romantic socializing, she said in 1994: "Now I'm getting into that area of my life. It's generally men who are much stronger and don't have a problem with power issues that are attracted to my kind of strength. . . . Dealing with fame is hard for friends and relationships, and it's hard for love interests. But I have no regrets. There are a lot of good things about fame, too. You have access to everything—movies, theater, Wimbledon tickets."

At this point in time, by Rosie's choice and media discretion, most of the public knew far more about O'Donnell's favorite TV shows (daytime: *The Oprah Winfrey Show*; nighttime: *Rescue 911*) than they did about O'Donnell's dating habits or objects of her affections. But that was quickly changing.

For the June 1993 issue of *Mirabella* magazine, Trish Deitch Rohrer interviewed Rosie O'Donnell at a Beverly Hills cafe. During the course of the profile she referred to Rosie's "good friend, singer Sophie B. Hawkins, who got O'Donnell into acupuncture and is talking to her about diet." In the April 1993 issue of *US* magazine in a mini-profile of 25-year-old Hawkins, this singer, in turn, referred to her comedian friend, saying, "I play baseball. Rosie O'Donnell's my coach. She's killer!"

Blonde, leggy Hawkins, whose raunchy rock music is a cross between Tina Turner and Melissa Etheridge and combines pop blues with rock, has recorded such albums as *Tongues and Tails* (1992) and *Whaler* (1995). (Her song, "As I Lay Me Down" from her second album was used in Rosie's movie, *Now and Then*, 1995.) At age fourteen, Hawkins had left home (her father was a lawyer, her mother a writer) to live with an African-American drummer then in his 40s. That was the start of her real music education which, in subsequent years, was as eclectic as her jammed-packed lifestyle, which included a stint as a construction worker. By the 1990s, after close relationships with members of both sexes, she preferred to call herself "omnisexual." She and Rosie became friends in the early 1990s, around the time that O'Donnell was doing the party circuit with Madonna.

In February 1995, Hawkins was interviewed by *Details* magazine. She told interviewer Brantley Bardin, "I know one famous person and that's enough for me." When he asked who, she answered "Oh, Rosie

O'Donnell" and then launched into a candid discussion of her friend. "When we first started hanging out it was very private, and then I realized she had this whole other world. So through her I met everybody I wanted to. And I didn't just meet them. Because Rosie is such a celebrity she has 'dinner' with them. But to me there's nothing satisfying about having dinner with someone every three months—it's because you're famous that you love each other so much. I really changed as a result of knowing Rosie and getting into a lot of extremely uncomfortable situations."

Hawkins then acknowledged that her rapport with Rosie had altered in more recent times: ". . . I can't hang with her in that realm of the famous. She's a real celebrity and she likes it." As to Rosie's friendship with Madonna, Sophie replied, ". . . that's where I learned all I needed to learn about what happens to famous people."

According to the July 2, 1996 issue of the *Globe*, O'Donnell's friendship with Hawkins had changed courses. The tabloid alleged that Hawkins, who was once "one of Rosie's strongest emotional attachments" was no longer so. *Globe* reporter Joe Mullins then quoted a source who said "Although they've both gone on to other relationships, Sophie is still having a tough time with the loss."

But that seemed to have been the tip of the iceberg, at least according to the *Globe*. In a September 3, 1996 article entitled "Rosie's Gay Marriage," reporter Diane Albright quotes sources who claim to have been familiar with O'Donnell's lifestyle from and during her early stand-up comedy years. One such person, listed as a show business talent manager, is quoted as saying, "Rosie told me almost from the moment we met, 'I'm a gay woman. . . .' She said, 'I have men friends, but there's never anything romantic going on.'" The source, according to Albright, also said that O'Donnell told him, "I've been with several women around the country, but I've never found that special woman I wanted to spend my life with." (This September 3, 1996 *Globe* article led the *New York Post* to report "Popular talk show host Rosie O'Donnell gets 'outed' in the new issue of the *Globe*.")

Meanwhile, Diane Albright, in a prior (July 23, 1996) *Globe* article ("Rough Rider Rosie") had detailed in text—with photos of the getaway holiday—about Rosie and Michelle Blakely and friends on holiday in Miami, Florida where O'Donnell owns a condo in a high-rise apartment building. The piece included photos of a very hefty Rosie and the petite blonde Blakely motorcycle riding and jet skiing at Key Biscayne. In case anyone should miss its gist, the article was subtitled

"Talk queen has gay old time on secret getaway with playmates." That piece labeled Michelle as Rosie's "ex-roommate," but in her follow-up story ("Rosie's Gay Marriage") for the *Globe* (September 3, 1996), Albright quotes a "friend" as saying "they're planning their lives together. . . . They share Rosie's New York high-rise condo, her fame and fortune and they both change little Parker's [Rosie's adopted son] diapers." According to Albright, "The 34-year-old funny gal and Michelle are also renovating a fabulous mansion that once belonged to Helen Hayes in Nyack, New York." (Reportedly, neither Rosie nor her representatives responded to these "outing" stories.)

In a later issue (October 29, 1996) of the *Globe,* in an article entitled "Talk Show Hosts' Real-Life Scandals," under the heading "Homosexuality" and subtitle "Queen of Nice has live-in galpal," the publication printed under the Rosie O'Donnell section heading "PER-SONAL SCANDAL": "*Globe* recently revealed that daytime TV's new Queen of Nice has a live-in galpal who's helping her raise her adopted son." This new mini-article also included a frequently published photo of Rosie riding a motorcycle with her passenger being Michelle Blakely.

And who is Michelle Blakely? According to *Theatre World* annual, Michelle was born on July 27, 1969 in Harrisonburg, Virginia and is a graduate of New York University. After playing in regional theatre and touring in the national company of the musical *Grand Hotel*, she made her off-Broadway debut in *Day Dreams: The Music and Magic of Doris Day* (1992) and her Broadway bow in the revival of *Grease!* (1994) which featured Rosie. Later, she would have a role in the Showtime Cable television movie, *Twilight of the Golds* (1997), which also featured O'Donnell.

In the months since her TV talk show debuted in June 1996, Rosie has occasionally referenced a "Michelle" on the air. (One might assume O'Donnell is referring to Michelle Blakely.) One such time, the multimedia star referred to "Michelle" having recently gone with her on holiday to Hawaii. On another occasion, when Charles Nelson Reilly was a show guest, O'Donnell reminded the actor/director that "Michelle" had worked with him at the Burt Reynolds Dinner Theatre in Jupiter, Florida.

• • •

More recently, fellow comedian Ellen DeGeneres was a guest on *The Rosie O'Donnell Show*. DeGeneres was making the round of talk programs to follow up on a prior news leak that on her TV sitcom, *Ellen*, her character of Ellen Morgan was planning to come out of the closet soon and be revealed as lesbian. This information caused a furor with network executives and ad agencies fearing a backlash from moral and religious leaders of the conservative right in the U.S. As such, it led to much speculation whether the controversial event would actually happen in the 1996-1997 TV season.

Coming onstage of *The Rosie O'Donnell Show*, Ellen DeGeneres joked that yes it was true that storylines on her series had been leading to a special revelation about her television alter ego. DeGeneres revealed—in mock humor—that yes, her character was actually, ". . . Lebanese." (This was DeGeneres' veiled, comical way of referencing the lesbian issue.) Ellen then launched into a satirical monologue, playing on the fact that recent *Ellen* scripts had been hinting at her now-it-can-be-told "Lebanese" nature (e.g., that her character ate hummus and baba ganoush, that she was a fan of actress Kathy Najimy and radio disc jockey Casey Kasem).

At one point in DeGeneres' on camera chat with O'Donnell, Rosie blurted out that she too was a big fan of veteran radio personality Casey Kasem. It led O'Donnell to say, "Maybe I'm Lebanese, too." DeGeneres replied, "I picked up sometimes that you might be Lebanese."

On the same episode of *The Rosie O'Donnell Show*, Rosie and Ellen also discussed recent supermarket tabloid articles in which the supposed "true facts" about their private lives were dissected for public consumption. DeGeneres insisted that these articles, especially one which indicated Ellen ate at particular gay-friendly restaurants were not true. The conversation led an amused but rather guarded Rosie to admit that such recent tabloid pieces involving her own offstage life were upsetting. Before going on to other matters, O'Donnell asked her guest, "How do you deal with the stress?" For the astute viewer—who also kept up with the tabloid press—the oblique discussion between Rosie and Ellen provided a great deal of food for thought.

At this time that is about all the information, or conjecture, that Rosie's wide and adoring public has about her love life, conventional or unconventional as it may be.

· 19 ·

I'm not aspiring to take Meryl Streep's roles. I don't want to do
Medea *after* Grease! *The people I relate to are like Vivian Vance . .*
. . I see myself as Rhoda, not Mary Tyler Moore.

Rosie O'Donnell, September 1994

*B*efore Rosie O'Donnell tackled *Grease!*, she entertained
thoughts of making the New York stage her real "home" and
of relegating Hollywood to a place to visit for making movies
or to see friends. However, her G*rease!* experience (especially those last
torturous months of monotony) had finally put to rest her childhood
ambitions to appear on Broadway. She was now ready to move on.

While singing and time-stepping in *Grease!*, Rosie had not been forgotten by Hollywood or by moviegoers. If the long-marinating *Car 54,
Where Are You?* and *I'll Do Anything* had come and gone quickly at theatres in early 1994, that year's summer blockbuster, *The Flintstones,*
had more than erased the memory of those two entries. Later, when
Exit to Eden was unchained for public inspection in October 1984, its
poor reception did nothing for the careers of the other principal players. However, Rosie, always the shrewd self-promoter, had used the
shaky R-rated vehicle to gain tremendous media attention.
(Apparently, the naughty but amusing image of her cavorting in a
leather bustier was now etched forever into the public's mind.)

Thus, while Rosie was on a sabbatical from motion pictures, the film
industry had made two key judgments about the comedian's value to a
big screen project: (1) O'Donnell was a tremendous asset in publiciz-

ing a movie —before, during and after its production, and (2) Rosie was developing a sizable, loyal following at the box-office.

Meanwhile, O'Donnell was being closely monitored by television executives. She had already shone as the emcee of VH-1 *Stand-Up Spotlight* over several years and was an irrepressible, heartwarming personality when a guest on morning interview and talk shows. Now, she was fast gaining a reputation as a darling of the late night talk show circuit.

On January 5, 1994, she made her debut on TV's *The Late Show with David Letterman* and the response had been extremely favorable both with viewers at home and with the *Letterman* staff. As Daniel Kellison—then a *Letterman* segment producer and later to become O'Donnell's executive producer on her own 1996 talk show—would observe, "Very few people can come on *Letterman* the first time and destroy the audience. Rosie did it. . . . We could call her two hours before the show and say, 'A guest just fell out. Can you help us?' She'd say, 'I have nothing to talk about.' Then 45 minutes later, after telling you what happened at lunch that day, you're on the floor."

While Rosie had been back East, she saw a great deal of her sister, Maureen, and her two nieces living in New Jersey. O'Donnell mingled far less with her brothers who were preoccupied with their own careers and families and lived further away than did her sister. As for her dad who was based in North Carolina with his wife Mary, Rosie still was unable to forget the past and establish a close new bond with him. Like her father, she was full of pride and unhealed wounds from past hurts. Nevertheless, he was her father and she still craved his approval. She especially wanted him to acknowledge that she was doing well in her career. But for reasons best known to him, Edward O'Donnell could not or would not verbalize his feelings about her achievements. As Rosie confided to Al Roker on his cable TV talk show: "I'll call him and he'll say his friend has seen a movie [I'm in] or—you know, like, I'll call him and he'll, like, be 'You know, sweetheart, Mr. O'Malley saw you on *Letterman*.' I'm like, 'Oh, he saw'—'Yeah, he said you were funny.' So he'll never admit it. He's very sort of stoically Irish, unemotional. But my sister and my two nieces are very, very proud. They usually come with me to all the things and they've been on TV [with me]."

As before *Grease!*, *Rosie* was still undergoing sporadic therapy. (She told one interviewer—"Do you think I've got it all together? Are you out of your mind?") She explained "Just because I have stability in my career doesn't mean I don't have the same insecurities as everyone else."

Part of her rationale for the sessions was hopefully to erase some of her childhood angst and to explore the reasons for her lack of any enduring romance. As for being an "emotional eater" she had long ago acknowledged that was her reality. More recently, she'd concluded that ". . . my days of Weight Watchers and diet programs are over." To her mind now, if she continued to fluctuate between 140 to 170 pounds or higher, so be it. She'd had more than enough of ritualistically weighing herself, then being depressed, and in the next moment, despite or because of the scale's verdict, going on a junk food binge. From now on, she declared, everyone, including herself, would have to accept her as she was—like it or not.

One of those who did accept O'Donnell just as she was, was Buster her new long-haired Chihuahua puppy. (She would later acquire a second one, named Valentine.) However, Rosie was somewhat embarrassed to admit this new addition in her household. She said, "Because it's very Zsa Zsa Gabor to own a Chihuahua and people laugh when they see I have a Chihuahua. I think that . . . they assume I'll have a pit bull or something, you know, something that could kill you, a Doberman, you know." She also admitted, "No, I don't put him on a leash. He doesn't like the collar. I just sort of take him everywhere and in a very annoying sort of movie star way, you know. I, like, carry him around, and people go, 'This is a restaurant, you can't have your dog,' and, like, 'I'm Rosie O'Donnell!' And then they let me in. . . . I just do it, because—. . . . I feel like I can [do this], maybe for another year, until people are sick of me, and then, you know, I'll have to keep him home."

• • •

One of the movie offers Rosie received during *Grease!* was to join Hugh Grant, Julianne Moore and Tom Arnold in the screen comedy, *Nine Months* (1995). If she agreed, O'Donnell would be playing Arnold's wife in this Twentieth Century-Fox production. That, in itself, was ironic because for a long time Rosie had been mistaken frequently by many people as being Tom's real life ex-wife, Roseanne. For whatever reason, O'Donnell declined the project and was replaced by Joan Cusack.

Instead, Rosie chose to appear in *Gaslight Edition*, later retitled *Now and Then* (1995). There were several elements to the project that appealed to Rosie. Very much a feminist, she was intrigued to be in this movie directed by a woman (Lesli Linka Glatter), produced by women (Demi Moore, Suzanne Todd, Jennifer Todd) and based on a semi-autobiographical story by a female scenarist (I. Marlene King). Then too, making the film would be a fun time with her actress friend Rita Wilson. It would also be a chance to work with Demi Moore and Melanie Griffith and a reunion of sorts with young Gaby Hoffman (who had also been in *Sleepless*). Others in the new production would include Cloris Leachman, an alumnus of O'Donnell's favorite TV series (*The Mary Tyler Moore Show*) and fast-rising actor/comic, Janeane Garofalo. (The latter, who made her start like Rosie in stand-up comedy, was being touted in the film industry as the new, slightly younger Rosie O'Donnell.)

Production for *Now and Then* began in early November 1994. Location shooting was undertaken in the Savannah, Georgia area, which was to stand in for a small Midwestern town. The low-budget feature was to be a nostalgic account of four thirtysomething women reuniting in their hometown when one of their number (Rita Wilson) gives birth to her first child. For this maiden effort by Demi Moore's production company, Demi, Melanie, Rita and Rosie were cast as story "book ends," appearing as the adult versions of their adolescent selves. Moore was a bohemian novelist, Griffith a much-married movie star, Rita a housewife and Rosie was the down-to-earth local physician. The bulk of the storyline was to be devoted to the young counterparts of the quartet as they struggle through childhood to adolescence during the hot, eventful summer of 1970 in Shelby, Indiana.

For Rosie, the location shoot was an opportunity to become friends with two very established stars (Moore, Griffith) who had made their way successfully in the male-dominated film industry. With such a subordinate-sized role to play oncamera, O'Donnell had ample chance to observe the filmmaking process, especially the directing (which she hoped to undertake one day soon) and the producing (which appealed to her need for control and order). As was her wont, Rosie spent a good deal of time with the young performers. When asked what they did together, she said, "We hang. We play Twister."

One evening during the shoot, while Demi's actor husband, Bruce Willis, was visiting the site, they all (Demi, Bruce, Melanie, Rita and Rosie) went bar-hopping. Their destination was Club One, a Savannah nightspot which featured Lady Chablis, the grand dame transvestite made famous in the best-seller book, *Midnight in the Garden of Good and Evil* (1994). Rosie would later recount this adventure into the bizarre: "I'm from New York City. I've seen the best of them. It wasn't exactly the highlight of my trip. Melanie was a bit star-tled—I don't know how many drag bars she's been to. Rita rolls with the punches. Demi's fascination with the whole thing was more enter-taining to me than the drag queens."

If that evening's escapade was exotic, another memorable night in Georgia was unforgettable for Rosie. Earlier that day O'Donnell, who usually had a cast-iron stomach, had eaten something that badly dis-agreed with her. She was in such pain that she hastened—moaning and groaning—to the emergency room of the closest Savannah hospital. It was quickly determined that she had food poisoning. Once treated, it was suggested that she remain overnight for observation. Rosie agreed reluctantly. However, as the evening wore on she had no peace of mind, as the staff kept trooping in to catch sight of a movie star and request-ing her autograph. By early morning, the comic could take no more. She surreptitiously called Demi to come rescue her. The commando squad of Moore and Griffith arrived by 3 a.m. and they sneaked a much-relieved, if exhausted, Rosie out of the fan kingdom from hell.

Now and Then would be released in October 1994 to very mixed reviews. For one thing, it was highly promoted as a feature starring the four adult women when, in reality, the bulk of the screen time was given over to the quartet of young (and very talented) teen performers. For another, it was most unfavorably compared to a similar coming-of-age story, *Stand by Me* (1986), which dealt with adolescent boys. However, that popular Rob Reiner-directed feature was judged a far more impressive telling of the rites of passage than this later artificially sentimental new release.

Edward Guthmann (*San Francisco Chronicle*) insisted, "You have to be a tin-hearted grouch not to find something to like in *Now and Then*." Unfortunately, there were plenty of "grouches" among the fourth estate: John Anderson (*Los Angeles Times*) judged *Now and Then* to be ". . . a memory film that derails into a smoldering heap before leaving the station." Yardena Arar (*Los Angeles Reader*) alerted her readers: "But, apart from catching up with the rising young stars, there's no compelling reason to go out of your way for this one." FX Feeney (*Los Angeles Weekly*) was even less charitable: ". . . the grownups in the picture—particularly the four bankables—feel freakish and exaggerated. The movie dies when they hold center stage, but merci-fully, these scenes constitute a fraction of the picture." For Roger Ebert (*Chicago Sun-Times*), "*Now and Then* is all made up of artificial bits and pieces." Ebert also admitted, "I would have liked to be a fly on the wall during the production meetings for *Now and Then*. . . . What was the purpose of the wraparound bookends with the big names?"

Rosie's reviews were a mixed bag as well. Anderson of the *Los Angeles Times* commended her " . . . nice wry delivery when the infrequently funny line comes her way." However, Caryn James (*New York Times*), who found the picture "a little dull and much too predictable," called attention, in particular, to the transitions between the young to the mature actresses: "The only odd leap is that the tomboy Roberta, convincingly played by Christina Ricci . . . grows up to be Rosie O'Donnell; a physical jolt that makes you think a changeling must have been put in Roberta's place at 13." (Later, *Movieline* magazine, in a feature entitled "100 Dumbest Things Hollywood's Done Lately" would list as #89: "Rosie O'Donnell was cast as the grown-up version of Christina Ricci in *Now and Then*.")

That wasn't the only thing about O'Donnell's role as Dr. Roberta Martin that was unusual. Her screen character had been neutered between the initial filming and the post-production. According to Rosie: "The woman I played was quite assuredly a gay woman. I was very happy because it was a movie for women and about girls' friendships, which I think there aren't enough of. The lesbian storyline made it an interesting role to act and said something interesting about how people are accepting of each other. So there was a scene where they say, 'How's Susie?' or whatever my girlfriend's name is. And I say, 'Oh, she's fine . . .,' and Rita Wilson's character interrupts and says, 'You know, they're thinking of adopting now. It's perfectly fine. It's very progressive.' Well, in looping, they changed it to "How's Michael?' or whatever. I was told it was taken out because it was confusing to the audience. I walk into Rita's house at one point and say, 'You home?' and the audience thought that we were a couple. So they said it was confusing. And I'm like [dryly], 'Oh, really?'"

Despite the relooping of dialogue and persistent snipping of footage, it is still evident in the release print of *Now and Then* that Rosie's character is not heterosexual. For example, John Anderson (*Los Angeles Times*) would point out: "Roberta has become a doctor, who also excels at sports (her dubious sexuality is delivered with something like a wink)." Even the official press kit for the movie details O'Donnell's character as "the unconventional town doctor."

While the reviews for *Now and Then* were certainly not likely to bring in a paying audience, word-of-mouth built this release into a movie "with legs" as they say in the industry. The combination of the

Courtesy of Photofest.

As giggly housewife and mother Betty Rubble in the live-action comedy feature *The Flintstones* (1994).

In dominatrix disguise with fellow undercover police officer Dan Aykroyd in *Exit to Eden* (1994).

Director Lesli Linka Glatter with stars Rosie O'Donnell, Rita Wilson, producer Suzanne Todd and producer/star Demi Moore on the set of *Now and Then* (1995).

Explaining the facts of adult life to Timothy Hutton (left) and Matt Dillon (right—hidden) in *Beautiful Girls* (1996).

As nanny Ole Golly with her charge (Michelle Trachtenberg) in
Harriet the Spy (1996).

Courtesy of Sygma Photo Agency.

With friend Michelle Blakely and Rosie's son, Parker Jaren, in
New York City (1996).

Rosie O'Donnell's new home (the former Helen Hayes estate) under renovation in Nyack, New York.

Relaxing on the TV stage of "The Rosie O'Donnell Show" (1996—).

Courtesy of Photofest.

The star of "The Rosie O'Donnell Show".

marquee names of the adult stars and the strength of the young actress-es' performances made this $12 million production into an over-$27 million grosser at the domestic box-office.

One other benefit of *Now and Then* was that it gave O'Donnell fresh material for her club and cable TV stand-up gigs. In them she would share hilarious anecdotes from the making of *Now and Then*. Among the riffs are Rosie's side-spilling imitations of husky-voiced Demi Moore and the squeaky-toned Melanie Griffith. The latter comes in for a good-natured ribbing about her penchant for four-letter words (as in "I want a hot *fuckin'* dog").

Now much in demand by filmmakers to add a needed jolt of energy to their movies (both on camera and during their promotion), Rosie signed to make *Beautiful Girls* (1996). Originally James L. Brooks (who had directed Rosie in her *I'll Do Anything* cameo) was to helm *Beautiful Girls*. However, because of a contractual conflict he dropped out and Ted Demme replaced him for this Miramax release. As with *Now and Then*, it was another ensemble production (Matt Dillon, Uma Thurman, Timothy Hutton, Michael Rapaport, Mira Sorvino, Lauren Holly, *et al*). Once again, Rosie was typecast as the smart-mouthed, unmarried local who has never left the home turf. At least, this time she had a change of profession, moving from physician to the owner of a beauty salon and her peppery character was Italian.

Director Ted Demme, the nephew of director Jonathan Demme (*The Silence of the Lambs, Philadelphia*), came from a background of MTV videos and had recently guided stand-up comic Denis Leary through the well-received *The Ref* (1993). When Demme took over *Beautiful Girls*, he liked the idea of having Rosie in his new venture. As he explained, "After working with Denis Leary and realizing how much fun it is to work with a comic/actor that can think on his feet and bring a character to life, the idea of working with Rosie O'Donnell was excit-ing to me. And she's such a great improvisational actress. Gina's got two really great speeches in the movie and I knew that Rosie'd kill them. . . . The thing about Gina that's great is that I really wanted her to be the guys' best friend and the girls' best friend. She grew up with all of these guys, knows everything about all of them and has really great insights into the girls. And Rosie definitely brought that to the role." During the course of production, he would say of O'Donnell: "Funnier than almost anyone I've ever met and she's from Long Island and drinks beer with me." On another occasion when asked to sum up each of the prin-cipals in his cast, Demme summarized Rosie as "Brazen. Ballsy. Irish."

In preparing *Beautiful Girls*, Demme described the film, "It's got a lot of *Big Chill* [1983] elements in it. It's got a little of a *Diner* [1982] thing going on too, but the thing I love about this movie is that being thirty-two, I really love the idea of making a movie about thirty-year-olds. You see all these movies about twentysomethings." He also had a clear vision of how it should look on the screen. "I gave a mandate to my cine-matographer, my set designer, my costume designer. I said, 'I don't want a new fucking thing in this movie. I don't want to see anything that's not at least ten years old. I want all the shit to feel really worn in, like this town has been here forever. It's going to look like this ten years after this, nothing is changing in this town, it's just the way it is.'"

To stand in for the fictional town of Knight's Ridge, Massachusetts, Demme chose Stillwater, Minnesota, a favorite site of moviemakers in recent years (*Fargo, Grumpier Old Men, The Cure*, etc.). With its curves along the Main Street, its river bluffs, it had just the feel he wanted. However, one thing he was counting on was missing. Snow! It was essential to the storyline which takes places in February *and* because several of the characters (Matt Dillon, Michael Rapaport, Max Perlich) plow sidewalks and driveways as their wintertime living.

Rosie would recall of her time on *Beautiful Girls*: "There's no snow . . . . The director is like suicide watch. Every day I'd been up there since January—we'd be at the bar at the—night at the Hyatt. He'd say, 'Rosie, it looks cloudy out there, doesn't it? It looks like it's going to—Rosie, don't you think it's going to snow?' And there'd be the weatherman, 'Hi. It's Minnesota and there's no snow for the rest of the season.' He's crying, 'Give me some. . . .' So now they're shooting corn flakes and—and Styrofoam all over the streets, but there's no snow. It's hard to believe."

If the weather wasn't cooperative, the cast was pliant to their direc-tor's demands. Since Demme wanted this ensemble movie to be like the first one-third of *The Deer Hunter* (1978), he had *all* the cast and crew arrive on location before filming actually started. He did this ". . . because it was really important for everyone to get down. So we rented out a theater and screened *The Deer Hunter*. We got a few cases of Rolling Rock, Irish whisky, some popcorn. And we were all so blown away by it. When you see the film in its entirety you remember how heavy it is—all the Nam shit—but the first third of it is such a great buddy movie and they were all inspired by it."

When production moved from Stillwater to Minneapolis, several of the cast, including Rosie stayed at the Marquette Hotel. With such a divergent, intriguing bunch of actors, Holly Sorensen (*Premiere* magazine) trooped to the Minnesota location to get a firsthand take on this shoot. There she came upon cast members and crew outside the local Veteran of Foreign Wars building waiting for a camera set-up to be completed. Rosie was dancing on the lawn, a coatless Matt Dillon was smoking a cigar, while hyperactive Michael Rapaport was about to toss an extra, playfully, into one of the last bits of hard snow. Sorensen soaked up details about Dillon, the woman magnet and of the then current romance between co-players Timothy Hutton and Uma Thurman. In talking with Ted Demme about his cast, the director observed, "I think women are more mature than men. Women have this chip implanted in their bodies that makes them smarter. Hands down. Even on this set, when the guys start acting like guys, the girls are like, 'Get over it.'"

Beautiful Girls was released in February 1996, but there was not a lot of endorsement for its derivative plotline. This focused on New York-based pianist, Willie Conway (Timothy Hutton) returning to his home town for his ten-year high school reunion. He is drifting in life, unable to push his career or commit to his attractive, urban lawyer girlfriend (Annabeth Gish). Once home he finds himself strangely attracted to the teenage next-door neighbor (Natalie Portman) and simultaneously drawn to a visiting beauty (Uma Thurman).

Willie finds that his high school buddies who have remained in their home base are no further along in becoming mature adults than he. Matt Dillon's Tommy Rowland, once king of the hill, has passed his glory days. He still pursues his now-married high school sweetheart (Lauren Holly) rather than settling down with the super loyal woman (Mira Sorvino) who deeply loves him. Michael Rapaport's Paul Kirkwood is so obsessed with the fantasy of dating a super model that he ignores his frustrated, waitress girlfriend (Martha Plimpton) who, in turn, has taken up with an older man, a butcher.

Reviewing the new release, Ralph Novak (*People* magazine) slammed, "Self-Pitying Louts would be a more accurate title for this lame comedy built around a feckless group of old high school buddies. . . ." Mike Clark (*USA Today*) was less harsh: "the movie lacks the stature of consistency to be truly beautiful—but you know, it is kind of cute." Janet Maslin (*New York Times*) gave it back-handed praise: ". . . its ensemble cast is as affable as anything on television these days." Then she went on to cite its faults: ". . . the film duly notes that beauty is only skin deep, then crams as many great-looking actresses as possible into its cast . . . The other bit of dishonesty is endemic to this film and every other feel-good ensemble story like it: the notion that a brief reunion may just change the lives of almost all the principals in a few days' time."

But there was one aspect of *Beautiful Girls* that most everyone applauded. Rosie in her brief screen footage outperformed everyone without a doubt. Joe Baltake (*Sacramento Bee*) caught the essence of her essentially brief role: "The link holding this amazing cast together, both the men and the women, is Rosie O'Donnell, who, as Gina Barrisano, the owner of the local beauty parlor, serves as Greek chorus and voice of reason. Her response to things: 'Get on with it.' Gina is here to gently (well, maybe not so gently) remind the guys that there are some very desirable women in Knight's Ridge and to wise up the women about the screwed-up guys' unreasonable idealistic demands and their cockeyed notions of what's beautiful and sexy and what isn't."

Others were in total agreement about Rosie's appearance. Susan Stark (*Detroit News*) reported, ". . . O'Donnell offers an exuberantly profane guide to real women—no parts excluded—for benefit of Dillon and Hutton. Both are thunderstruck. Viewers would be, too, if they could quit laughing at O'Donnell's boisterous account of the truth beyond *Playboy*." Ed Morales (*Village Voice*) enthused, ". . . *Beautiful Girls* is saved from its somewhat moronic torpor by the relentless O'Donnell, who counter-acts the banal neo-homeboyisms of the snowplow crew with a withering feminist harangue. In one momentous encounter, she pulls a soft-core pornzine from a convenience store rack and proclaims, 'This shaved pubis is bullshit!'" For Amy Dawes (*Los Angeles Daily News*), "Rosie O'Donnell as a beauty salon owner who has washed her hands of men and has nothing to lose, gives an applause-worthy tirade as she barges through town with two chagrined guys in tow, like a tugboat blasting off steam."

Rosie's attention-grabbing minutes on screen led Manohla Dargis (*Los Angeles Weekly*) to editorialize on the film's smug, chauvinistic underpinnings. She, like many reviewers, utilized Rosie's very strong performance as a focal example in her dissection of the movie's mixed blessings. Dargis decided, ". . . *Beautiful Girls* is even a worse cheat when it comes to Rosie O'Donnell's Gina, a ball-buster who tosses off the film's funniest barbs, and a few genuine sparks. . . . For most of the scene, the spotlight stays fixed on O'Donnell, who walks and talks as if she were spitting rivets—her words ricocheting off the walls, her heels rhythmically nailing the floor. It's easy stuff, the righteous anger and grinding, one-note delivery, but O'Donnell is fun to watch, especially since there's more than a shudder of her stand-up rage in Gina. . . ."

But what bothered Dargis was the one-dimensional unisex nature of O'Donnell's screen character: "Funny, but not consequential—or sexual. Gina, after all, doesn't have a boyfriend or a husband, or anything approaching an intimate sexual relationship with a man (much less a woman). She's funny, she's fat. She's funny in part because she's fat, at least by the standards of skin magazines—as well as those of the movie itself. And, as a result, Gina stays a joke, a woman alone whose indignation is ultimately answered by ridicule. When she winds up her harangue with, 'You guys as a gender have to get a grip,' Willie and Tommy smile indulgently, sheepishly. She totters across the street, the camera dogging her. Nice tits says Willie, nice ass says Tommy."

Beautiful Girls cost $12 million to make, but only grossed $10.40 million in its first six weeks of domestic release before dropping off the box-office charts. That Rosie's performance should generate so much critical response and moviegoer word-of-mouth said a great deal about the impact this performer had on viewers. By now, there was little doubt. Rosie O'Donnell was a movie personality whom the film industry obviously needed and the public very much wanted.

· 20 ·

The other day I was in the park with my nieces, who are two and four. I was playing with them, and these two women said, "I can't believe this! It's something I never thought I'd see!" I said, "What?" "That you're such a mother!" I laughed. "Why don't you think you'd ever see that?". . . . [T]hey had such a vision of me which was very different.

Rosie O'Donnell, August 1994

*H*aving abandoned Broadway and reapplied herself successfully to the movies, Rosie found herself turning again to her show business roots—stand-up comedy. It was all in preparation for her first *HBO Comedy Hour* special which was set to air in April 1995.

At an AIDS charity fund-raiser in the fall of 1994, Rosie had realized how rusty she'd become in doing a true stand-up turn. She remembers all too vividly how she fumbled through the performance, forgetting how a joke or cue words should lead into the next comedy bit: "I got up there to do 20 minutes and realized that I didn't know my act. Luckily, my sister was in the audience and she would go, 'Pez dispenser!' Then I could do the joke [involving breath mints]."

To get back in form, Rosie took her act on the road. Her first new engagement was in November 1994 in her old stomping-ground of Boston where she performed a six-day gig. O'Donnell was the first to admit, ". . . the first night was hard. I forgot my act. I couldn't finish. I was nervous. But once you're up there, it's like surfin', once you're in the wave. The tough part is paddling out there, waiting for the wave to hit." Before long, she could report that she was enjoying herself. "I remember what it felt like. When you're away from it, it's easy to forget. But when you do it, when you're on stage for that hour, you're like, 'Wow, this is a great way to live.'"

By now she'd realized she had to revamp the material and approach in her act because of her changed status in lifestyle. This was because audiences associate a performer's real life with his/her stage persona. So Rosie went to work ". . . I do a bit on each movie. I tell 'em what it's like to be famous. The thing is, when you get rich and famous, you're no longer like your average audience member. They have a perception of me that I'm different than them. When I go to McDonald's, people go, 'What are you doing here?'. . . I go to the mall and people can't believe it. . . ."

Her next major stop, after a brief holiday in Maui, was at Merv Griffin's Resorts Casino Hotel in Atlantic City. There, during the Thanksgiving weekend, she performed her 70-minute act in the Superstar Theatre three times for a reported $50,000 fee. Tickets were $40 each and Mario Cantone—a very confrontational comic—was her opening act. Not everyone was overjoyed by her much-anticipated arrival. Chuck Darrow of the *Camden (NJ) Courier Post* reported, "Comic-actor Rosie O'Donnell is the biggest booking in Atlantic City this fall. And that tells you all you need to know about how uneventful things will be in casino showrooms during the next three months. . . ."

However, the public flocked to Rosie's laugh-filled shows. Lori Hoffman (of Atlantic City's *The Whoot!*) was on hand to chronicle the performance: "Her humor is gentle without being too sweet, based on being a child of the TV generation. She never knows when totally useless trivia about TV commercials will pop into her head. She tosses in the occasional one-liner and barb, but mostly her routines are stream-of-consciousness musings from rich comic sources like Catholic school, her weight, celebrities in the news, and of course, TV, TV and more TV." (Rosie would return again to Merv Griffin's Atlantic City casino hotel in late May 1995 for the holiday weekend and had, by then, an exclusive contract with his resort for appearances in this East Coast gaming city.)

Part of Rosie's reshaped act contained scathing commentary on Woody Allen (then going through his scandal-soaked break-up with actress Mia Farrow) and O.J. Simpson (on trial for allegedly murdering his ex-wife and her boyfriend). O'Donnell included the controversial material in her routine despite objections from her management. She detailed, ". . . my agent said to me, you know, 'Don't do it. It's too edgy. It's too controversial and you're not that kind of a comedian.' I said,

'Well, you know what? Maybe I am taking a stand. I against murder and incest.' Call me crazy. . . ." She then added that when she performed ". . . they are the two bits that get the biggest reaction. People scream. There was like—there's like a three-minute applause break after the Woody Allen joke." As a result of audience approval, she kept the anti-Simpson and Allen material in her act for many months to come.

In between completing her movie assignments in *Now and Then* and *Beautiful Girls*, she performed in Las Vegas, Reno and Lake Tahoe in early 1995. In mid-March that year she was at the Sands Hotel Casino in Vegas at the Grand Ballroom where tickets for her show were each $35 plus taxes. O'Donnell enthused, "I like playing casino showrooms. You don't have to localize the jokes—you know, tell Houston jokes because you're in Houston. Casino audiences are from everywhere. And when you finish your show in a casino, there's always someplace you can go from there—to the slot machines, some of the restaurants, whatever."

Also in March 1995, Rosie made one of her most vivid television cameo appearances. It was for the 67th Annual Academy Awards being aired by ABC-TV. David Letterman was the master of ceremonies and not doing that well. However, one of his choicer moments occurred when he did an extended routine revolving around his one line of dialogue in the screen comedy, *Cabin Boy* (1994). His "timeless" words in that film had been "You want to buy a monkey." After giving his rendition of these words, there were extreme variations on the bit pre-recorded by several performers including Martin Short and Rosie. In tough-talkin' jive, O'Donnell repeated the requisite phrase in New York-ese ("Wanna buy a monkey?") Then as a post-script she added—in mock anger—"Yo mama, look, you buy the friggin' monkey." It brought down the house and left TV viewers around the world agog, even though the word "friggin'" which she mouthed very distinctly was bleeped out.

O'Donnell's *HBO Comedy Hour* was taped in Boston at Faneuil Hall's Comedy Connection. It was the first time she had done an hour of stand-up comedy on TV. Noting the upcoming event, she expressed, "Well, it's always a lot of fun doing shows for HBO because you can just sort of do what you [are] thinking and not have to edit for a network TV." The finished results were aired on HBO on April 29, 1995 at 10 p.m. with several subsequent airings. The event was well received, but because of an HBO policy rule she would not be eligible to do another such special for sixteen months.

When the Emmy Award nominations for the 1994-1995 season were announced in July 1995, O'Donnell was not initially included in the category of outstanding performer in a variety or music program. However, when Dennis Miller was disqualified on a technicality from consideration in that category, Rosie and her special were elevated instead. Weeks later, she and such rivals as Julie Andrews were losers to Barbra Streisand. Rosie's reaction to being beaten by her biggest idol was to say—in mock horror and surprise: "I lost to Barbra Streisand . . . what a fluke!"

• • •

If anything, fame had made Rosie more restless than ever before. She was constantly anxious for new creative challenges. As early as 1993 she had drafted a film script titled *Girl Hoops*. It dealt with a former basketball star who drops her college scholarship when she becomes pregnant, but, years later, returns to the game as the coach of a high school's girl team. The Disney studio had taken an interest in the project and optioned it. But it eventually stalled at the starting gate. By the end of 1994 the undiscouraged Rosie was involved with *Friends for Life*, a project she had not written, but which producers Nora Ephron and Linda Opes agreed she could direct for a possible release by Tristar. It was a comedy drama about three 30-year-old Long Island women who question the directions of their lives. An optimistic O'Donnell hoped to convince Meg Ryan, Demi Moore and Joan Cusack to star in it.

When asked about her background for handling such a challenge, Rosie explained that she had been building up to this moment for several years. "I told Penny [Marshall] when I did . . . [*A League of Their Own*] with her that that's what I wanted to do—direct. She's like, 'So watch and learn.' Everyone I have worked with has been very helpful and supportive in that way. Garry Marshall [director of *Exit to Eden*] told me, 'Your main job is to not get fired. If you don't get fired then you did good.'" Warming to her subject, Rosie would add, "I'm going to do . . . [directing] for a year and if it's successful and good, I'm going to do another one. People don't believe me, how I can be able to give up acting." But she reasoned it would not be that hard ". . . because I'm a stand-up comic, where I have an outlet when I want to perform."

However, time has passed and, to date, *Friends for Life* remains unproduced.

For more than a year, Rosie had intended to pull up stakes in California, which meant selling her Studio City home. Even though *Grease!* had come and gone, she had not changed her mind. Her rationale was "In LA it's only about show biz. . . . That seems to be the only topic of conversation at dinner. I lived in New York [at the time of] . . . the release of *Exit to Eden* and it was so different. I didn't even know I had a movie opening; whereas in LA it's a countdown." Finally, on March 16, 1995, escrow closed on the sale of her Bellingham Avenue home. She had paid $415,000 for the property in June 1990 and now, because of the declining real estate market, she had to sell at a $115,000 loss.

Rosie was philosophical about the real estate loss because she felt that in other areas of her lifestyle, she was being relatively conservative. "With all the money that I've made, I don't spend it in a way that people think I do. I go on vacation. I go jet skiing, regular skiing, and I buy toys. I have a huge Happy Meal collection. I have a Barbie Doll collection. I read books. I don't really have any luxury items. But my life is luxurious to begin with."

The Studio City sale did not leave Rosie homeless. She still had her New York City co-op on the 12th floor of a high-rise building on the Upper West Side and another condo, this one in the South Beach section of Miami, Florida.

• • •

It was getting to be tradition that Rosie would do the unexpected and, generally, carry it off successfully. Her latest such act floored those who only knew her as an entertainer, but it was no great shock to those close to her. They had only wondered what took her so long. Rosie adopted a baby.

O'Donnell already had tremendous experience in tending to the needs of infants and children. As a youngster she had taken care of her younger brother and sister. For many years in Commack on Long Island she had earned spare money by baby-sitting. The yearning had always been there ("I always knew I'd have children in my life. It was a given for me.") However, she kept postponing doing anything about her desire.

What made her change her mind in the spring of 1995? She explained her rationale on national television: ". . . since I was 16 I've been on the road and I'm 33 now. And I see with my nieces that they're the priority in my life. I schedule my movies around their birthdays and I try to get time off for their little dance recitals and stuff. And when they looked up at me—my four—four-year-old niece looked up at me and said, 'Aunt Ro, work, work, work' because I was on the phone and she wanted me to play. And it broke my heart and I thought, you know, 'You've got to really change your direction or'—you know, I figured I'd be 50 years old with awards and me going, 'Yeah, that was my life.' But on Christmas morning they don't mean very much, you know?. . . So I think 33 is a good time to change gears."

Being a single woman without a male relationship, Rosie still might have chosen artificial insemination as an option. However, for her, it was not. She reasoned, "I really had no ego investment in recreating myself. Nor did I feel the need to dive into my gene pool or go fishing there, because there is a tremendous amount of illness in my family, a tremendous amount of alcoholism."

Having made those choices, she knew there would be disapproval from those who believed a single woman should not adopt a child. Her answer would be: ". . . I don't think that . . . you have to be in a happy heterosexual marriage in order to be a good parent." Furthermore, she reasoned, there were her three brothers who could provide a role model, even at a distance. She stressed, "I, by no means, am trying to prevent parenting male influences around him."

Once she had begun the complex adoption process through her Los Angeles attorney, Rosie came to understand that her fame had opened many doors—and quickly. "Without a doubt, it helped me get my son. I'd be lying to say it didn't. I don't know in what capacity it helped, because I didn't ask to cut the line. . . . So, when they called me and said, eight months after I was fingerprinted, 'We have a son for you.' I wasn't going to say, 'You know, why don't you go find another family; I think I should wait.' I said, 'Bring him home.'"

Her son-to-be was born in Florida on May 25, 1995. He was a premature baby and weighed seven pounds. Within an hour of the delivery, her lawyer brought a picture of the infant to O'Donnell. Rosie, at first, was panicked: ". . . he looked like a smushed-up tomato! I called my sister. I said, 'My son is a smushed-up tomato all red and blotchy!' She said, 'All babies look like that.' Now I think he's the most gorgeous child I've ever seen." The adoption provided for a full disclosure of the birth mother to be given to the child at the age of eighteen.

The infant was named Parker Jaren (P.J.) by Rosie. On one occasion,

O'Donnell said that she selected the first name because of *The Hardy Boys* TV series and one of its actors, Parker Stevenson, had been a big favorite of hers. At another time, she insisted, "I didn't name him after anyone in particular. I wanted a name that would work if he were a surfer, or a supreme court judge. So Parker it is." As to his middle initial of "J," Rosie would explain, "When my brother Timmy was little, we called him T.J., and in fact all the males in my family have the middle initial J. My dad's Edward J., my brother's Eddie J., Danny J. and Timmy J. and so Parker J." In actuality, Rosie would soon nickname the infant "Boo-Boo." (On June 6, 1995, actress Meg Ryan would host a baby shower at her Los Angeles home for Rosie. Others at the party included Geena Davis and Carrie Fisher.)

In several different and unexpected ways, having Parker in her household (which for the moment was still in Los Angeles), had a tremendous effect on Rosie. For one thing: "It changed my priorities in a moment without even trying to." For another, "I was surprised that a human being can function on as little sleep as I did for the first three months. I was surprised to wake up every two hours, 'cause that is how they torture people in other countries!"

Not long after Parker arrived, Rosie celebrated Mother's Day. It was the first time since her own mother's death twenty-two years ago that she could acknowledge the holiday ". . . without feeling a lingering, omnipresent gloom. It was the first time I literally wasn't overwhelmingly sad, where I felt joy and levity and something close to pride." She also confided, ". . . beforehand I was much more of a pessimist about my life and maybe my longevity. You know, my mom died when she was young, and I always thought that might be my fate. . . . Since having my son, I don't think that anymore. I think I'm going to live to see him grow up. It's like you grow another heart, like someone kicks down a door that was sealed shut, and then the whole world—sunshine, flowers—falls through. I have such joy that I didn't think was possible." And not least of all, becoming a mother also made Rosie ". . . feel more connected to my mother, as a grown woman who is facing her own mortality with a small child."

One of Rosie's primary goals was to provide her son with what she had not had as a youngster, a feeling of safety. She defined this with, "You know, the world can always be unsafe, but your home has to be a safe place. And [growing up] mine wasn't. But he has a safe, loving home where he's known, accepted, appreciated and loved. And that's really important to me."

Despite all her child-rearing experience, O'Donnell was the typical nervous first-time mother. She turned to those of her celebrity friends who were parents. One was Rita Wilson. "She came over with her mother. . . .To me, he was this tiny little boy. He wouldn't eat. I was so scared. But Rita's mother got him to drink a whole bottle. I kept saying how nervous I was, and she's from Greece, and she said 'Rosie, they throw babies in the trash bin and they live for four days. You can't kill him! Don't worry.'"

There was also actress Kate Capshaw, wife of Rosie's *The Flintstones'* producer, Steven Spielberg. Regarding Kate, O'Donnell would enthuse, "I have to give her credit. She provided everything I needed in any way, shape or form. During the first three months, I thought she should establish 1-800-CALL KATE for new mothers. You'd say anything to her, like, 'I don't think these are the right-size diapers,' and suddenly you'd hear beep-beep-beep, and a truck would be pulling up. And a delivery man would say, 'Here's 95,000 diapers from Ms. Capshaw.'"

There was one particular occasion where Rosie was especially grateful for Capshaw's experienced efficiency. O'Donnell recites, "My son came home from the hospital apparently circumcised. I'm changing him and going, 'It doesn't look circumcised.' I thought maybe there was some genital configuration that changes at puberty; I didn't know. So Kate came over and said, 'Why didn't you have him circumcised?' and I said, 'I did.' And she was like, 'You didn't.' And now I'm like, crying, 'I did . . . I really did. . . . ' So she called the head of OBGYN at Cedars-Sinai, who is also a moyl [i.e., a religious man in the Jewish faith who performs circumcisions], and he came over and performed a bris [i.e., circumcision] the very next day, which was the eighth day, which is the appropriate time in the Jewish religion."

Then there were other matters to deal with; in particular, the press. Since Rosie was so newsworthy these days, it was considered a great coup among the paparazzi to take pictures of O'Donnell and P.J. As such, one day, says Rosie, "I was sitting with a friend, and we looked out the window, and there was a guy standing in my yard with a camera. And I said, 'What are you doing?' And he said, 'I'm sorry. But they offered me this much money. I'll leave, but people will be back.' He ended up getting some pictures, they didn't show [Parker's] face, which was nice of him." Over the following weeks, the public heard several variations of Rosie's Close Encounter of the Bad Kind with the overanxious press. O'Donnell admits to having distorted the baby photo story for comedy purposes when she appeared on *The Late Show with David Letterman*: "I said I wrapped up my puppy, which wasn't true. Actually, a friend of mine came over who has a baby who is about a month older. And I said, 'Give me your baby.' So I took her baby outside. I didn't want the guy at the *Globe* to get in trouble."

Meanwhile, Rosie herself was being extraordinarily camera-happy with the blond-haired infant. She would admit later, "Okay. I took a picture of him every day for a while, but so you won't think I'm a total Kathie Lee Gifford ass, I only do it every month now."

· 21 ·

It was a 23-day shoot [on Harriet the Spy, *1996], and I saw my son an average of one hour every day. I knew on the second day that I would not make another film for a long time. That's not the kind of parent I want to be. . . . I didn't have a mom, and I am a single parent. I want to be consistent, provide him with stability. I don't want him to have to sleep in a hotel room; I want him to sleep in his own bed every night. I want him to be around his cousins, his dogs, and his toys. So I tried to think of a job that would allow me to do that.*

Rosie O'Donnell, July 1996

A few months after adopting Parker in May 1995, Rosie flew with her infant to Toronto, Canada where she was to shoot a new movie. The film was *Harriet the Spy* (1996) and was based on Louise Fitzhugh's beloved children's novel (1964). When *Harriet the Spy* was first published it had won the *New York Times* Outstanding Book Award and since then had sold over 2.5 million copies. O'Donnell was very familiar with the story because "I read the book when I was in the fifth grade. It was my sister's favorite book, and I stole it from under her pillow. . . . She was mad because I used to dog-ear the pages and she's a bookmark kind of girl. So she knew I was reading it." On another occasion, Rosie would expand on why she liked the story: "It encourages young girls to be independent and artistic and intellectual and strong." O'Donnell envisioned this film as the kind of kids-and-family, Disney-style movie she had loved as a child. For Rosie, "It's not sugarcoated Disney, yet it's also not as dark as, say, *Welcome to the Dollhouse* [1996]. But it shows kids accurately in the '90s, how cruel they can be to each other."

Yet another reason for Rosie accepting the Ole Golly role in *Harriet the Spy* was that she was becoming increasingly dissatisfied with the type of movie roles she was being offered. This Canadian-shot project might just be the key for expanding her career in a new direction, illustrating to casting directors that her so-called brash personality was suitable for children-oriented movies of all sorts.

For many years, the film rights to *Harriet the Spy* had been kicking around the Hollywood studios as a possible screen vehicle. Now it was finally to be produced by Nickelodeon Movies (a newly formed branch of the Nickelodeon Cable Channel), Paramount Pictures and Rastar Productions. Canadian Bronwen Hughes was set to direct the project for a tight budget of under $15 million. The story was updated in some aspects from the 1960s to the 1990s and the setting was changed from Manhattan's Upper East Side to Any City, USA. To cut the overall cost, several bigger-name actors such as Lily Tomlin had been passed over in favor of O'Donnell to play Ole Golly the nanny. Another consideration in choosing Rosie was her recent victory (for *The Flintstones*) in Nickelodeon's Kids Choice Awards. Such an endorsement from the youth market had not gone unnoticed by Nickelodeon.

Hughes would later state why she had wanted O'Donnell cast for the pivotal adult role: "There were very few actresses who fit the bill and Rosie was at the top of the list. The bill was that the Golly role had to be the single adult human in Harriet's world that she related to most closely. . . . Rosie combines a wit and a wisdom and a hipness that is a great combination for the kid audience to relate to." As to milking the Golly part in favor of the story's central character, a young girl named Harriet: "There was the idea of making the scenes with Golly as strong as possible so her influence would be felt throughout, but that was it. The movie, like the book, is about Harriet."

Michelle Trachtenberg, 11, who had done some 100 commercials and was a regular on two TV series (Nickelodeon's *The Adventures of Pete & Pete* and ABC-TV's soap opera, *All My Children*), was selected for the primary part of the precocious adolescent who dreams one day of becoming a writer. It is her eccentric nanny, Ole Golly, who suggests that the sixth grader keep a diary in which she should record all her daily, detailed observations of life about her. The girl takes the advice to an extreme and becomes Harriet the nosy spy. As such she fills her diary pages with revealing notes about her classmates and about the neighborhood eccentrics (including the bizarre Agatha K. Plummer played by Eartha Kitt).

Meanwhile, Ole Golly, due to a misunderstanding with her employers and feeling her job in rearing Harriet is done, leaves the Welsch household. As such, Harriet's world collapses. Later, the girl's diary notebook is found by her snooty school rival. The latter reads aloud Harriet's embarrassing private thoughts—full of critical assessments—that immediately make her an outcast at school. Harriet's self-obsessed, yuppie parents, now concerned about their child's plight, send for Ole Golly. The mentor returns to save the day.

Although Rosie was playing an all-knowing, poetry-quoting character, she was the first to admit that it did not reflect her real self. "I don't think I ever quoted Keats, like that 'all you know and all you need to know' thing. When my character says that, and Harriet asks what it means, I wanted to say, 'Hell if I know.'" On the set, O'Donnell found great pleasure in playing with the young cast, giving them shoulder rides, airplane swing twirls and engaging in thumb wrestling. Co-star Michelle Trachtenberg had her own favorite on-the-set moments: "We all loved cherries, and one day, Rosie decided it would be fun if we spit the pits at each other! We had a point game: shoulders and up was 10 points, waist to shoulders was 5 points, and below the waist was 3 points. It was so much fun! But we had to make sure the pits were clean, so wardrobe wouldn't get upset." This ongoing spitting competition and its ilk would lead Rosie to say later, "I'd much prefer to do movies with kids than adults because they only work a few hours a day and they'll have cherry pit fights with you, which Demi Moore [her *Now and Then* co-star] won't do. You know, you spit on a kid, they like you for life."

When *Harriet the Spy* was released in July 1996 it led the *Los Angeles Times* to commend it as "... an appropriate mix of the improbable and the impractical." *Daily Variety* judged it a "sweet-natured morality tale" while the *Washington Post* found it a "low-key, reasonably charming take" of the famed children's story. On the other hand, the *Los Angeles Daily News* countered, "Maybe it's a case of too many well-meaning cooks, but this movie is not nearly as happening as its noisy, busy, hyper-cool style wants it to be." The *New York Times* warned, "If the movie's refusal to be contemporary in ways that knowingly wink at the audience is a sign of its integrity, that refusal could be a commercial impediment."

As for Rosie's performance—in an essentially oversized supporting part dominated by her presence and personality—she also received diverse reactions from the reviewers. *Drama-Logue* enthused, "Rosie O'Donnell as Golly is the sane, humorous grown-up that every child hopes to have in his or her life—O'Donnell combines surety with a great sense of fun." *Entertainment Today* endorsed, "The on-screen rapport between Trachtenberg and O'Donnell is superb—their scenes together are the most endearing part of the film. . . . [N]ot since *The Sound of Music* have we seen a nanny have such a profound effect on child-rearing." *Daily Variety* praised Rosie for providing "the right balance of eccentricity and maturity" and pointed out ". . . when O'Donnell quits the story, her presence is very sorely missed."

Less favorable to Rosie were *People* magazine who cited O'Donnell as ". . . declaiming her lines as if flinging snowballs." *Entertainment Weekly* gave O'Donnell a backhanded compliment, calling her "Likably restrained." On the other hand, the *Los Angeles Reader* complained that ". . . O'Donnell chews up the scenery as a latter-day Mary Poppins. . ." *USA Today* in its 3-star review rated Rosie "an amiable presence" but added ". . . it's not clear what she's doing in the movie. Whatever it is, it's not acting."

For all its faults and its limited appeal to an adult audience *Harriet the Spy* did surprisingly well at the box-office. In its seven weeks on the industry's 50 top-grossing films chart, it amassed $25.05 million at the domestic box-office. A good deal of the movie's success was attributed to Rosie.

On the downside, *Harriet the Spy* demonstrated very forcibly to Rosie that the demands of serious moviemaking made it very difficult for her to do both her acting job properly and also to be a good mother who was there for her child, to tend to his needs and to bond with him. Being a very hands-on mother, she didn't like the idea of entrusting his day-to-day care to another. As such, the *Harriet the Spy* work experience gave her strong reasons to consider other viable career paths, ones that would allow her to have a more regular schedule and to devote part of each day to her infant son. It was a new concept for the adult O'Donnell to adjust her life to the needs of another, but there was no question she would do it for Parker and with a happy heart. Being a truly full-time mother to her child was far too important for her to fudge on the crucial issues. As she would explain, "I want to . . . put him to bed at night, be there when he takes his first step, goes to kindergarten, the whole thing." After all, Rosie knew all too well what it was like to spend so much of one's childhood without positive parental supervision. Nonetheless, workaholic O'Donnell had already committed to many other job assignments.

During the same period that Rosie made *Harriet the Spy*, she did a cameo assignment as a nun in *Wide Awake* (1997). Described as a "darkly sweet comedy," it starred Denis Leary, Dana Delany (who co-starred with Rosie in *Exit to Eden*) and Joseph Cross. Scripted and directed by M. Night Shyamalan, the Miramax movie deals with a ten-year-old boy (Joseph Cross) from Philadelphia who searches for God after his granddad's death. Rosie was cast as Sister Terry. She is the youngster's teacher who is more adept at playing baseball with the boy than in answering his philosophical musings on life and death. Much of the picture was shot in and around Philadelphia, and some of O'Donnell's sequences were filmed on the Ivy League campus of the University of Pennsylvania, in particular, the Chinese Rotunda and the Buddhism Gallery at the college's Museum of Archaeology and Anthropology.

After her offbeat *Wide Awake* assignment, Rosie next accepted a role in *Twilight of the Golds* (1997), a made-for-cable television movie based on Jonathan Tolins' 1993 Broadway play. The impressive cast for this Showtime Cable project included, besides Rosie, Faye Dunaway, Garry Marshall, Jennifer Beals, Brendan Fraser (who had a cameo in Rosie's *Now and Then*), Jack Klugman, Kathleen Marshall (one of Garry Marshall's daughters) and Michelle Blakely (Rosie's *Grease!* co-worker and friend). Shot between February 13 and March 22, 1996 in Los Angeles, it focused on a dysfunctional Jewish family in which the son (Brendan Fraser) is gay and the daughter (Jennifer Beals), who is married, learns from genetic testing that her child-to-be has a 90% chance of being born homosexual. The primary question posed within this sitcom comedy and moralistic drama was whether the pregnant daughter should go through to term.

When *Twilight of the Golds* was premiered (before its cable debut) at the 32nd annual Chicago International Film Festival in mid-October 1996, Duane Byrge (*Hollywood Reporter*) judged that the movie, despite its "carefully" assembled drama, ultimately suffers from "artificiality" and that its intense philosophical discussions eventually "take on the gray flavor of a symposium." However, Byrge had high praise for the cast, especially Faye Dunaway and Garry Marshall as Jennifer Beals' parents and pointed out that O'Donnell ". . . is characteristically a hoot as Suzanne's [Beals] abrasive, infertile co-worker."

• • •

In the midst of her moviemaking Rosie found time to attend the September 1995 Emmy Awards. O'Donnell had front-row seats "so I had to smile for 3 hours straight." Wearing an outfit designed by

Richard Tyler, she sported some fancy baubles. (Per Rosie: "Yes, 400gs for the necklace, 90 for the ear bobs. Wild huh!") But as a new mother, she made only a brief appearance at one after-Emmy show party and then hastened home to Parker. The next day she left for a brief vacation in Miami, Florida. While down south, Rosie continued to choose not to visit her dad in North Carolina, even though that year, 1995, he had undergone open-heart surgery. Reportedly when tight-lipped Edward O'Donnell was asked by a reporter to comment on his lack of rapport with his famous daughter he responded with, "What does our relationship have to do with anything?"

Regarding her father's interaction with the press, O'Donnell insists, "My father calls me twice a week to tell me somebody's at his door again. 'Honey, what should I do. . . .' 'Dad, you just don't talk to them. . . .' 'I didn't say anything and they said I said something last week. . . .' 'I know you didn't say anything, Dad, just ignore it . . . ' but it's hard! He's a retired man living with his wife, far away from here, and they're outside his house. Kind of creepy."

More recently, Rosie has said of her current state of rapport with her parent, "My dad and I aren't really in each other's lives too much and I think the tabloids make more out of it than it is. You get to a point in your adult life where you need a certain amount of communication and intimacy and you're no longer a child who has to put up with being treated in a way you don't really want to. That's the gist of it, and they can make it into this and that. . . . I speak to my father on the phone occasionally, it's not like we're estranged. He's just, not right now, a functioning part of my life and that's kind of a mutual decision by both parties and it seems to be working better. So I don't keep saying 'Well, you don't do enough for me,' and he doesn't keep saying, 'Well, this is all I can do.'"

• • •

Previously, on December 15, 1994, Rosie had made a guest appearance on the TV sitcom *Living Single*. She was seen as Sheri, a girlhood pal of Khadijah (Queen Latifah) hired to work at *Flavor* magazine. (That segment led *Entertainment Weekly* to quip, "After the ignominy of *Exit to Eden*, Rosie may have a lot of TV work in her future.") On October 11, 1995, Rosie could be seen on the short-lived CBS-TV teleseries, *Bless This House*, starring Cathy Moriarity (her coworker from *Another Stakeout*) and comedian Andrew Dice Clay.

O'Donnell was cast as Clay's sister who is dating a guy (Michael Rispoli) of dubious intentions. (This appearance prompted *Entertainment Weekly* to jab, "Just what this show needs—more screaming.") This was followed by a guest appearance on Garry Shandling's HBO-Cable series, *The Larry Sanders Show* (November 15, 1995). Rosie played herself as a most-annoyed guest waiting backstage to go on the talk show-within-the-show, only to discover that her expensive car had been mangled in the parking lot. For her shrill but effective performance, Rosie would receive an Emmy nomination, but did not win the Award. On the February 26, 1996 episode of *The Nanny*, Rosie would be reunited with her *Car 54, Where Are You?* co-star to appear on the latter's hit sitcom. O'Donnell made a forceful presence as a fast-talking, street-savvy cabbie.

On a television roll, Rosie would host the CBS-TV special *Catch a Rising Star's 50th Anniversary...Give or Take 26 Years* (April 24, 1996), a tribute to the famed Manhattan stand-up comedy forum, where she'd performed in past years. That same month she would also co-host TNT-Cable's Hollywood documentary, *The Good, the Bad and the Beautiful.* She was a guest on the opening episode of the syndicated series, *Night Stand* in early May 1996. This was followed by her joining Whitney Houston as co-hosts of the *9th Annual Kids' Choice Awards* on Nickelodeon Cable on May 11, 1996. As well, Rosie was a presenter on *The 23rd Annual Daytime Emmy Awards* that gave her an opportunity to mingle with her soap opera star favorites. When Linda Ellerbe presented *The Body Trap* (May 29, 1996), a Nickelodeon Cable special geared for the teen (and under) market, O'Donnell was a guest demonstrating that not all women who succeed in today's show business are stereotypically svelte and traditionally beautiful.

However, O'Donnell's most impressive TV appearances in the 1995-1996 season were not in comedies, dramas or talk shows—they were in the world of commercials. In a stroke of near genius it had been decided to team Rosie with her pal Penny Marshall in a series of *Laverne and Shirley*-type spots on behalf of the Kmart store chain. With scripts by Rosie, the ten humorous skits/ads began appearing throughout the U.S. as of November 12, 1995. The ads were Kmart Corporation's biggest holiday ad splurge in over five years. For these hilarious ad spots, aimed at the blue collar market, it was estimated that O'Donnell could earn as much as a million dollars. These Kmart plugs were so wildly successful that Rosie and Penny did another batch in the summer of 1996.

Some months later, when Penny Marshall was a guest on Rosie's TV talk show, the two reminisced about their foray into the world of TV spokespersons. With prompting by an amused O'Donnell, Marshall detailed how, while shooting the spots, she had asked Kmart executives, "You don't mind if we take a few things, do you?" According to Marshall she took "a microwave oven, refrigerator, cappuccino machine, roller blades and lots more." Rosie evidently had gone home nearly empty-handed.

During all of this professional activity, O'Donnell found the time to do stand-up comedy at a few major club venues. From November 10-12, 1995, she was at the MGM Grand in Las Vegas, which was followed, eleven days later, by an appearance at the Fox Theatre in Detroit. For New Year's Eve 1995, interested New Yorkers could purchase $30 to $40 tickets to see Rosie perform at Radio City Music Hall at a special eight o'clock evening show.

When George Burns became too ill to fulfill his highly publicized 100th birthday stage appearance at Caesars Palace in Las Vegas in January 1996, Rosie was brought in as a substitute. At the time she had already planned to be in the gambling capital to promote her upcoming new TV venture at the annual conclave of National Association of Television Program Executives. Despite his ailments, Burns found the strength and interest to telephone Rosie backstage at Caesars Palace during her engagement. It was the first time she had ever talked to him. He told her a few jokes, asked how her upcoming TV program was selling market by market. An over-awed Rosie told Burns that it would be an honor if he would consider being her first guest on her June 10, 1996 debut TV program. He said, "I don't know, Sweetheart. I'll try to do it. But I've gotta go see Gracie [Allen—his late wife]." Burns would pass away on March 9, 1996 at his Beverly Hills home.

Months later, in recounting this very moving conversation with the legendary George Burns, one of show business' great legends, Rosie would say, "Well, he didn't make our show; but he did keep his date with Gracie. And maybe he did make the show after all. I'd like to think so."

· 22 ·

This is going to be enjoyable and easy for me, the staff and the guests.
I'm looking for a fun, enjoyable ride during the first five or six years
of my son's life.

Rosie O'Donnell, June 1996

*O*ne of Rosie's most often repeated anecdotes in mid-1996
involved the time in 1995 when she had again substituted
for co-host Kathie Lee Gifford on TV's *Live with Regis and
Kathie Lee*, an hour show telecast live daily from New York City.
According to O'Donnell: "I arrived there at 8:45 a.m. and came home
at 10:20 a.m. Kathie Lee was talking about leaving the show, so I called
my agent and said, 'Should she really leave the show I would like to do
it.' My agent said, 'You don't want to do that. Are you crazy?' I said,
'No, I really do want to do it; it's a great gig. It's fun, it's interesting,
you get to talk to celebrities. It's not depressing, like Ricki Lake and
the guy who slept with the mother's father or whatever.' So my agent
said, 'Let's see if they'll give you your own show.' I said, 'Okay, try it.'
And they did."

Rosie's rationale was that, if Kathie Lee, the wife of ex-gridiron star
Frank Gifford, could be both a (morning) TV talk show host and give
birth and raise two youngsters in recent years, O'Donnell could certainly do the same. The fact that Gifford had typically brought her
pre-school children to the studio to be supervised in a special nearby
nursery seemed a workable concept for O'Donnell. It suggested to
Rosie a feasible way to have the best of both worlds—motherhood and

221

full-time career. It was certainly a more realistic option than taking Parker on the road while she undertook stand-up gigs, or bringing him with her to movie locations, or leaving him at home with a nanny while she endured the lengthy daily grind of starring in a TV sitcom.

Actually it was not a fresh idea for Rosie O'Donnell to host a TV talk show. Back in the fall of 1993 when David Letterman left NBC-TV for CBS-TV and the Fox network had canceled Chevy Chase's new chat show, Rosie had been considered as one of the possible replacements. However, at the time, she'd been preoccupied with movie and other assignments. As a result, NBC eventually hired Conan O'Brien while Fox abandoned the talk show concept as part of its late evening programming.

Later on, when Rosie was doing *Grease!* on Broadway, Warren Littlefield, the president of NBC Network Entertainment, had let it be known that he wanted Rosie to come work for NBC. According to O'Donnell, "He asked me what I wanted to do and I said I'd love to do *The Tonight Show* the weeks that Jay Leno had off." Reportedly, Littlefield tentatively agreed. However, no deal was forthcoming. Apparently, Leno, who had not been consulted on the concept, made it clear that he only took time off when his staff needed vacation, and that, if he had his choice, he would work all year round. Rosie was disappointed and, as she has noted, has not been on Leno's chat show since.

Further on into 1994, David Letterman's staff had also bandied the notion of Rosie becoming a regular substitute host for Letterman when he vacationed. But, says Rosie, "That came at a time when Dave was coming down a bit in the ratings and I think he thought people would read something into it." However, along the way, Rosie did have a few opportunities to display her talent as a talk show host. On August 3, 1993 she had filled in for Kathie Lee as co-host of daytime's *Live with Regis and Kathie Lee*. In addition, for four nights in mid-June 1995, O'Donnell had substituted as the host on NBC-TV's *Later with Greg Kinnear*.

Now, here she was in the fall of 1995 finally considering the ways and means of entering the talk show arena. As on so many other occasions in Rosie's career, she picked just the right time to make a move, in this case to chat TV. Equally as important, she was wise enough to have settled on a format variant that was refreshingly different in the latter half of the 1990s and one that would prove to have enormous appeal to both the TV industry and to home viewers.

Talk shows had been a staple of American television for decades.

The genre dates back to May 16, 1950 when NBC-TV debuted a nightly hour-long program called *Broadway Open House*, with Jerry Lester and Morey Amsterdam, two veteran comedians, as alternating hosts. That show had gone off the air in August 1951, but the concept was not forgotten. Two years later, a brash young personality from Los Angeles moved to Manhattan where he began hosting his own late night program, *The Steve Allen Show* (July 27, 1953) over WNBC-TV. It developed such a following with TV watchers that, the next year, NBC turned the program into a national property. And so, on September 27, 1954, *Tonight!* was launched as a 105-minute nightly entertainment package. It quickly caught on with the public.

Over the next two years, Allen refined the format for *Tonight!* However, by 1957, the multi-talented personality was so overloaded with television and other projects that he quit *Tonight!*, claiming burnout. After a few fumbles, NBC came up with a new *Tonight* host, the antic, highly emotional comedian/actor, Jack Paar, who quickly turned the art of conversation into a nightly pastime. In the next years his evening program thrived. However, after several brutal skirmishes with network censors for daring to speak his mind on TV about controversial subjects, he made good his repeated threats to quit his evening series. In March 1962 he left the airwaves. Paar was replaced by game/quiz show host and comedian, Johnny Carson.

A brand-new era of TV began on October 1, 1962 with *The Tonight Show Starring Johnny Carson*. With Ed McMahon as his announcer/sidekick and Skitch Henderson (later Doc Severinsen) in charge of the studio band, the late evening series became truly an American institution It rolled on very successfully, for the most part, until May 22, 1992. Then the unbelievable happened. Carson actually retired from his throne as king of the talk shows. He was replaced by a protégé, Jay Leno.

During the thirty-year reign of the mighty Johnny Carson the networks launched many competing versions of *The Tonight Show*. They featured such diverse personalities as Joey Bishop, Dick Cavett, David Frost, Alan Thicke, Garry Shandling, Dennis Miller, Chevy Chase and Joan Rivers. None of them survived the competition in the long run. Others, like Mike Douglas, Dinah Shore, Merv Griffin (who'd also tried the evening show approach previously) and Virginia Graham, found that they could maintain decent national ratings by airing in the daytime and gearing themselves to a viewership primarily of housewives. A few, like David Letterman and Tom Snyder, existed by airing in the wee hours of the morning after *The Tonight Show.*

Meanwhile, former journalist Phil Donahue began a new form of American TV talk show. His program, *The Phil Donahue Show*, debuted on WLWD-TV in Dayton, Ohio in 1967. It not only used a studio audience who were encouraged to ask questions of the guests, but Phil also took phone calls ("Is the caller there?") from at-home listeners. Phil's program grew steadily in popularity and, by the mid-1970s, he'd relocated to Chicago to host his show from that metropolis. Its format was so appealing to home viewers that it led to a rash of such similar shows over the coming years. These newcomers would be hosted by the likes of Regis Philbin (much later joined by Kathie Lee Gifford), Dr. Ruth Westheimer, Sally Jessy Raphael, Vicki Lawrence, Geraldo Rivera, and, Donahue's most formidable competition, Oprah Winfrey. Later came such other hosts as the very politically conservative Rush Limbaugh, the trash talking Howard Stern and such other Rivera-type hosts such as Montel Williams, Richard Bey, Jerry Springer, Jenny Jones, Maury Povich and Rolanda.

By the early 1990s, the Phil Donahue-type show had seemingly exhausted every conceivable type of acceptable shock topic (drug addiction, homosexuality, incest, obesity, etc.) and the surviving contenders of these programs were fighting hard to be the first to present anything remotely new as a daily topic for their audiences. (Ironically, while some of his distilled clones carried on, Donahue would quit the talk show business in the mid-1990s, increasingly frustrated at finding fresh topics and suffering from declining ratings.)

On September 13, 1992 the syndicated *The Ricki Lake Show* debuted on national TV. It differed in format from the Geraldo Rivera wannabes in two respects: Lake, an accomplished screen actress, had a winning, warm personality and, more importantly, was in her mid-twenties. Her program, taped in Manhattan, had vitality (emanating from her and from her equally young guest panelists and audience members who represented a very broad ethnic mix). The show was an almost instantaneous hit. Typical of the television business, in the forthcoming seasons, a bunch of similar, youth-oriented talk shows would appear on the scene, each anxious to grab a share of the lucrative marketplace. These Lake-alikes featured such twentysomething hosts as Charles Perez, Danny Bonaduce (of *The Partridge Family*), singer Carnie Wilson, Gabrielle Carteris (of *Beverly Hills 90210*) and Tempestt Bledsoe (of *The Cosby Show*). Most of the new arrivals fell by the wayside after one season or less on the air.

During 1995, as politicians prepared to woo the public's votes for the upcoming 1996 presidential elections, they set their sights on the bad effects of all of this trash talk TV. They labeled such programming a moral outrage that should be cured by several means: pressuring sponsors not to support such shows, encouraging viewers to channel surf elsewhere, and, most appealing of all to them, creating legislation to institute government censorship. All such critics pointed, in particular, to an unfortunate situation that occurred as a result of a taped (but never aired) segment of *The Jenny Jones Show* in which a young man admitted to having a crush on an unsuspecting male friend. The latter was so upset by this unwelcomed public disclosure that he later shot and killed his would-be suitor.

In a wave of self-reform, many of the existing talk shows proclaimed that they would embark on self-censorship and be born-again good hosts of responsible talk television. None was more fervent than Geraldo Rivera who many remember as once having been the worst offender of confrontational chat TV. Meanwhile, while people in power criticized and threatened, American television still offered many hours of these daily confessional talk shows. It seemed as if there would or could be no alternative to such programming, which networks, syndicators and local stations found so financially lucrative and easy to produce over the decades.

It was at this juncture that Rosie came up with the notion of wanting to do a TV talk show. On a cross-country flight she discussed her concept with her agent, Risa Shapiro, at ICM, and that got the ball rolling. From the start, O'Donnell was convinced she did not want to do nighttime programming. She believed she did not have the edge to attract the college-type audience of a *Letterman* show. She also insisted that her potential daytime program would not be trash TV. As she would say, "I could never do a show like Ricki Lake or Jerry Springer. I'd say: 'You're an idiot. Why are you sleeping with your sister's husband!'" As Rosie stressed, she did not want to participate in a "humiliation festival" genre on television. (Not that she didn't watch trash TV talk shows. When asked if she did, she told respected TV journalist Tom Shales, "Always! Always! Welcome to my life.")

Instead, Rosie wished to headline a viewer-friendly show. She noted, "We're going after that eclectic brand of variety in the afternoon. When I was a kid, I used to run home from school and watch Merv Griffin with Captain & Tennille, Zsa Zsa Gabor, and Totie Fields. It was a wonderful program that I watched ever since I was six with my grandma." What she especially remembered about Griffin's and the other afternoon talk programs (e.g., Mike Douglas, Dinah Shore, *et al*) was "You never saw anybody on Merv Griffin appearing nervous. It appeared everyone was his friend and nobody felt in dangerous territory." Such a show was the type she knew, liked and would feel most comfortable in doing. And her instincts told her that American TV audiences were quite ready for such a programming change of fare.

Thus, in November 1995 what had been only rumors in the TV industry for weeks became reality. Rosie signed a deal with Warner Bros. television for a new talk show. However, it would be an offering with a difference from those now on the air. The trade paper *Hollywood Reporter* described this difference: "The show is the latest in a growing brigade of new daytime projects being offered in first-run syndication for 1996 that aim to offer stations and advertisers alternatives to much of the current programming that has brought criticism for politicians, deep concern from many stations and a shunning from major advertisers."

The package had been put together by Rosie's representatives at ICM, who, in turn, met with Jim Paratore, president of Telepictures Productions (which produced, among others, *The Jenny Jones Show* and *Extra*, the flash entertainment news half-hour program). Paratore liked Rosie's pitch from the start. He says that he knew his instincts were right on when both his 72-year-old mother and his 19-year-old daughter approved of O'Donnell's proposed format. As he explained, "She appeals down to that generation but she also appeals up to the Baby Boomers."

Since Paratore's Telepictures Productions was affiliated with Warner Bros., Rosie's show ended up being marketed by that conglomerate's subsidiary, Warner Bros. Domestic Television Distributors. (Other companies who had been in the very competitive running to distribute O'Donnell's show included Sony, Disney and Rysher Entertainment.) According to Bob Sanitsky, who specializes in syndication packaging at ICM which represents Rosie: "It was the most fluid process of deal-making that I've ever seen. The timing was just perfect. There was just an insatiable appetite on the part of the studios." Rosie's contract with Warner Bros. guaranteed her at least an initial 39-week run. Her four-year deal was worth an estimated $4 million to the comic/actor. In addition, through her Kid Ro Entertainment Company, she would receive extra revenue from her percentage participation in the show's profits.

By January 1996, Rosie was in Las Vegas at the big NATPE (National Association of Television Program Executives) to promote the sale of her show to TV stations around the country. She bally-hooed, "Lots of people watch *The Tonight Show* and *Letterman* in the evening, so there's no reason why they won't also watch in the after-noon." She promised TV station executives that on her program "there will be no fist fights." In the coming months *The Rosie O'Donnell Show* would be cleared for airing on 166 stations covering 93% of the coun-try. It was a hit even before it was launched on the air!

As of March 1996 Rosie had completed her moviemaking commit-ments and was focusing almost exclusively on preparing her show which was set to debut on June 10, 1996. The reasons for starting mid-year, rather than in the more traditional fall, were, according to Jim Paratore of Telepictures "No. 1, the history of talk-variety is that it is a slow build. No 2, some things are going to work and some things aren't going to work, so it gives us a television version of an off-Broadway run. We hit Broadway in the fall. Thirdly, we will get a bigger bang from our marketing dollar in June, when we're not competing against the flood of the network and syndicated [fall] season."

By now, whenever O'Donnell was asked the inevitable question of why she was abandoning moviemaking to have more time with her son Parker, she would say, "The reason is indefinable but quite easy to feel. I don't worry about answering so much now. I just ask a question myself. I say, 'Do you have kids?' When they say no, I say, 'That's why you're asking.'"

A staff had to be quickly assembled for the pending Rosie show. Daniel Kellison, 31, was chosen to be executive producer. He'd been with David Letterman for several years after attending New York University. He was the one behind the scenes on Dave's TV show who had the knack for getting guests to do the unusual. For example, he'd inveigled British actor Peter O'Toole (of *Lawrence of Arabia* movie fame) to ride on stage on a camel and feed it a beer, he convinced in-hiding author Salman Rushdie to deliver a top 10 list to Letterman when Dave was on location in London, and he had encouraged Drew Barrymore to dance on Letterman's desk and to pull up her blouse and flash Dave with her bare breasts. It was Kellison who persuaded Rosie to sing "Oklahoma!" to Dave on one of her many Letterman appear-ances. Kellison, now aboard, would soon be supervising a 30-person staff, only a few of whom were over the age of 40.

When word went out that writers were needed for the upcoming

O'Donnell show, a great many applied and most were vetoed. One rejected applicant was quoted as saying, "She's being called Der Fuhrer. I knew I was sunk when she said without a trace of humor: 'Pickles! Be funny about pickles for 30 seconds. Go!'" Others insisted that they were being passed over if they had worked for programs Rosie had not liked. Still others claimed that during the staff-writer audition process Rosie would demand "Quick! Name the funniest word in the English language!" or require the applicants to provide lengthy essays on "Why I think I'm Funny." One passed-over candidate complained, "I've never had to explain why I'm funny. It was like taking the SAT Test all over again!" (However, since Rosie was not only the star of her program but its executive producer as well, whatever she decided was how it was to be.)

Eventually, Randy Cohen, 48, would be appointed as head writer for the new talk show. Cohen had spent seven years (and 950 shows) with Letterman. He was put in charge of a writing staff of five, including Kate Clinton, 47, an openly gay stand-up comic whose own performance material is aggressive and political. At the start of his task, Cohen would enthuse of Rosie, his boss, "She's our generation's Eve Arden; a tough-talkin' dame with a heart of gold." But he had a concern. "The watchword around here from the start has been nice. I mean, determinedly nice. And frankly, that worried me a bit, because by its nature, comedy attacks, you know? Good comedy is necessarily critical of something, and if you're busy trying to make everything 'nice,' where does that leave the comedy?"

As the writers honed their brand of material to suit O'Donnell's style and attitudes, they presented samples to Rosie. She would detail, "Sometimes the [jokes] are too biting. Kate, for example, writes brilliant political jokes every day and I'm like, 'Strom Thurmond? No one cares, I can't pronounce it, let's forget it.' Sometimes on the jokes [the staff] hands me I write 'XL', which means, 'No, but I love it.' Because they're funny but mean, and I don't wanna do mean." According to Rosie staff writer Janette Barber, ". . . her policy is, if she wouldn't say the joke in front of the person it's about, she won't do it."

Very much in charge of what would be said and/or done on her show, Rosie would say, "I do feel bad when I kill a joke" to which head writer Cohen would retort, "Oh, don't worry about Rosie—that guilt passes very quickly. It's like the first time a cop kills a bad guy—for the first one there's remorse, but then you get used to it. So do we." As time wore on, Cohen would admit of his new boss: "It's been instructive in this sense: Rosie loves pop culture. I'm that much older than her that the stuff she loves—all the cheesy '70s TV shows and movies—are the things I think have contributed to the fall of Western civilization. I have to be ironic to joke about it, but there's no irony in Rosie—she's pure."

To direct the daily program, Bob McKinnon formerly of *Today* and *Good Morning America* came aboard. John McDaniel, who had played keyboards for Patti LuPone and had been musical director for the 1994 Broadway revival of *Grease!* (in which O'Donnell appeared) was hired to be the show's music director and lead the five-piece studio band. (It would be McDaniel who would create the show's theme song.) Another of the O'Donnell staff would be Joanna Philbin, 23, the daughter of talk show maven Regis Philbin. Not to be overlooked, O'Donnell's sister Maureen continued on as Rosie's business manager. (This would change in the summer of 1996 when Maureen had her third baby and decided to remain at home in New Jersey to care for the infant. Maureen's brother-in-law took over as Rosie's business manager.)

From the beginning, it had been agreed that Rosie's program would be taped in Manhattan, now her new home. It worked out that the show would be taped at 30 Rockefeller Plaza in Studio 8G, the former 175-seat setting for the Phil Donahue Show. As part of the enticement package for O'Donnell to do her daily show, some $20,000 was expended to create a special soundproof office/nursery off the studio set, where Parker could play and/or rest while his mother was earning their daily bread. Kathleen Ankers, who had been Letterman's stage designer since 1980, was brought in to create a set for Rosie that would have a Broadway theatre feel.

As the weeks passed, Rosie quickly discovered the differences between doing a daily TV program and a big feature film. She has recalled, "I was in a meeting [with Warner Bros.] executives and publicity before the TV show was on the air and somebody said, 'Now, we're gonna have a problem with Rosie's chin—how are we gonna light her chin?' I was sitting right there, and they're discussing how difficult it is to light me and my weight! And I thought, on a movie set, they would do everything they could to protect you from hearing anything that might undermine your confidence."

In promoting herself and the show to the media, she explained repeatedly how her program would differ from the rest of the crowd: "I think that comfortable, sort of friendly feeling isn't around that much in the talk show genre. So many times, a guest will come out and Jay Leno will say, sarcastically, 'That's a nice shirt. Where did you get that shirt?'

Every time I see that, I think that Johnny Carson would never have done that. . . . I'm hoping the celebrities will think this is a safe environment. I'm hoping to get them in and make them look good." Demonstrating that she was keeping a sense of perspective, she offered, "What I'm doing is not brain surgery. And not every show I do has to be a home run. I just want to get on base and do the best I can."

As the June 1996 air date approached, it was decided to do five test shows that most likely would not air. As an inducement to draw audiences who wouldn't have the opportunity to wave to family at home, trinkets were given to several of the show-goers—silly items such as a fish-flavored water for cats, a rabbit leash, etc. At the end of the taping, producer Kellison brought down several guests who asked for a different gift and Rosie did an impromptu bit while doing the exchanges.

Behind the scenes, the staff learned from a trial-and-error process. Cohen would admit, "If there was a mistake I learned in that first practice show, it was that I had the writers do too many of what we call 'desk pieces,' where Rosie would deliver some jokes at her desk. When we did that audience thing, I thought, 'Yes! That's why we're here.' We're creating a more intimate show and she's great with the audience. It wasn't like the desk pieces weren't funny, but we're not there to have our bright little words said. We're there to create an arena where Rosie will thrive."

As the shakedown continued, Kellison would assess, "For weeks, I've been looking for the disaster, but it's never come. The biggest change we made after doing the practice shows was changing from three guests a show to four, just to make the pace better. But nothing has really gone wrong. No one hates each other. The staff has just plugged along."

Finally, after a weekend in Washington D.C. for Rosie to participate in the Stand for Children Rally, Monday, June 10 arrived and it was time for the first live show. Said a game Rosie, "You've just got to do it to do it. Like the Lottery. You've got to be in it to win it. Right now, we're lucky. We're at least in it."

• 23 •

I'm also the executive producer [of The Rosie O'Donnell Show*], so there's nobody on the show that I will hate. And I'm only mean to people who have committed heinous acts, or crimes against nature.*

Rosie O'Donnell, June 1996

*I*t was ten a.m., Monday, June 10, 1996 and on the eighth floor of 30 Rockefeller Plaza it was D-Day for the premiere of TV's *The Rosie O'Donnell Show.*

In studio 8G each member of the audience had been provided with a container of low-fat milk and a Drake's cake (one of Rosie's favorite snack foods) to take the edge off anyone's possible hunger. (This would become a show tradition.) Comedian Joey Kola had done his warm-up session with the studio viewers and had selected one of them who would perform the on camera introduction of Rosie and announce the names of that day's show guests. (This would become a show policy.) Now it was time to start. The show's animated opening credits, deliberately created in the 1960s style of the title credits used to start each episode of the sitcom *Bewitched.* In the new variation, a happy-faced, stout cartoon stick figure of Rosie bobs around, distracted by a tempting pie, then cradling a baby in her arms and finally reciting rhyming lines involving the lineup of the day's show guests.

Next, with an introduction shouted out by the designated studio audience member, Rosie in her trademark pants suit breaks forth from behind the stage curtains. She saunters onto the stage doing a rhythm step, waves enthusiastically to the cheering audience, modestly

231

motions to them to stop their applauding ("don't applaud unless you want to—this isn't Sally Jessy Raphael"), thanks the day's announcer, and launches into her boisterous monologue bits. Among her opening remarks that day were "Today, women who sleep with their in-laws. . . . Just kidding!" Then she says "Please say hello to Doc Severinsen and the NBC Orchestra." Pause. Then with a "just kidding," she introduces John McDaniel and his band (soon to be called the McDLTs, a pun and in homage to McDonald's fast food chain and its penchant for naming foods with words beginning with "Mc"). Thereafter, Rosie takes her place at the host's desk.

The next minutes of the show would soon become standard procedure. Rosie chats with John McDaniel who is seated at the piano, then picks up a newspaper which she lets the audience knows holds an assortment of jokes taped to each page. She delivers a string of jokes, some winners, some not. (It would become part of the show's formula for Rosie each day to hold up a newspaper and then a magazine from different cities and recite what station in that area was airing *The Rosie O'Donnell Show* and at what time.) The jokes done, she tosses the publication onto the floor behind her. (Whenever Rosie would stumble reading a joke from the teleprompter or from the cheat cards on her desk, her favorite cover-up would be "I'd like to buy a vowel!")

As it would develop, her final joke for the opening segment of the show would be attached to the desk and soon, she would make a daily habit of announcing, "The final joke. And how do I know it's the final joke?" And, in unison, the audience would chant with her, "Because it's taped to the desk." All these customs would give the talk show a folksy, predictable feel, all part of O'Donnell's goal to be an extremely audience-friendly program.

Originally, comic Brett Butler had been planned as one of the opening show's primary guests. When she canceled, George Clooney was substituted. When this contender for the Sexiest Man Alive title walked onstage he came bearing gifts. Clooney presented Rosie with a bouquet of roses and a bottle of champagne. (It would quickly become a tradition on the program for guests to arrive with a shopping bag in hand to present O'Donnell with tokens of their affection. It might be a gift for little Parker asleep in the studio nursery next door. Or, it might be an intriguingly rare nostalgia item for Rosie to add to her on-the-desk memorabilia collection. Or, if too big, she'd take it home for her ever-expanding assortment of show business merchandise she'd gathered over the years.)

Among Clooney's first words to Rosie are "I'm here 'cause Madonna couldn't make it." (The very pregnant Material Girl had postponed her show visit until after the October 1996 birth of her baby.) This relaxed banter immediately set the stage for equality between guest and host, with nothing being sacred. It was an atmosphere that would prevail on the show. (A parallel informality between Rosie and the studio audience would be quickly established as she began her almost daily ritual—whenever the mood hit her—of launching harmless, brightly colored Koosh balls into the audience. These spongy balls quickly became favored collectors' items for the studio audience. As time went on, it became customary for the more "hip" show guest to be given a Koosh launcher and to try their hand at "pelting" the audience with the light-as-air ammunition. Still later, Rosie would start using Koosh ring tosses to amuse herself and the audience.)

Later in the debut program, out came one of O'Donnell's favorite performers from her beloved world of soap opera—Susan Lucci of *All My Children*. In their mellow, back-slapping chitchat Rosie immediately distinguished herself from most of her talk show peers, especially the likes of a David Letterman who apparently never had a kind word to say about TV shows. In contrast, Rosie has freely admitted that she has always been a TV addict and confirmed moviegoer. As she would chat on the air with guests or with John McDaniel, it was evident that she had an extravagant but quite sincere enthusiasm for the "mundane" diversions provided by TV and movies. She would demonstrate her huge capacity for absorbing the most minute detail about TV programming in the days and months to come. It was this love and knowledge of show business (trivia) that would endear Rosie not only to her guests (who felt that she admired them instead of disdaining them as did other hosts) but to home viewers as well. People could relate to this down-to-earth host who liked a lot of simple things that they did, including junk food.

Having Susan Lucci as a guest on the debut program reflected several policies that would become integral to *The Rosie O'Donnell Show* formula. If Rosie had a penchant for a particular entertainment genre (e.g. soap operas), then she would book many soap opera actors for her program. O'Donnell's philosophy was that if she liked something, the odds were an awful lot of people out in TV land felt the same way.

Rosie's chat fest with Lucci also demonstrated O'Donnell's knack for job networking even when on the air. For example, during their conversation, Rosie said, "I'm so self-indulgent with you. You wanna go to lunch after the show?" O'Donnell's obvious rapport with Lucci led to Rosie being asked later to make a special guest appearance—as Naomi the rambunctious maid—on ABC-TV's *All My Children* (July 30, 1996).

Yet another bit of business during the show would be Rosie verbalizing her wish list of guests for future episodes. So if she were chatting on camera with a guest or John McDaniel about, say, Barbra Streisand, Rosie would suddenly look up and mouth or say aloud to the camera, "Barbra. Are you listening? Call me. Come be on the show." This gambit worked amazingly well and would lead to such people as Virginia Graham, Miss Piggy, Elton John and Shirley Jones volunteering to trek onstage as a Rosie guest in the months ahead.

Rosie also had no qualms about making it known to one and all that she was a staunch Democrat, a big enthusiast of President Bill Clinton and opposed to 1996 presidential hopeful, Bob Dole. Thus she would crack political jokes at a moment's notice, such as about seeing two car bumper stickers on the way to work. One read: "Clinton in '96" and the other: "Dole is 96." This would establish a program forum for Republican bashing and Clinton boosting. Later, for a time, in the name of "fairness," Rosie permitted a member of her writers' staff to come out and recite a pro-Republican joke. But no one said that O'Donnell couldn't make faces while it was being delivered—and she would!

To add that personal touch to her stage presence, Rosie, as on the debut show, would joke about her show business friends. Of Madonna she would crack, "She sleeps with her trainer. I ignore mine." It became standard practice for the very relaxed Rosie to drop names of celebrities with whom she'd recently socialized.

It also was a part of the star's shtick to be self-deprecating—but in a positive way if that is possible—about her excessive love of junk food such as Ding-Dongs and goat cheese pizza, her oversized figure and even her hairdo (which went through several transformations in coloring to lighten and better showcase her face). In the shows ahead, Rosie would constantly refer to herself as an obsessive fan of this or that celebrity and say "It's sick" or characterize her mind full of TV trivia or Broadway show tunes as a wealth of garbage information. She would also institute a studio audience game called Stump Rosie in which she was asked to sing the title song to a given TV series. If O'Donnell missed, the audience member earned a complimentary dinner for two at a Manhattan restaurant.

In case there were any lulls on the show, Rosie would frequently punctuate the silence by pressing one of several buttons on her desk-side control panel. It would launch one of an assortment of brief, frequently changed, pre-recorded messages that might say, "Good one Rosie!" (if she had delivered a particularly fine joke) or might be a snippet of a song made famous by one of that day's show guests. Many of these messages were recorded by Gary Owens, famous as the over-exaggerating announcer on the classic *Rowen and Martin's Laugh-In* TV series.

At the end of the premiere show on June 10, Rosie pulled out her Polaroid camera to snap candid photos of herself with George Clooney and Susan Lucci. It immediately established the image of O'Donnell the unabashed star-struck fan who adores mingling with her show business favorites. It was all part of the package which made it so easy for home viewers to relate with Rosie and to live vicariously through her hobnobbing with current show business luminaries.

At last, Rosie and crew had made it through their debut TV show! Except for glitches with the cue cards and sporadic audio problems, the program had aired with no noticeable hitches. Within the next few days, reviews of Rosie's new show began appearing everywhere.

Syndicated columnist Liz Smith championed, "You don't feel like you have to take a shower after you watch Rosie and guests do their stuff." *TV Guide*'s Jeff Jarvis endorsed, "Rosie's show isn't about freaks. It's about fun. It's a nighttime talk show brought to daytime, complete with show-biz guests, music, and a happy studio audience. And it's funny because Rosie has a hailstorm sense of humor and because she has the simple ability to enjoy her guests. . . . Rosie avoids others' pitfalls. She doesn't try to be sly, as David Letterman does (it was David's smirk that kept him from succeeding in daytime). She doesn't try to please everyone, as Jay Leno desperately does. She doesn't try to save the world with her smile, as Kathie Lee Gifford does. . . . And Rosie doesn't try to sling sleaze, as every other daytime talk show does. . . . She may just be the first person to take the night out of *Tonight*. And in the process, she's making the daytime a nicer place."

Mike Duffy (Knight-Ridder/Tribune Information Service) reported that Rosie ". . . may be the most natural daytime talk-show host to enter our living rooms since Oprah Winfrey went national a decade ago." Todd Everett (*Weekly Variety*) pointed out, "O'Donnell projects a lot of nervous energy and is quite funny. . . her most striking feature may be her seeming accessibility; she seems closer to the audience than any other host in memory. . . . O'Donnell is a far better interviewer than any of the late night variety show hosts in recent memory; for one thing, she seems to know who her guests are." Matt Roush (*USA Today*) applauded, ". . . so what's new? A complete lack of self-importance. . . It couldn't be more refreshing if it tried. . . . Rosie's greatest strength may be her unembarrassed love for TV. She knows whereof she watches. She should be doing her show from a couch, not a desk. Let's hope TV never goes to her head to such a degree that she stops tuning in."

Rick Marin (*Newsweek* magazine) insisted, "Not since Merv Griffin oozed his way through the '70s has there been this level of raw celebrity sycophancy on TV. Who'd have thought we'd be praising a talk-show host for being 'the new Merv'? but it's such a relief from the freak-of-the-week sideshows on Jenny Jones, Ricki Lake, Sally Jessy Raphael and their ilk. . . ." For Laurie Stone (*Village Voice*), "O'Donnell is all gut, and viewers are responding to her authenticity. She is New York: gooney for Broadway musicals, hip to queerness and the polyglot melt. . . . O'Donnell isn't sexual but is plenty libidinous, diving into appetite, hoisting her smarts and bents. The large women of daytime, Oprah [Winfrey], Carnie Wilson, and ex-fatty Ricki Lake—are humiliated by their bodies. O'Donnell calls herself fat and neither weeps nor apologizes for liking food. . . . She's hog-happy with her hungers, whether for Drake's cakes or TV trivia—O'Donnell is Joan Rivers without the self-loathing. . . . Rosie, clearly, has made friends in entertainment, and audiences are responding with similar affection for her big, smart, heartfelt, unembarrassed presence."

Emphasizing O'Donnell's special appeal to the very young, Naomi Serviss (*Newsday*) observed, "What other live show can you take kids to where they'll see a good-natured, normal-looking celebrity? None. On most shows you have to be at least 18, and who wants to attend one of those confessional 'my dysfunctional family is worse than yours . . .' shows anyway?" According to Serviss, "*The Rosie O'Donnell Show* loves kids, with staffers scanning ticket holders looking for wee ones to make announcements and showcase artistic talents and singing skills." In analyzing Rosie's special attraction to the young, Serviss notes, "She is the child raised by the Village of Vintage TV, inhabited by Mr. and Mrs. Brady, the Partridge clan, the ubiquitous Mary Tyler Moore, Rhoda, and Mr. Grant. . . . Maybe that's why kids exposed to her goofy, Koosh-ball-hurling antics and her show-and-tell giggly style fell in love with her. . . ."

When all was said and done (and there was amazingly little panning by critics anywhere of Rosie's program), perhaps Michele Greppi (*New York Post*) phrased it best, "Rosie's like those potato chips. You can't watch just one [episode]. And you want to share them with your friends."

If reviewers around the nation were tossing bouquets to Rosie, how were the home viewers responding to this new meat-and-potatoes type host? The show built from a 3.2 rating on its June 10 debut to a 3.9 in the national Nielsen ratings by mid-July 1996. In the New York marketplace, during its first 30 days, Rosie's program would average a 6.0 audience rating and a 23 share of households watching her show during that time period. This was compared to a 5.0 rating and 19 share for the well-established *Live with Regis and Kathie Lee* morning talk show. In the Nielsen 34 metered national market, O'Donnell's show bowed with a 4.4/16 rating/share, making it the highest-rated premiere of a daytime talk show of the 1990s. Within a month of its debut O'Donnell's vehicle had risen to being the 5th highest rated daytime talk show in the U.S. (Oprah Winfrey's daily talkfest was generally rated in the top spot for the category.)

Rosie's startling TV success led Michael Freeman to write in *Adweek* magazine, "Not everyone can have or clone a Rosie, but her success illustrates the point that if you have something different to fill a new audience niche, anyone can build a hit." He also commented on O'Donnell's advertiser-friendly and squeaky clean show: "Rosie and Oprah [Winfrey] are two strong examples of how a show can successfully balance the scales between achieving high ratings and maintaining a quality environment."

An even surer sign of the show's success occurred when stations around the country began upgrading the time slot of *The Rosie O'Donnell Show* from odd hours to more beneficial positions such as mid-morning or mid-afternoon, which meant that advertising fees to sponsors could be raised. In Philadelphia, the country's fourth biggest TV audience market, the show was switched from 2 a.m. to 11 a.m., while in Baltimore (market #23), the program was switched from 10 a.m. to a prime 4 p.m. time spot, positioning it before the early evening hour. As a result of the terrific critical and viewer response, when it came time for stations to renew their agreements to air Rosie's show for the upcoming 1996-1997 season, Warner Bros. Domestic Television Distribution was, according to the *Hollywood Reporter*, "playing hardball" with stations and licensing fees were frequently tripled or quadrupled by what the outlets had paid for the debut season. The trade paper also reported that stations were being requested to upgrade *The Rosie O'Donnell Show* to evening news lead-in-positions or, perhaps, risk losing the property to a marketplace rival.

In booking program guests—before, during, and after her escalating ratings and glowing reviews —Rosie adhered to a special guideline. As she explained, "You know, when Joan Rivers had her show she made a mistake: On her first show were Elton John, Cher and all these people who were friends with her. And the next day, it was like she had the third lead from *Bosom Buddies*. I think you shoot yourself in the foot by doing that. My friends will come on when they have something to promote."

As Rosie and her program progressed through their initial weeks, there were high points, such as comedian Fran Drescher and, in particular, her parents—Mort and Sylvia—who provided via a remote from Florida reviews of restaurants offering great dinner bargains. There were also low moments, such as Tony Danza (especially when singing), or some so-so interludes, as when actor Matthew Broderick began to philosophize about his career. However, the real highlight of the early run of *The Rosie O'Donnell Show* occurred on June 14, 1996 when singer Donny Osmond (of Donny and Marie 1970s TV variety show fame) appeared as a guest.

When Donny first came on stage, an obviously enthusiastic Rosie proudly displayed her Donny Osmond lunch box and doll. Obviously wanting to get beyond those long-ago teen idol years, Donny wished to focus on the here and now. Later, he mentioned that for an upcoming July 4th celebration show at Brigham Young University he was to make his entrance hanging from a helicopter. Rosie, riveted by her childhood fantasy man, popped up with "I'm willing to go be your stunt double for that, 'cause I don't want you to get hurt." To which a bemused Donny replied, "It's okay. It's going to be fun. It's going to be great—plus the helicopter can't handle that much weight."

Zaftig Rosie, well-experienced at hiding her true feelings, looked a bit askance, but definitely did not go ballistic. Meanwhile, there was a noticeable gasp from the studio audience when Donny made the unwarranted crack. Next, she and Donny did a duet of his and his sister's old novelty song: "I'm a Little Bit Country, I'm a Little Bit Rock and Roll." End of session. However, that was hardly the end of the matter.

On the next show, Rosie attempted to smooth things over with a few weak jokes about Osmond's verbal slam. Whenever she'd mention Donny's name—and she was milking the incident already—the audience groaned. Somehow, it became a *cause celebre* in the media and everyone was rooting for Rosie against the ungracious Donny. (Later, when asked what was the worst moment on her early shows, Rosie would reply, "Donny Osmond calling me fat on national TV. . . . I thought he'd become Howard Stern!") Within days, a repentant Osmond had sent Rosie flowers and a note saying, after all, he had just been kidding. Not willing to let the matter rest, O'Donnell made Donny's negative remarks a recurring bit on future shows.

Finally, after much on-air discussion of whether he would or would not show up in person to apologize, Donny returned to *The Rosie O'Donnell Show* on Friday, July 26, 1996. Much to the audience's approval, Rosie did not make it quick or easy for the shame-faced singer. First she brought out his sister Marie who proceeded to relate stories of how Donny had embarrassed or made fun of her when they were young. Then when Osmond himself trooped out on stage, he presented Rosie with another bouquet of flowers. Playing to the audience, she said in mock shyness, "I guess it's okay for fat people to get flowers, huh?" As a final token of submission, she told Donny not only must he sing to her "Puppy Love" (one of his records from decades ago), but (1) he must put on a dog costume which she proceeded to hand over to him and (2) he had to get down on bended knee while he crooned to her. After doing all this, Donny was forgiven.

Weeks later, as a coda to the episode, Rosie confided on air to viewers that for the Osmond apology segment, "We had the highest ratings ever. We had such high ratings that I'm now requiring all my guests to call me fat and then come back and apologize. Because what the hell if we can get big ratings I'll do it—sure it will hurt me, but for the show, damn it, it'll be worth it."

Almost from the start, there were no shortage of guests who wished to appear on *The Rosie O'Donnell Show*. With the program's growing popularity, it was a marvelous forum to promote new movies, TV series, books and CDs. Visitors could count on a fawning Rosie to gush about whatever they were hawking. As Rosie said, her goal as host to her guests was to follow the example set by one of her predecessors: "I think Johnny Carson was the best at it. He understood that it was his job to assist and it was the guest's job to shoot and score. When they looked good, he looked good. I think a lot of talk show hosts today forget that."

Frequently, Rosie would encourage the guest celebrity to perform a duet with her, and often—to the visitor's amazement—Rosie would remember all the words to their trademark songs while they did not. O'Donnell's session with Cher was a case in point. Cher found herself following the lead of Rosie as they harmonized on one of her popular songs ("Gypsies, Tramps and Thieves") from the past. Occasionally, a guest would not get along with O'Donnell in their musical turn. Such an instance was the August 7, 1996 show on which talented but grungy-looking Meatloaf was her musician visitor. As they began their joint number, Rosie screwed up the words to his song so that his vocal entrance was thrown off. He promptly pulled at her to make her stop mid-lyric, attempted to French kiss her (a routine he used in his music video of the song) and then had her start anew to his satisfaction. Viewers—by now confirmed Rosie-ites—would have none of this and the Internet newsgroups were abuzz at Meatloaf's unappreciated behavior on the program.

On the same episode as Meatloaf, dieting/exercise guru Richard Simmons was also a guest. Since it was "Suck-Up to Barbra Streisand Day" (Rosie hoped her show's theme might prod the entertainer to make a future guest appearance), Rosie and Richard exchanged Streisand trivia. They also matched one another in their knowledge of lyrics to Barbra's song repertoire. At one point, Richard kissed Rosie and she screamed in loud, high-pitched (mock) horror: "You French kissed me!" It just wasn't her day!

If Rosie could and did fawn shamelessly over guests, it was nowhere more evident than on August 23, 1996 when former talk show host Mike Douglas made a rare public appearance by coming to visit Rosie on air. This past king of daytime TV was clearly very touched that the audience remembered him so well. He was nearly teary-eyed at O'Donnell's adulation. The same held true when Bette Midler, "the Queen of All Things," appeared on Rosie's daytime showcase on September 16, 1996. As with so many other favorite celebrities, Rosie could recount particulars, down to the dates and places, when she had seen these entertainers perform and even had treasured ticket stubs and programs to prove it. Frequently, she'd recall bits of their act that even the subjects had completely forgotten. This day, Bette looked on with amazed bewilderment as O'Donnell's admiration poured forth. Reflecting on her own compulsive nature toward cherished stars, Rosie retold an instance from 1984 when she was just getting started in stand-up. She had learned what Midler's concert touring schedule was to be for the forthcoming season and, in turn, booked herself at comedy clubs in the same cities at the appropriate dates. Rosie recounted that she even went so far as to cancel gigs so she could see the Divine Miss M perform "one more time." She also showed home viewers an autographed photo of Midler, which Rosie, the now repentant "obsessive fan" admitted she had actually signed herself years ago.

If such vicarious elbow-rubbing with the rich and famous entranced Rosie's legions of TV viewers, they were equally—if inexplicably—intrigued with her moments of public self-deprecation. Few others on today's TV scene would dare, let alone succeed, in devoting minutes of the day's program to whether or not she should pull out a chin hair, or what color she should restreak her hair, or how many double chins she actually had.

One of the several no-nos on Rosie's TV offering has been her steadfast refusal to follow in the tradition of Kathie Lee Gifford who has used her own talk show with Regis Philbin as a forum to talk about and show off her two youngsters, almost from the day each was born. Thus O'Donnell has vetoed all requests to bring Parker on stage or to even discuss his daily activities on the program. She reasons: "Fame is tough enough on me. On a child, it can be impossible. If I talk about how my child was toilet-trained on TV, years later when he's a teenager people are going to remind him about it." (As a send-up of show business personalities, such as Lucille Ball, who have, over the years, hired young actors to play their "real-life" children on their TV series, Rosie concocted a funny recurring skit. Over the course of several days on her talkfest she had three different actors—one about two years old, another age six and a third about sixteen—each make a one-shot guest appearance on a different episode. It allowed for her tongue-in-cheek comment, "Gee, they grow fast." That was her amusing answer to those who wanted to see her "son" on the program. Still later, her adult "son" would appear on the show—now a male stripper!)

Attempting to make *The Rosie O'Donnell Show* a fail-safe operation, there were bumps to be ironed out with the behind-the-scenes crew. By mid-August 1996, it was announced that the show's stage manager had departed, as had the head researcher Aimee Baker. Director Bob McKinnon had decided to move over to *In Person with Maureen O'Boyle*, the new talk show being produced down the hall from Rosie's and also distributed by Warner Bros. Baker reportedly said, "I've been in the business for ten years and I've worked for Oprah and Bob Costas, and I've work with executive producers who are far more experienced than he [Daniel Kellison] is. I didn't like his management style." Kellison's public response was ". . . there are personality differences on every show you work on. You hire 60 people and not everyone works out." One anonymous source at the time was quoted with saying, "You come in every day to work and you don't know whether Rosie is going to praise you or scream at you." Evidently, to insure that she would not be confused with the anonymous complainer, Baker would soon tell the press, "I think she's [i.e. Rosie O'Donnell] great. I didn't see eye-to-eye with Dan."

(Later in 1996, a dozen other staff members would depart *The Rosie O'Donnell Show*. According to a *National Enquirer* follow-up article on these staff changes, Rosie ". . . terrorizes employees, fires people left and right—and forces workers to sign a gag order so they can't talk about her behavior. . . . She has a habit of picking up things and throwing them while she's having a little fit. It doesn't matter to her if the object just misses someone." In the wake of these staff changes, Daniel Kellison left *The Rosie O'Donnell Show* in December 1996. He was replaced by Hilary Estey-McLoughlin, who had been vice president of development for Telepictures Productions, the producers of Rosie's talk program.)

Sometimes the ruffled feathers on Rosie's show would derive from the pressure of the competition among the talk shows to grab topical guests. After the 1996 Olympics in Atlanta, Georgia, the prime chat programs all bid to be the first to have this or that champion athlete on their particular program. The appearance of such sports figures was always a sure and quick way to win rating points with TV viewers. However, it wasn't always easy to accomplish. O'Donnell's show was no exception. Rosie's executive producer admitted, "There's a mini-battle that goes on behind the scenes in the jockeying for the athletes. It's hustling, it's wheeling and dealing. It's a wrestling match to get them on. . . . It is competitive, but no not in a malicious way. It's just fine to get someone exclusively, especially when you're the newcomer." What turned the tide in O'Donnell's favor in several instances, besides an aggressive on-Atlanta-site O'Donnell show segment producer, were that so many of the young sports figures were Rosie fans and, when not in a match or working out, frequently would watch her daily TV show at the Olympic Village. So, during the week of August 5-9, 1996, O'Donnell was able to welcome to her show such young American medalists as swimmer Amy Van Dyken, track and field star Jackie Joyner-Kersee and soccer champ Mia Hamm.

After the initial staff changes, the day-to-day running of Rosie's gab fest franchise ran fairly smoothly—that is until Tuesday, September 10. The day before, the show had been "introduced" by studio audience member Ed Rendell, Mayor of Philadelphia. (His appearance was part of a promotion to celebrate the upgrading of *The Rosie O'Donnell Show*'s time slot in the city of brotherly love.) The next day, while doing the live show, a call came into the studio. The person on the phone claimed to be Mayor Rendell and said he wanted to speak with O'Donnell on the air. His call was put through to a surprised Rosie. The caller then proceeded to say, "Howard Stern says you're a fat pig, you know that?" A stunned Rosie responded, "Who did what?" The caller replied, "Howard Stern says you're a [big] fat pig." Rosie tried to cover over for the studio audience by saying, "Really interesting. Thanks for calling!" Before hanging up, the haranguer again called her a "fat pig."

This actual conversation was heard by those station affiliates with a live (10 a.m. EST) program feed. (Other stations which showed the program in a later time frame were given a hastily edited segment version in which the rude caller's comments were bleeped out and the title box at the bottom of the screen was changed from "On the Phone: Ed Rendell" to "CRANK CALL.") As it developed, the crank caller turned out be a prankster who went by the nickname of "Captain Janks." He had taped the conversation with O'Donnell as a stunt to be played back on Howard Stern's radio show. (Years ago, the shock talk jock and Rosie had squared off in different corners when he rudely expressed his lack of appreciation for her talents on several public occasions.)

Since Rosie's executive producer, Daniel Kellison, had final responsibility for the call being put through, O'Donnell expressed her immediate and extreme displeasure to Kellison during a show break. Later, a member of Rosie's staff contacted the police and a citation was issued to the offender (traced by his phone number when he called Rosie's show). As such, Captain Janks faced a $147 fine, but seemed unfazed.

On a far happier note was another saga which ended in an on-the-air phone call. For days ... weeks ... months, Rosie had been professing her adoration of actor Tom Cruise on the air, always insisting that her admiration for his film work was "not sexual." She would tease that his actress wife, Nicole Kidman, should beware of Rosie "on the prowl." One day, O'Donnell received flowers and a note from Cruise thanking her for her many kind words. Thereafter, Rosie's daily dose of effusive puppy love reached a semi-climax when O'Donnell announced she had been selected to emcee the 11th annual Moving Picture Ball of the American Cinematheque. The festivities were to be held at the Beverly Hilton Hotel's ballroom in Los Angeles on September 21 and Tom Cruise was this year's honoree. To say the least, Rosie was beside herself with anticipation which she played up to the hilt. She took to having a daily countdown on camera, tearing off the number of days left from beneath his photo that sat on her TV set desk.

The long-awaited night came and proceeded well. The capper to the evening came when Rosie, proclaiming herself the ultimate "obsessed" Tom Cruise fan, proved her point by pulling at the front of her black dress so that the area above her left breast was suddenly exposed. There in plain view was a (faux) tattoo which read "Tom." It earned a huge laugh from the audience! Two days after the eventful tribute, a still-glowing Rosie flew back to New York. On her Tuesday, September 24, 1996 show she told all about her night out with "Tom." She even sang a parody ode to Cruise based on the melody to "Big Spender." On stage there were enlarged photos of Rosie and Tom together and video footage of Cruise embracing her on the dais at the tribute. Meanwhile, during the hour program, Rosie received onstage a bouquet of flowers from Cruise along with his note thanking her for having hosted the big event.

Later, while the Tuesday program was still in progress, O'Donnell was informed by a staff member that she had an urgent phone call and she simply must take it. Recalling all too well the recent "fat pig" episode she shuddered at the thought of being humiliated again. Should she or shouldn't she take the call? She confided to viewers that she had already worked out a routine with musical director John McDaniel that if anything like that caller episode should happen again, or anyone in the studio audience should ever begin to heckle, he and his musicians were to start playing—immediately and loudly! Reluctantly, Rosie agreed to take the call. It turned out to be the real Cruise (as the studio audience and home viewers could immediately hear). Once again, he reiterated his appreciation to Rosie for flying to the coast and emceeing the event.

Playing to the studio crowd, Rosie ended the conversation with her sentiments that any time there should be another such award event, Tom Cruise definitely should not hesitate to call O'Donnell because "I'm just a phone call away."

And Cruise did call Rosie again. This time it was to arrange to appear on her talk show on December 10, 1996 as part of his promotional tour for his new movie, *Jerry Maguire*. To mark the momentous event, a near-giddy Rosie had a daily countdown to "my Tom's" appearance on her program. For O'Donnell, having Cruise as a show guest was the apex of her debut season as a TV talk show host, and it garnered her the highest ratings for *The Rosie O'Donnell Show* of the year.

· 24 ·

I'm not really shocked [by the degree of success]. That probably sounds egotistical, but I don't believe that there's any person who's successful who never thought he would be, because you have to see it before you can live it. I remember being in third grade and writing autographs on my loose-leaf paper that said, 'Best wishes, Rosie O'Donnell.' I really did. . . . I always knew that I would do this in some capacity, so it really doesn't shock me.

Rosie O'Donnell, November 1994

*A*s 1996 rolled onward, *The Rosie O'Donnell Show*, with its love fest between host and guests and host and audience, continued to gain momentum in the ratings and to win additional critical endorsements. It seemed as if O'Donnell could do no wrong. *Newsweek* magazine, in its July 15, 1996 issue had labeled Rosie "Queen of Nice" and the unique appellation stuck. As *Newsweek*'s Rick Marin explained her royal title, she gets ". . . credits for singlehandedly saving daytime TV from itself. She's taken the trash out of talk by making nice, not nasty. And for that she should be given a Nobel Prize, or at least more Twinkies." He also pinpointed a prime reason for O'Donnell's mass appeal: ". . . under the gruff exterior, fans sense a softy, someone just like the best friend she played in *Sleepless in Seattle*. And they love that she's now the doting single mom of an adopted 1-year-old son."

Everything about Rosie's talk show intrigued the public. If she mentioned conversationally on the air that she was having difficulty locating a particular brand of baby diapers or a particular candy bar, lo and behold the next day, the manufacturer would inundate O'Donnell's studio with boxes of the product. Knowing O'Donnell was a fanatic about TV show merchandise from the 1970s, fans would go to great lengths to send her rare samples for her collection.

Then there was the smoky fire which broke out in the early morning of October 10, 1996 at NBC-TV's 30 Rockefeller Plaza headquarters. O'Donnell's chat program was one of those that had to vacate the premises for the time being. The media went wild covering the event, wondering aloud what Rosie fans would do for their daily talk show fix if she had to miss telecasts. For the first few days thereafter, previously taped episodes were used. Then Rosie's crew found temporary headquarters at the Ed Sullivan Theatre, home of *The Late Show with David Letterman*. For their first telecast (October 14, 1996) from the Ed Sullivan Theatre, Rosie opened the program with a song of appreciation to Letterman. It was sung to the tune of "The Telephone Hour" from the musical *Bye Bye Birdie*. O'Donnell's music director, John McDaniel sang along with the host.

• • •

Despite her huge current TV success, levelheaded O'Donnell is shrewd enough to realize that the viewing public is and has always been fickle. They can love you one minute and then the next you are forgotten. Further on this point, she has explained, "For a while, everybody likes the underdog. Now I am the underdog. I did this movie. Nobody knew who I was. People go, 'I remember her from *Star Search*. She's one of us. She looks like us. She's sort of the normal one. Oh, God, she got in a movie. She did good. Oh, wow! She's in another movie. . . .' But you know, after a while you're not the underdog anymore. Then you're the one who always gets up to bat and hits. Then they're like, 'Enough, already. Oh, you think you're so great now?'. . . Especially if you change, if you start to become different than what it was they fell in love with to begin with. It's hard to maintain that. Your life changes. . . . They only want the truth. Your act has to change as your life changes. . . . You need to find a way to make your new life more relatable, otherwise the audience is lost, and they end up resenting you."

For O'Donnell the best—and only—way for her is to continue being herself and trusting her instincts which so far have done very well by her. Sometimes her gut feelings prompt her to do an about-face. For example, in early 1996 it was touted that Rosie had made an agreement with Warner Books (a corporate division of her TV show distributor and the publisher who had put out Madonna's 1992 book, *Sex*) to write a humorous book on her observations in life. By the spring of

1996 it was rumored that her projected manuscript would be a more serious offering, one that dealt with, perhaps, her role as a single mother. One thing, it would not be, however, was a tell-all book because relating some painful episodes in her life would infringe on the privacy of others. Then, by August 1996, Rosie confirmed the writing project was delayed. She explained, ". . . I had a deal to write one, but I will put it off for a while 'cause the prospect is a bit daunting for now." She later added that the primary reason for postponing the book was that the media was so relentless in hounding Rosie's family and friends for news about her. O'Donnell says, "I really have found it so intrusive that I felt to write a book and give details and facts would only provoke them more in a certain way." She does suggest that ". . . in a few years from now I think I'll be more ready and willing to write stuff."

One thing she didn't change her mind about was staying in the New York City area. Although she had a co-op apartment in an Upper West Side high-rise, she decided in early 1996 to purchase a suburban home. The one she settled on was along the Hudson River in Nyack, New York, about twenty miles and sixty minutes north of the city. She had been told about the property by her good friend Madonna who had looked at this piece of real estate, but then decided the brick wall surrounding the house and yard was not sufficient to insure privacy. On the other hand, Rosie was excited by the real estate and purchased it for a reported $770,000. (One report circulated that the impulsive O'Donnell had actually paid as much as $850,000 for her new address, having acquired the parcel from the owner of an adjoining home who had himself just purchased the real estate for $750,000 as an investment opportunity.)

The 22-room, three-story Nyack mansion, known as Pretty Penny, was the former estate of the late stage star, Helen Hayes, of whom Rosie claimed to have been a huge fan. Hayes and her playwright husband, Charles MacArthur, had purchased the riverside property in 1931. (MacArthur had died in 1956 while Hayes passed away in 1993.) Wanting her expansive new home to reflect her own tastes, O'Donnell had it redecorated from top to bottom. One of Rosie's celebrity neighbors at her Nyack address is actress Ellen Burstyn who lives just around the corner.

While preparing and appearing on each day's *The Rosie O'Donnell Show* is Rosie's primary career focus, she seems to be everywhere at once. She is a frequent emcee and/or participant at charity fund-raisers all over the country. It had become almost a second career for Rosie. As an avid supporter of President Bill Clinton she and fellow talk show host Conan O'Brien were among those invited to attend a White House state dinner on June 13, 1996 in honor of the visiting Irish president, Mary Robinson.

When the Democrats threw a huge fund-raising gala on August 18, 1996 at Radio City Music Hall in honor of President Clinton's 50th birthday, Whoopi Goldberg hosted while Rosie was among the guest performers (including Tony Bennett, Carly Simon, Aretha Franklin) requested to entertain the 6,000 donors who had each paid $250 to $500 per seat at the two-hour show. Wearing a tux and white sneakers, Rosie made her entrance onto the music Hall stage and told the partisan audience of Clinton's 1996 Presidential rival, "[Bob] Dole sucks."

A Very Brady Sequel, the follow-up to 1995's *The Brady Bunch Movie*, was released in September 1996. Peripatetic Rosie had a guest cameo in this amusing, if tenuous satire of the classic *The Brady Bunch* sitcom. In the storyline O'Donnell appears in an auction scene with Zsa Zsa Gabor. Rosie snapped a few wisecracks at and about the much-married Gabor. Most impressive is O'Donnell's well-tailored outfit, chic coif and, especially, her makeup which made the 34-year-old comic look quite beautiful.

If exposés on the supposed true nature of motorcycle-riding Rosie's personal life were a mainstay of the supermarket tabloids in the summer of 1996, O'Donnell did her best to shrug them off. She continued to be seen about town and on holiday with her good friend, actress Michelle Blakely. O'Donnell made time to fly to Los Angeles on the weekend of July 27, 1996 to attend the baby shower for her pal, Madonna. The party was held at the home of Debi Mazar (the actress who had been a regular on such TV series as *Civil Wars* and *L.A. Law*). Among those who attended were actress Sharon Stone. It was circulated that Rosie had been thrown into Mazar's pool by playful friends. (However, Rosie clarified later on her TV show, that was not true.) Supposedly, the big topics of discussion at the shower were natal care (upon which the experienced Rosie could advise the Material Girl) and how long after giving birth should Madonna wait before having sex. The consensus, it was reported, was six weeks.

From the West Coast, Rosie, accompanied by Michelle and Parker, flew to Hawaii, to the island of Maui. Who should have the resort suite next to theirs but actor Joey Lawrence, his parents and fellow actor siblings. Ten years before, Rosie had been a regular on the TV sitcom, *Gimme a Break* with Joey and Matthew Lawrence. Chatting with the Lawrences certainly gave O'Donnell ample opportunity to assess just how much had happened for and to her professionally and personally in just the past decade.

And what will the next decade be like for Rosie O'Donnell?

There will, of course, be TV's *The Rosie O'Donnell Show*. In mid-October 1996, it was announced that the "rockin'" program had been renewed in all its U.S. outlets through the year 2000. Stations were already in a bidding war to continue to air *Rosie* in future seasons and, as such, had to agree to substantial fee hikes. For example, in smaller markets, the weekly station fee jumped from $6,000 to $70,000 while in the biggest markets, the price went from $25,000 to $160,000 per week. According to Jenny Hontz in *Daily Variety*, "A new show has never before been renewed for such an extended period, especially in the nation's top markets. . . . The show's performance stands out even more when compared with the new crop of first-run shows on the air, most of which are failing badly."

For another thing, O'Donnell will continue to do guest shots on TV such as her work on the October 9, 1966 episode of *The Nanny*. On that sitcom segment, Fran Drescher's character becomes a short-lasting child-care consultant on *The Rosie O'Donnell Show*. Rosie also made an appearance on the series *Muppets Tonight* in the fall of 1996 and returned to *The Late Show with David Letterman* (October 22, 1996) where she sang a rousing "Give My Regards to Broadway." On *Vanessa Williams & Friends: Christmas in New York* (December 1, 1996), Rosie sang a duet of "White Christmas" with Elmo, the puppet of TV's *Sesame Street* fame. On December 14, 1996, O'Donnell hosted *Saturday Night Live* with Whitney Houston and did comedy sketches with special guest Penny Marshall.

For yet another, there will undoubtedly be more feature films in her near future. Not that long ago, Rosie had insisted that a primary reason for abandoning her film career in 1996 and moving into talk TV was to have far much more time to spend with her son Parker. However, in late September 1996, the *Hollywood Reporter* published that Rosie was in "final negotiation" with Miramax Pictures to star in a movie based on her screen treatment, *Double Wish*. The movie would focus on Rosie's character as "a sort of Mary Poppins with attitude." There is also the possibility that O'Donnell will play the tough prison matron in the screen version of *Chicago*, the Broadway musical which was revived very successfully in 1996. That Rosie is seemingly doing a contradictory about-face in her stated thinking on the subject of moviemaking proves merely that the very human Rosie, like most successful movie personalities, cannot easily abandon a field of endeavor that provides so much creative, emotional and financial satisfaction.

There is also O'Donnell's ongoing dream of one day soon directing a motion picture. Regarding this professional goal she says, "If I could—could get nearly as good as Penny [Marshall], if I could be half as good as Penny, if I could . . . work as a director, which I hope I will be able to, then that would be thrilling for me because, you know, you—you work three months on the location and then you have, like, nine months to edit it and . . . it's easier to have a life. . . . " She also has said of being behind the camera: "If I were in Jodie Foster's position with that kind of power, I'd direct all the time. I don't think I'd act any-more. Not because I don't respect it, but creatively it doesn't fulfill me as much as I would like it to. When you're an actress, you're not selling the character. You're selling you. 'Like me. Buy me. Come see me.' And that gets toxic. Which is why I started writing. I'd like to have the piece of art I make be something I can hand to someone else. And have it not be me."

In yet another area—that of avid participant on televised award shows—Rosie continues to gain in stature. For example, at the MTV Video Music Awards (September 4, 1996) O'Donnell (dressed in a gray-green pants suit with an intriguing collar) was "merely" a presen-ter. However, it's more than likely that O'Donnell will soon be called upon, as have other major comedians, to host one or more of the prime entertainment industry award shows that pepper the TV schedule. In fact, Whoopi Goldberg, who has emceed the Oscars twice (1994, 1996) said that she will not return to the Oscars in 1997 in that capac-ity. When asked who'd she suggest as a replacement, she recommended O'Donnell. "There isn't anybody else who can do it in my opinion but Rosie." However, the producers of the Academy Awards felt different-ly. They selected comedian Billy Crystal (who had done the hosting chore several times before) to emcee the March 1997 Oscar festivities.

• • •

From the motherless youngster in Commack, Long Island to the multimedia star of today has been a long trip for the career-driven Rosie O'Donnell. Unlike many others, she has adapted to her success with far less trauma than most. She admits, "You could go crazy with all this attention, but I think I was really fortunate to do my first [sic] film with probably the most famous woman in the world. I've tried really hard to maintain my essence, which is what got me here in the first place. . . . I'm very direct, and it gets me in trouble. I'd rather have people say it like it is. I think I'm tactful, but I'm not as gentle as I could be. I'm abrasive in some ways, and I'm often not conscious of it."

In early October 1996, in yet another testament to her public appeal, Rosie was named the most popular female entertainment figure in a voters' poll conducted on *People Magazine Online* for its Icon Awards. In this Internet-based competition, O'Donnell competed in the finals against Gillian Anderson, Sandra Bullock, Teri Hatcher and Meg Ryan. At the time, the Internet-based *People* Online's Laura Smith Kay took occasion to point out, 'Genuine' might describe O'Donnell's on-line worshipers [who operate the various Rosie O'Donnell unofficial web sites]: "They . . . differ from the usual celebrity spotters that sprout on the Net. They seem to be more interested in talking about Rosie, or repeating some of her best lines, than, say, cataloging her every life event or posting every latest photo."

Showing just how far up in the popularity scale Rosie had risen, TV journalist Barbara Walters chose Rosie as one of the lucky ten for her ABC-TV television special *(The 10 Most Fascinating People of 1996)*. Others selected and interviewed on this December 6, 1996 special were Israeli Prime Minister Benjamin Netanyahu, astronaut Shannon Lucid and Rosie's favorite actor, Tom Cruise.

Regarding Rosie's still-expanding celebrity status—which she strove so hard to obtain—she recognizes, "Once you get fame you can never give it back. And it infiltrates every area of your life. It affects everything. People come up and . . . it dehumanizes you. They think you're not human anymore. . . . You try to maintain some of your humanity to keep yourself sane, and yet. . . ." She also acknowledges, "It's sort of a hard thing, but you can't really complain because you knew going in it would be like this. And you get to be a millionaire, so what can I say?"

In her current off camera life, Rosie has become the dedicated mother. Besides the obvious joys and fulfillment of parenting, Rosie admits it has provided another perk: "When I go out alone in the city, sometimes it can be difficult. Now, when I take my son to the park, mothers stop me as a mom, not as somebody on TV or movies. . . . They ask how old he is, how he's doing. I'm able to connect with people on an innate maternal level. My fame has been superseded by my parenting, which I love. . . . I'm in the sorority now." She would also like to adopt more children. (In fact, O'Donnell is so enthusiastic about single motherhood that she encouraged and helped actress Kate Jackson in recent times to adopt a child of her own.) When asked the inevitable question about whether she'd let her son (or other future children) go into show business, Rosie admits, "I'm going to tell him what my parents told me. When you're old enough to drive yourself to the audition, you can go."

As for her family, O'Donnell still maintains the emotional distance with her geographically far-away dad. (She now says, "He's not a horrible man, my dad, he's a good guy trying to do the best that he can.") As before, Rosie is much closer with her siblings: Maureen and her husband and their three children live in New Jersey; Tim, who recently had his second child, lives in Florida; Eddie—who has one child—is based in New York City; and her lawyer brother, Danny, also is a Manhattanite.

Regarding her religion, Rosie told Patricia Harty of *Irish America* magazine not long ago: "I think that my Irish heritage is ingrained in me in ways that I don't even fully comprehend yet, but I know that it comes out. As far as my Catholicism, although I'm not a practicing Catholic at the moment, I know that when I drive past an accident, before I realize what I'm doing, I cross myself, so there are things that are ingrained in you that come . . . from your childhood, the foundation of how you were raised. It definitely had a profound impact on me."

As to O'Donnell's comedic stock-in-trade—i.e., her full figure—she admits her compulsions still win out over common sense and that her chubbiness remains a great escape: "I'm an emotional eater. I'll have a feeling and before I know it, I've got that second Dove bar in my mouth going: 'I think I'm upset about something!'" Besides, she says, "I'm a naturally big woman—and women love that about me. . . . I'm a mom now with my own little boy to bring up. Why do I need to run around looking like some starving super model. . . . I honestly believe that my weight is part of my popularity. Thousands of heavy women can identify with me. They see me heavy but enjoying life and having fun. . . . Look what happened to Oprah [Winfrey] when she finally lost weight—she lost more rating points than pounds. . . . She got so involved in her glamorous image, she forgot about the average women in her audience who were the real key to her success."

And, finally, looking both backward and forward at her hugely successful career, Rosie O'Donnell predicts that one day she'll be saying, "It's been a wonderful ride." According to Rosie: "You know, you get on a big wave and you ride it till it hits the surf, and then when you're done, you say, 'Thanks, that was great.'"

· 25 ·

It's my [TV] show and I'll do what I want.

Rosie O'Donnell, 1997

O n Friday, May 16, 1997, Rosie O'Donnell celebrated the first anniversary (from the date of her initial tapings) of her hugely popular syndicated TV talk show. To honor the milestone, she had as that episode's special guests the three celebrities (actor George Clooney, soap star Susan Lucci, and Grammy-winning singer Toni Braxton) who had appeared on the first aired installment of her television program.

In retrospect, the first year of *The Rosie O'Donnell Show* had been amazingly successful with audiences and critics alike, leading to consistently high ratings (especially when she spent two weeks taping from Universal Studios in Los Angeles with an array of celebrity guests), increased advertising revenue, and tremendous visibility for Rosie, the program's irrepressible star. (It also led to a renewal of her show's contract into the year 2000 with hefty salary and incentive escalations for star/producer O'Donnell.)

If, during the show's "freshman" year on the air, singer Meatloaf had been one of the low points as a guest, the on-the-air contretemps with singer Donny Osmond had been a controversial high spot. Ratings had soared when the still baby-faced entertainer returned to Rosie's venue—wearing a dog suit—and apologized for having suggested that

O'Donnell was overweight. Then there was the time when Rosie's pal Madonna—who recently had given birth to her first child—had "dared" to appear first thereafter on Oprah Winfrey's rival TV talk show. (Madonna made "amends" by appearing on Rosie's show in January 1997 and graciously listening to all the parenting advice O'Donnell, the seasoned mother, offered her equally famous single-parent guest.)

Then, too, there was the occasion when Elizabeth Taylor canceled her scheduled visitation to *The Rosie O'Donnell Show* because she was suddenly scheduled to undergo brain surgery. This cancellation prompted rumors that O'Donnell was quite miffed by Taylor's "snub," and, to retaliate for the alleged "slight," Rosie supposedly refused to appear on an upcoming TV special celebrating Taylor's sixty-fifth birthday. (Rosie eventually taped a cameo for the star-studded *Happy Birthday, Elizabeth*, which aired on ABC-TV on February 24, 1997).

Later, on October 30, 1997, there was another major no-show on Rosie's syndicated TV program when pop singing star Whitney Houston canceled at the last minute. Supposedly, Whitney bailed out forty-five minutes before Rosie's scheduled live taping, claiming a stomach flu had incapacitated her from coming on air to plug her TV special *Cinderella*. An obviously displeased Rosie said—on air— "Whitney is not here—she's ill. I hope she's *very* ill." Matters were not helped when later that same day, Houston accompanied her husband, singer Bobby Brown, to a taping for his appearance on the *Late Show with David Letterman*. Days later, a still-fuming O'Donnell informed *Entertainment Weekly* regarding Houston's bothersome non-appear-ance: "Oh, yeah, it definitely screwed up the show . . . It threw [every-thing] off. I've been on live TV for a year and a half, and I've never missed a show. Most people show up, especially when they have a movie that they're producing and starring in to sell."

However, not all the conflicts on *The Rosie O'Donnell Show* involved persnickety guest talents (or "creative differences" with pro-gram staff members who defected on their own or were asked to quit the enterprise). Sometimes big business was the culprit. For example, Scope, a major national manufacturer of mouthwash had the "nerve" to suggest in a promotional article that Rosie O'Donnell was on its self-created list of America's "least kissable" celebrities. Never a shrinking violet, O'Donnell responded to that distinction during one of her daily TV shows. To emphasize her displeasure to her TV fans, while gargling with rival brand Listerine, she suggested her loyal viewers should avoid using Scope. This action on her part prompted Listerine to enter the fray by offering to pay $1,000 to charity each time a guest on *The Rosie O'Donnell Show* kissed its famed host on air. The on-going gimmick lasted for several weeks and, before the campaign ended, a buoyant Rosie had collected over $500,000 for charity!

As a far more positive note on *The Rosie O'Donnell Show,* one installment (February 7, 1997) found Rosie proudly playing host to her Commack, Long Island high school classmates and teachers with an hour filled with nostalgic anecdotes. Earlier, O'Donnell had one of her prime fantasies come true when, on December 10, 1996, movie superstar Tom Cruise finally appeared on her TV talk program. For days before Cruise's well-hyped appearance (to plug his new movie, *Jerry McGuire)* O'Donnell was a-twitter wondering aloud to her TV viewers what she should wear or say when her beloved Tommy did show up for the much-heralded show taping.

When the greatly-anticipated T. C. Day finally arrived, a highly-excited Rosie advised the studio audience that *my* "boyfriend is right around that corner." She emphasized, "He's my one and only. I love him." Becoming more excited, she bubbled, "Please welcome the most perfect man on the planet, my Tommy!" As he walked on-stage, it was a toss-up who was more noticeably nervous—host or guest. Between repeated hugs and kisses, O'Donnell asked her famed visitor if his wife, actress Nicole Kidman, was okay with Rosie's obsessive fan behavior. An ever-beaming Cruise replied, "Absolutely." (Later, enormously-devoted Rosie admitted to her handsome guest: "I'm just a moment away from being totally insane and living outside your house in a sleeping bag.") Further on into this televised love fest, effusive Rosie acknowledged, "I know that you're just a guy who's an actor, and you have a wife and family. But, somehow, you make me really happy." (This drew great applause from the largely-female studio audience.) To cap the momentous event, at the end of their program segment, O'Donnell and Cruise adjourned to her on-stage photo booth where they posed together for candid snapshots. This led the enthralled Rosie to point out to her viewers, "I just wanted to say, dreams come true on *The Rosie O'Donnell Show. . .*"

If having super stud Tom Cruise appear on her TV show tremendously excited Rosie (and led to high viewer ratings) the ultimate happened when O'Donnell's show business "god," Barbra Streisand, finally agreed to spend an hour on-air at *The Rosie O'Donnell Show*. Rosie had been begging the famed singer to guest on the program since the talk show debuted one-and-a-half years ago. Whether engaging equally fanatical Streisand devotee Richard Simmons in Barbra trivia contests or having a "Barbra Streisand Day" on her show, O'Donnell was unrelenting in urging the legendary entertainer to visit *The Rosie O'Donnell Show*. (Repeatedly on her talk forum, obsessive Rosie would discuss Streisand with guests, sing snippets of Barbra's trademark songs, and, looking directly in the camera, would enunciate, "Barbra, can you hear me? Come on my show!")

Regarding her forthcoming appearance (November 21, 1997), Streisand admitted that part of her resolve to do Rosie's TV show was based on the fact that fans on several of Streisand's Internet Web sites "wanted her to do it." The diva also explained to the media that O'Donnell "has been very kind and supportive of me, and I really appreciate that. But don't make me out to be a saint. I'm promoting my [new CD] album [*Higher Ground*]."

As the longed-for Streisand visit grew closer, Rosie told viewers that she was desperately trying to lose twenty pounds to look more fit for her idol. She also confessed that because she was so nervous about the pending occasion, she had constant diarrhea.

To prepare for the pending momentous event, Rosie—without fanfare—rearranged her TV stage set. Starting a few weeks before Streisand's arrival, O'Donnell changed the arrangement of furniture so that guests now sat to Rosie's left. This was to accommodate quietly the singer icon who always insisted she photographed more flatteringly from her left side than from her right.

Come the actual taping, Rosie was quickly reduced to tears in the presence of her idol. Through teary eyes O'Donnell recalled on air how she and her mom, both devoted Streisand fans, listened to her albums and went together to see all of Barbra's movies. (Regarding her emotional devotion to Barbra, Rosie told the press, "It's so connected with my mom, she loved [Streisand] so much, had all her records, used to listen while she cleaned house and cooked dinner.") When the TV host showed no signs of regaining her composure on air, an obviously choked-up Streisand reached over, asked "Are you OK?", helped to wipe away Rosie's tears, and held O'Donnell's trembling hand. (Streisand herself got teary at this highly-charged meeting.)

As the interview progressed, Rosie admitted to her flattered visitor, "I have no conscious memory of my life without you in it." (On another occasion, O'Donnell would admit that she had cut school classes to buy Streisand albums the first day they were released.) Before the exciting TV hour was over, Rosie also played host to Streisand's fiancé, actor James Brolin. Becoming boisterous, O'Donnell prodded—unsuccessfully—for the very affectionate couple to reveal to viewers when their much-speculated wedding would finally occur. This was as daring as the ultra-respectful Rosie got in questioning her famed guest. O'Donnell reasoned, "I would never in a million years say or ask anything that might offend her. But there was no area we were not allowed to go in."

Following the thrilling meeting, O'Donnell told *USA Today* columnist Jeannie Williams, "She was everything I ever dreamed she'd be and more, so warm and kind to me, all at once like a friend, a sister, a mother . . ." The dream visit also garnered for Rosie her highest to date TV show ratings (10.2) and share (26). That Friday talk show episode finished first in its time slot in twenty-six of thirty-eight metered markets in the United States.

Substantiating Rosie's ultra successful TV year, on May 21, 1997, three weeks before her first anniversary on the air with *The Rosie O'Donnell Show*, O'Donnell won an Emmy Award as Best Talk Show Host, beating out talk diva Oprah Winfrey (who, in turn, beat out Rosie in the Best Talk Show category). At the prestigious TV Awards, televised from New York City's Radio City Music Hall, Rosie cried as she accepted her Emmy. She reminisced to the audience that, as a child, she had sat in the upper balcony of this famed theater watching the annual Christmas Show with her mother and sister. "I feel as though they have guided me in my life," she said weepily as she collected her trophy.

A few days later, on June 1, 1997, Rosie was back at Radio City Music Hall, this time as host of the 51st Annual Tony Awards. A great enthusiast of the Broadway theater, O'Donnell had plugged the upcoming Tonys for weeks on her TV program. To further insure a larger viewing audience she and the Awards producers especially had booked celebrity presenters who would be very well known to television watchers. A highlight of the two-hour festivities occurred in the opening production number when O'Donnell joined enthusiastically in a marathon medley of songs-and-dances with members of several nominated and current Broadway musicals. As a result of Rosie's hosting chores, the Tony Awards jumped some 35% in the Nielsen Ratings compared to the prior year's event. It further enhanced O'Donnell's reputation as a media darling and made many wonder why she had been passed over (in favor of Billy Crystal) for hosting the Academy Awards in March of 1997.

Not only was Rosie a favorite participant at TV Award shows, but she seemed to pop up everywhere in a variety of on-air forums. For example, she dueted with Elmo, the *Sesame Street* puppet, on Vanessa Williams' *Christmas in New York* special (December 1, 1996), hosted *Saturday Night Live* (December 16, 1996), and returned (February 14, 1997) as the boisterous maid Naomi to the daytime soap opera *All My Children.* Among other TV appearances that season, she hosted the *10th Annual Kids Choice Awards* (April 19, 1997) and was the featured guest on *Larry King Live* (May 28, 1997). Having only recently learned that her mother had actually died in 1972 of breast cancer (not liver cancer, as her dad had told her), Rosie made time to appear in the Lifetime-Cable documentary, *Say It, Cure It* (October 5, 1997). O'Donnell was a featured guest in this "wake up call" on prevention and early diagnosis of breast cancer. Added to this media mix were Rosie's ongoing (and highly popular) TV ads with Penny Marshall for the Kmart store chain as well as O'Donnell's voice-overs commercials for the California Prune Council.

During 1997 O'Donnell was also very well represented in other performing arts media. Her made-for-cable movie, *Twilight of the Golds,* aired on Showtime-Cable in March 1997 to respectable reviews. When the family drama was released theatrically in the fall of 1997, *Drama-Logue* judged that Rosie, in her role as the heroine's (Jennifer Beals) best friend, was "tart and funny." Another of O'Donnell's features, *Wide Awake,* made in 1995 (and in which she played a nun!), was rescheduled for theatrical release several times in 1997, but was continually postponed. Meanwhile, now that both Madonna and Goldie Hawn had been signed to appear in the upcoming screen version of the Broadway musical *Chicago,* it was rumored that O'Donnell might play the featured role of the rowdy prison matron in the new film. (It was also circulated that if Rosie could not fit the project into her schedule, Bette Midler would take the splashy part.) If O'Donnell was ambivalent about the *Chicago* screen part, she was very keen on doing on-camera the life story of stocky comedienne Totie Fields who died in 1978 at the age of forty-eight.

Having put off writing her scheduled book of observations and/or autobiography, Rosie, nevertheless, emerged as an author in 1997. For many months, as a recurring segment on *The Rosie O'Donnell*

Show, she'd been reading kid jokes sent in by youngsters. This actually led to *Kids Are Punny,* published by Warner Books, which became a near instant best-seller, with proceeds going to charity. This triumph prompted talk that Rosie would "edit" a sequel to the successful first joke book and might even supervise a forthcoming cookbook.

Not to be overlooked is O'Donnell's heavy-duty participation in the world of cyberspace. On America On-Line she has her own Chat Room and is a frequent major interviewee on Internet forums. She's also smartly focused her staff on creating a rash of games which debuted on her show's two Web sites in the fall of 1997. Perhaps the most favorite item on the TV talk program's official Web site is ROSIE'S SCRAPBOOK, which offers hundreds of film clips, sound bytes, and still shots of the show's landmark moments. An estimated 250,000 users visit that Internet location monthly. Twice that number drop by America On-Line's ROSIEO, which boasts message boards, chat rooms, and listings of the guests/highlights from each aired show.

As if all this were not enough activity for O'Donnell, she finds time to continue her charity work, emcee fundraisers, and even helped to found All for Kids, a new charity devoted exclusively to children in need. (One of her money-raising efforts for this charity was her endorsement of the newly-launched Rosie O Doll.)

• • •

As Rosie's fame has accelerated, so has her media visibility. Back in 1994 when she co-starred in *Exit to Eden* and had to wear such revealing on-camera costumes as a leather bustier, 5' 7" O'Donnell dieted down to a svelte 150 pounds. Soon thereafter she jumped back to her usual weight of 170 pounds. Still later, as her *The Rosie O'Donnell Show* gained in success in late 1996 and early 1997, the now more-confident star blossomed to an unwieldy 210-plus pounds. She told one source, quoted in an April 18, 1997 *National Enquirer* article, that she saw no reason why she should diet: "I'm not going to be an Oprah Winfrey yo-yo, going up and down, up and down!" She added, "Some people smoke and some people drink too much. I eat. Everyone's got a crutch. All I know is I'm miserable when I'm thinner. I want to enjoy life—and I'm doing it. Is that such a big crime?"

Regarding Rosie's social life, the tabloids persisted in featuring O'Donnell as a star attraction. Alan Smith, in his article "Rosie Dumped by Live-In Girlfriend" *(National Enquirer,* January 28, 1997), reported that O'Donnell's "two-year relationship with former *Grease* star Michelle Blakely broke up at Christmas. The two had been fighting bitterly because Rosie refused to sign a 'galimony' agreement to support her—and turned down pretty Michelle's marriage proposal." Smith also noted, "Michelle recently moved into a Manhattan apartment of her own—and expressed one major regret. 'I love Parker [Rosie's adopted son] like he was my own child . . . I miss him every moment of every day.'" A few months later, when Rosie was in Los Angeles taping segments of *The Rosie O'Donnell Show,* O'Donnell and Blakely allegedly attempted a reconciliation that failed to gel.

Later, in the *National Enquirer* of June 17, 1997, Alan Smith reported of O'Donnell, who continued to live both in her new high-rise apartment on Manhattan's Upper West Side and in her Nyack, New York mansion: "Rosie O'Donnell has found new love right under her own roof—she's flipped for her son's nanny! The talented talk host's new live-in girlfriend, 40ish blonde Kate Fitzgerald, is helping Rosie get over the heartbreak of losing her longtime lesbian lover Michelle Blakely." In the article Smith quoted a source as stating that Rosie said, "Michelle was the love of my life. Kate is helping me put the pieces of my broken heart back together." Much of this same data was "confirmed" in Rod Gibson's July 8, 1997 *Globe* article, which discussed her eating binges (leading to size 18 dresses) to compensate for her romantic frustrations and that "Lonely Rosie relies on women for her close relationships . . ." Later on, in an article entitled "Rosie In Steamy Love Triangle" *(National Enquirer,* September 9, 1997), Alan Smith noted that Rosie and Michelle, who had continued to remain in touch over the months, had been trying to find a new path of compatibility together, one which could leave Kate out in the cold.

While the tabloids continued to prominently chart Rosie's supposed romantic life, the establishment publications generally remained noticeably silent on the subject. This dichotomy prompted the *Village Voice's* Michael Musto to editorialize in his column of March 18, 1997: "It's been downright comical to see magazine after magazine (except for the tabloids) tripping over each other writing long-winded treatises about Rosie without a single reference to her romantic life. And these are the same mags that will report practically anything personal about anyone remotely famous in the name of fair play and good copy."

On the other hand, there was one subject that *all* the media felt at ease in discussing—Rosie's single parenthood. Since adopting her now-two-year-old son Parker, O'Donnell had thrived on motherhood and kept insisting that she wanted to add to her family. As such, on November 12, 1997, Rosie announced on her TV show that she had adopted another child, Chelsea Belle. (A few months earlier Rosie had told Gail Buchalter of *Parade* magazine that since there was no man in her life, "I would never get pregnant artificially. I'm certainly not condemning anyone who does, but I have no genetic investment in a child. Any baby you put in my arms will be my baby. Girl or boy, it makes no difference.")

Seven-pound, five-ounce Chelsea Belle was born on September 20, 1997 and was about two weeks old when O'Donnell received her. One of Rosie's nieces suggested that the green-eyed infant be named Chelsea (after President Bill Clinton's daughter?) and the baby's second name was suggested by O'Donnell's son Parker, who was fascinated by the lead character (Belle) in his favorite movie (*Beauty and the Beast*). Reportedly, the adoption was not arranged with a particular mother and Rosie was just informed when a baby became available. According to O'Donnell's publicist, Liz Smith: "Not even the people on her show knew about [the adoption]. Rosie said she wanted some time to herself so she and Parker could get used to having the baby around."

As single mother Rosie informed TV journalist Barbara Walters, she was confident she could handle both her talk show chores and her parenting duties because of her healthy support system of family and pals. She insisted, "I'm going to be okay." She also admitted that she wanted to have yet more children. And, in a request to her many fans, Rosie urged that instead of gifts for Chelsea, well-wishers donate to the Toys for Tots charity.

• • •

The second season of *The Rosie O'Donnell Show* got underway on Monday, September 8, 1997 with a trio of guests: singer Billy Joel, actor Joe Lando (*Dr. Quinn: Medicine Woman*), and stand-up comic Paula Poundstone. The latter had been contracted recently to be a special correspondent for the TV talk show and, as such, to provide recurring humorous segments over the upcoming season. By now, O'Donnell's TV ratings had solidified into continuously very impressive numbers, as she and Oprah Winfrey (who shared the same time spot in many TV syndication markets) vied for being the daytime television show champ. On-camera, Rosie continued to play host to established (especially the likes of her frequent show guest Whoopi Goldberg) and new talent. O'Donnell still lobbed Koosh balls into the studio audience and peppered the program with appearances by her classic TV idols. (In this vein, Mary Tyler Moore paid a special visit to Rosie's forum on November 7, 1997, to host a game playoff between Rosie and another expert on trivia from Moore's classic 1970s sitcom.)

As this point in her career, Rosie, now in her mid-thirties, seems assured of a major position in the public limelight. In late 1996 Barbara Walters included Rosie in her TV special on the Ten Most Intriguing People of 1996, while *People Magazine* listed O'Donnell as one of The 25 Most Intriguing People of the Year. *Entertainment Weekly* picked Rosie as 1996 Entertainer of the Year. At the February 1997 11th Annual American Comedy Awards, Rosie was named the Funniest Female Leading Performer in a Television Series. In the spring of 1997, *Entertainment Weekly* selected Rosie as #8 of the Top 50 Funniest People. Later, *Time* magazine named O'Donnell one of the year's 25 Most Influential People. Clearly everything was continuing to come up Rosie!

Above and beyond her parenthood and her burgeoning career (which still includes her ambition to direct movies), Rosie is now very focused on her status as a children's advocate. She is on the board of directors of the Children's Defense Fund, has raised money for Hale House, has established the For All Kids charity, and has joined with the Chevrolet Division of the General Motors Corporation in the "Concept: Cure" program to raise money for breast cancer research. Through this exhausting activity she finds therapeutic release from the traumas of her own formative years: "In my own childhood, I felt neglect and that's a very profound and distinct wound that takes a lot to get over. But if you never had pain, you never have empathy. I recognize it when I see it in the faces of children in the clinics I go to or the kids who come to the show or in the letters I get." Summing up her life's mission, she says, "I want to make childhood safer for kids."

Rosie has also thought of entering politics. As she explained to syndicated columnist Liz Smith, she has considered becoming "an advocate for different causes on a legislative front. When I was a kid, Barbra

Streisand was the most famous person to me, the person I most wanted to be. When my mother was sick, I thought: 'If Barbra Streisand's mother had cancer and everyone sent in a dollar, they'd find a cure.' At 9 years old, I knew that with fame comes the power to change society—to cure diseases, to help people. When my mother died, I felt powerless—like there was nothing I could do to help. Now, I feel there are things I *can* do."

• Filmography •

FEATURE FILMS:

A League of Their Own
(Columbia, 1992). Color-128 mins. PG-rated.

Executive producer, Penny Marshall; producers: Robert Greenhut, Elliot Abbott; associate producer, Amy Lemisch; director, Penny Marshall; story, Kim Wilson, Kelly Candaele; screenplay, Lowell Ganz, Babaloo Mandel; production designer, Bill Groom; costumes, Cynthia Flynt; music, Hans Zimmer; song, Madonna and Shep Pettibone; camera, Miroslav Ondricek; editor, George Bowers.

Tom Hanks (Jimmy Dugan); Geena Davis (Dottie Hinson); Lori Petty (Kit Keller); Madonna (Mae Mordabito); ROSIE O'DONNELL (Doris Murphy); Megan Cavanagh (Marla Hooch); Tracy Reiner (Betty Horn); Ann Cusack (Evelyn Gardner); Anne Elizabeth Ramsay (Shirley Baker); Freddie Simpson (Ellen Sue Gotlander); Renee Coleman (Alice Gaspers); Robin Knight ("Beans" Babbitt); Kelli Simpkins (Marbleann Wilkenson); Kathleen Marshall ("Mumbles" Brockman); David Strathairn (Ira Lowenstein); Garry Marshall (Walter Harvey); Jon Lovitz (Ernie Capadino); Bill Pullman (Bob Hinson); Eddie Jones (Dave Hooch); Rae Allen (Ma Keller); Eddie Mekka (Mae's Guy in Bar); Lynn Cartwight (Older Dottie); Kathleen Butler (Older Kit); Eunice Anderson (Older Mae); Vera Johnson (Older Doris); Patricia Wison (Older Marla); Mark Holton (Older Stilwell); Barbara Erwin (Older Shirley); Marvin Einhorn (Older Ira); Shirley Burkovich (Older Alice); Dolores "Pickles" Dries (Lady in Bleachers); Joette Hodgen (Opera Singer); Ray Chapman (Ticket Scalper); Brenda Watson (Stacey Gustaferro); Lita Schmitt (Tonya Gilles Koch); Sally Rutherford (Julie Croteau); Lisa Hand (Shelley Adlard); Cheryl Jones (Vickie Buse); Shelly Niemeyer (K.C. Carr).

Sleepless in Seattle
(Tristar, 1993), Color-104 mins. PG-rated.

Executive producers, Lynda Obst, Patrick Crowley; producer, Gary Foster; associate producer, Delia Ephron; director, Nora Ephron; story, Jeff Arch; screenplay, Nora Ephron, David S. Ward, Arch; production designer, Jeffrey Townsend; costumes, Judy Ruskin; music, Marc Shaiman; music supervisors, Shaiman, Nicholas Meyers; song, Shaiman and Ramsey McLean; camera, Sven Nykvist; editor, Robert Reitano.

Tom Hanks (Sam Baldwin); Meg Ryan (Annie Reed); Bill Pullman (Walter Jackson); Ross Malinger (Jonah Baldwin); Rob Reiner (Jay); ROSIE O'DONNELL (Becky); Gaby Hoffman (Jessica); Victor Garber (Greg); Rita Wilson (Suzy); Carey Lowell (Maggie Baldwin); Tom Riis Farrell (Rob); Le Clanche Du Rand (Barbara Reed); Kevin O'Morrison (Cliff Reed); David Hyde Pierce (Dennis Reed); Valerie Wright (Betsy Reed); Frances Conroy (Irene Reed); Tom Tammi (Harold Reed); Calvin Trillon (Uncle Milton); Caroline Aaron (Dr. Marcia Fieldstone); Dana Ivey (Claire); Hannah Cox (Jessica's Mother); Rich Hawkins (Jessica's Father); Tamera Plank (Stewardess); Brian McConnachie (Bob); Stephen Mellor (Wyatt); Marguerite Schertle (Baltimore Waitress); Linda Wallem (Loretta).

Another Stakeout
(Touchstone, 1993). Color-109 mins. PG-13-rated.

Executive producer, John Badham; producers, Jim Kouf, Cathleen Summers, Lynn Bigelow; co-producer, D.J. Caruso; associate producers, Justin Greene, Kristine J. Schwarz; director, Badham; based on characters created by Kouf; screenplay, Kouf; production designer, Lawrence G. Paull; costumes, Stephanie Molin; music, Arthur B. Rubinstein; camera, Roy H. Wagner; editor, Frank Morris.

Richard Dreyfuss (Police Detective Chris Lecce); Emilio Estevez (Police Detective Bill Reimers); ROSIE O'DONNELL (Assistant District Attorney Gina Garrett); Dennis Farina (Brian O'Hara); Marcia Strassman (Pam O'Hara); Cathy Moriarty (Lu Delano); Madeleine Stowe (Maria); John Rubinstein (Thomas Hassrick); Miguel Ferrer (Tony Castellano); Sharon Maughan (Barbara Burnside); Christopher Doyle (McNamara); Sharon Schafer (Tilghman); Rick Seaman, Jan Speeck (Van Agents); Gene Ellison (Las Vegas Police Captain); Frank DeAngelo, J.R. West (Las Vegas Investigators); Frank C. Gurner (Unlucky); Steven Lambert (Killer);

Dan Lauria (Captain Coldshank); Donald Williams (Desk Sergeant); Bruce Barbour, Rick Blackwell (Police Officers).

Fatal Instinct
(MGM, 1993). Color-89 mins. PG-13-rated.

Executive producer, Pieter Jan Brugge; producers, Katie Jacobs, Pierce Gardner; director, Carl Reiner; screenplay, David O'Malley; production designer, Sandy Veneziano; costumes, Albert Wolsky; music, Richard Gibbs; choreography, Lester Wilson; camera, Gabriel Bereistain; editors, Bud Molin, Stephen Myers.

Armand Assante (Ned Ravine); Sherilyn Fenn (Laura); Kate Nelligan (Lola Cain); Christopher McDonald (Frank Kelbo); James Remar (Max Shady); Tony Randall (Judge Skanky); Clarence Clemons (Clarence); Michael Cumpsty (Laura's Husband); John Witherspoon (Arch); Blake Clark (Milo Crumley); Edward Blanchard (Restroom Patron); David Greelee (Restroom Stall Patron); Tim Frisbie (Guy in Bumper Car); Carl Reiner (Judge Ben Arugula) Eartha Kitt (First Trial Judge); ROSIE O'DONNELL (Bird Store Owner); Ronnie Schell (Conductor); Susan Angelo (Lana's Prosecutor); Doc Severinsen (Guest Musician); Joseph Attanasio (Jury Foreman); Savannah Smith Bocher (Juror); Laurie Lapinski (Frightened Woman); Michael MacLeod (Freckled-Faced Kid); Christopher Darga (Prison Guard); Harvey Levine (Blind Guy); Jacob Vargas (Flower Delivery Man); Alex Zuckerman (Jeff); Bob Uecker (Sportscaster).

Car 54, Where Are You?
(Orion, 1994). Color-89 mins. PG-13-rated. [Made in 1990.]

Producer, Robert H. Solo; director, Bill Fishman; based on the TV series created and produced by Nat Hiken; story, Erik Tarloff; screenplay, Tarloff, Ebbe Roe Smith, Peter McCarthy, Peter Crabbe; production designer, Catherine Hardwicke; costumes, Margaret M. Mohr; music, Pray for Rain, Bernie Worrell; song, John Strauss and Hiken; sound, Peter Shewchuck; sound designer, Dan Molina; camera, Rodney Charters; editors, Alan Balsam, Earl Watson.

David Johansen (Officer Gunther Toody); John C. McGinley (Officer Francis Muldoon); Fran Drescher (Velma Velour); Nipsey Russell (Captain Dave Anderson); ROSIE O'DONNELL (Lucille Toody);

Daniel Baldwin (Don Motti); Jeremy Piven (Herbert Hortz); Bobby Collins (Carlo); Louis Di Bianco (Nicco); Al Lewis (Patrolman Leo Schnauser); Barbara Hamilton (Mrs. Muldoon); Rik Colitti (Sergeant Abrams); Penn & Teller (Luthers); Tone Loc (Hackman); Coati Mundi (Mambo Singer); Ellen Ray Hennesey (Arleen); Sally Cahill (Brandy); Jackie Richardson (Madam); Daniel Dion (Officer Brown); Michael Ricupero (Officer Nicholson); Arlene Duncan (Officer Kagan); Jason Scott (Officer Simons); Santino Buda (Officer Rodriguez); Peter Keleghan, Conrad Coates (District Attorneys); Doug Innis (Tunnel of Love Attendant); Jackie Harris (Woman in Slip); Phil Jarrett (FBI Plainclothesman); Lee Arenberg (Ivan the Architect); Terry Howson, Eli Gabay (Henchmen); Joanna Bacalso (Beautiful Young Woman); Gina Darling (Nurse); Matt Robinson (Homeboy); Elena Kudaba (Mrs. Pirogi); Von Flores (Mr. Kim); Gina Vasic (Mrs. Manicotti); Khan Agha Soroor (Kahn); Maria Diaz (Voice of EDNA); Floyd Flex, Devon Martin (Rap Fellows); Majo Nixon (Sidewalk Preacher); Claude Salvas (Animal Rights Activist).

I'll Do Anything
(Columbia, 1994). Color-115 mins. PG-13-rated.

Executive producer, Penney Finkelman Cox; producers, James L. Brooks, Polly Platt; associate producers Richard Marks, Ian Deitchman; director/screenplay, Brooks; production designer, Stephen J. Lineweaver; costumes, Marlene Stewart; music, Hans Zimmer; sound, David M. Kelson; camera, Michael Ballhaus; editor, Marks.

Nick Nolte (Matt Hobbs); Whittni Wright (Jeannie Hobbs); Albert Brooks (Burke Adler); Julie Kavner (Nan Mulhanney); Joely Richardson (Cathy Breslow); Tracey Ullman (Beth Hobbs); Jeb Brown (Male D Person); Joely Fisher (Female D Person); Vicki Lewis (Millie); Anne Heche (Claire); Ian McKellen (John Earl McAlpine); Joel Thurm (Martin); Angela Alvarado (Lucy); Dominik Lukas-Espeleta (Ricky); Justina Hardesty (Essa); Robert Joy (U.S. Marshal); Maria Pitillo (Flight Attendant); Jake Busey (Burke's Fired Driver); Harry Shearer (Audience Research Captain); ROSIE O'DONNELL (Makeup Person); Ken Page (Hair Person); Amy Brooks (Shannon); Roz Baker (Taxi Driver); Suzanne Douglas (*Rainbow House* Star); Chelsea Field (Screen Test Actress); Courtney Perry (Audition Child); Justine Arlin (Studio Executive.); Woody Harrelson (*Ground Zero*

Hero); Patrick Cassidy (*Ground Zero* Villain); Joan Gianmarco, Tricia Leigh Fisher, Jerry Hauch, Jose Payo (Airplane Passengers); Joseph Malone (Assistant Director).

The Flintstones
(Universal, 1994). Color-92 mins. PG-rated.

Executive producers, William Hanna, Joseph Barbera, Kathleen Kennedy, David Kirschner, Gerald R. Molen; producer, Bruce Cohen; co-producer, Colin Wilson; director Brian Levant; based on the animated series by Hanna-Barbera Productions, Inc.; screenplay, Tom S. Parker, Jim Jennewein, Steve E. de Souza; production designer, William Sandell; costumes, Rosanna Norton; music, David Newman; song, Hanna, Barbera and Hoyt Curtin; choreography, Adam M. Shankman; special visual effects, Industrial Light & Magic; visual effects supervisor, Mark Dippe; Animatronic creatures, Jim Henson's Creature Shop, John Stephenson; sound, Charles Wilborn; camera, Dean Cundey; editor, Kent Beyda.

John Goodman (Fred Flintstone); Elizabeth Perkins (Wilma Flintstone); Rick Moranis (Barney Rubble); ROSIE O'DONNELL (Betty Rubble); Kyle MacLachlan (Cliff Vandercave); Halle Berry (Miss Stone); Elizabeth Taylor (Pearl Slaghoople); Dann Florek (Mr. Slate); Richard Moll (Hoagie); Irwin "88" Keyes (Joe Rockhead); Jonathan Winters (Grizzled Man); Harvey Korman (Voice of the Dictabird); Elaine & Melanie Silver (Pebbles Flintstone); Hlynur & Marino Sigurdsson (Bamm-Bamm Rubble); Sheryl Lee Ralph (Mrs. Pyrite); Jean Vander Pyl (Mrs. Feldspar); Janice Kent (Stewardess); Rod McCary (Store Manager); Laraine Newman (Susan Rock); Jay Leno (Bedrock's Most Wanted Host); Dean Cundey (Technician); Joe Barbera (Man in Mersandes); Bill Hanna (Boardroom Executive); Jim Doughan (Maitre D'); Alan Blumenfeld (Fred Look-a-Like); Sam Raimi (Cliff Look-a-Like); Messiri Freeman (Miss Stone Look-a-Like); Alex Zimmerman (Accuser); Andy Steinfeld (Aerobics Instructor); Bradford Bryson (Foreman); Lita Sevens (Woman at Chevrox).

Exit to Eden
(Savoy, 1994). Color-113 mins. R-rated.

Executive producers, Edward K Milkis, Nick Abdo; producers,

Alexandra Rose, Garry Marshall; director, Marshall; based on the novel by Anne Rice; screenplay, Deborah Amelon, Bob Brunner; production designer, Peter Jamison; costumes, Ellen Mirojnick; music, Patrick Doyle; music supervisor, Maggie Rodford; sound, Jim Webb, Kleith A. Webster; camera, Theo Van De Sande; editor, David Finfer.

Dana Delany (Mistress Lisa Emerson); Paul Mercurio (Elliot Slater); ROSIE O'DONNELL (Police Detective Sheila Kingston); Dan Aykroyd (Police Detective Fred Lavery); Hector Elizondo (Dr. Martin Halifax); Stuart Wilson (Omar); Iman (Nina); Sean O'Bryan (Tommy); Stephanie Niznik (Diana); Phil Redrow (Richard); Sandra Korn (Riba); Julie Hughes (Julie); Laurelle Mehus (Heidi); Tom Hines (Nolan); Allison Moir (Kitty); Deborah Pratt (Dr. Williams); Laura Harring (M.C. Kindra); James Patrick Stuart (James); Rene Lamart (Roger); Rosemary Forsyth (Mrs. Brady); Rod Britt (Mr. Brady); Barbara Marshall (Shy Student); Lynda Goodfriend (Linda); Nancy Debease (Nancy); Tanya Reid (Naomi); Sam Denoff (The Confused Golfer); Kristi Noel (Fantasy Secretary); Kathleen Marshall (Susan, the Stewardess); Frank Campanella (Wheelchair Walker); Mel Novak (Walker's Henchman); Dr. Joyce Brothers (Herself); Donna Dixon (Fred's Ex-Wife); Scott Marshall (Latte); Lori Marshall, Bill Fricker (Tourists); John Schneider (Professor Collins).

Now and Then
(New Line, 1995). Color-96 mins. PG-13-rated.

Executive producer Jennifer Todd; producers, Suzanne Todd, Demi Moore; director, Lesli Linka Glatter; screenplay, I. Marlene King; production designers, Gershon Ginsburg, Anne Kuljian; costumes, Deena Appel; music, Cliff Eidelman; sound, James Thornton; camera, Ueli Steiger; editor, Jacqueline Cambas.

Demi Moore (Samantha Albertson); Melanie Griffith (Tina Tercell); ROSIE O'DONNELL (Dr. Roberta Martin); Rita Wilson (Christina Dewitt); Christina Ricci (Young Roberta); Thora Birch (Young Teeny); Gaby Hoffman (Young Samantha); Ashleigh Aston Moore (Young Chrissy); Willa Glen (Angela Albertson); Bonnie Hunt (Mrs. Dewitt); Janeane Garofalo (Wiladene); Lolita Davidovich (Mrs. Albertson); Cloris Leachman (Grandma Albertson); Devon Sawa (Scott Wormer); Travis Roberts (Roger Wormer); Justin Humphrey (Eric Wormer); Bradley Coryell (Clay Wormer); Ric Reitz (Mr.

Albertson); Walter Sparrow (Crazy Pete); Tucker Stone (Young Morton); Hank Azaria (Bud Kent); Beverly Shelton (Eda); Carl Espy (Morton Williams); Brendan Frasier (Vietnam Veteran).

Beautiful Girls
(Miramax, 1996). Color-110 mins. R-rated.

Executive producers, Bob Weinstein, Harvey Weinstein, Cathy Konrad; producer, Cary Woods; co-producer, Alan C. Blomquist; associate producers, Scott Rosenberg, Joel Stillerman; director, Ted Demme; screenplay, Scott Rosenberg; production designer, Dan Davis; costumes, Lucy W. Corrigan; music, David A. Stewart; camera, Adam Kimmel; editor, Jeffrey Wolf.

Matt Dillon (Tommy "Birdman" Rowland); Noah Emmerich (Michael "Mo" Morris); Annabeth Gish (Tracy Stover); Lauren Holly (Darian Smalls); Timothy Hutton (Willie Conway); ROSIE O'DONNELL (Gina Barrisano); Max Perlich (Kev); Martha Plimpton (Jan); Natalie Portman (Marty); Michael Rapaport (Paul Kirkwood); Mira Sorvino (Sharon Cassidy); Uma Thurman (Andera); Pruitt Taylor Vince (Stanley "Stinky" Womack); Anne Bobby (Sarah Morris); Richard Bright (Dick Conway); Sam Robards (Steve Rossmore); David Arquette (Bobby Conway); Adam Le Fevre (Victor); John Carroll Lynch (Frank Womack); Sarah Katz (Kristen Rossmore); Camille D'Ambrose (Sharon's Mother); Martin Rubin (Chip); Nicole Ranallo (Cheryl Morris); Earl R. Burt (Bartender); Allison Levine (Waitress at Moonlight Mile); Tom Gibis (Peter the Eater).

Harriet the Spy
(Paramount, 1996). Color-101 mins. PG-rated.

Executive producer, Debby Beece; producer, Marykay Powell; co-producer, Nava Levin; associate producer, Julia Pistor; director, Brownwen Hughes; based on the novel by Louise Fitzhugh; adaptors, Greg Taylor, Julie Talen; screenplay, Douglas Petrie, Theresa Rebeck; production designer, Lester Cohen; costumes, Donna Zakowska; music, Jamshied Sharifi; camera, Francis Kenny; editor, Debra Chiate.

Michelle Trachtenberg (Harriet M. Welsch); ROSIE O'DONNELL (Ole Golly); Vanessa Lee Chester (Janie Gibbs); Gregory Smith (Sport); J. Smith-Cameron (Mrs. Welsch); Robert Joy (Mr. Welsch); Eartha Kitt (Agatha K. Plummer); Don Francks (Harrison Withers);

Eugene Lipinski (George Waldenstein); Charlotte Sullivan (Marion Hawthorne); Teisha Kim (Rachel Hennessy); Cecilley Carroll (Beth Ellen Hansen); Dov Tiefenbach (Boy with Purple Socks); Nina Shock (Carrie Andrews); Conor Devitt (Pinky Whitehead); Alisha Morrison (Laura Peters); Nancy Beatty (Miss Elson); Gerry Quigley (Sport's Dad); Jackie Richardson (Janie's Mother); Mercedes Enriquez (Windchime Lady); Mung-Ling Tsui (Mrs. Hong Fat); Ho Chow (Mr. Hong Fat); Byron Wong (Frankie Hong Fat); Paul Lee (Bruno Hong Fat); Kim Lieu (Paige Hong Fat); Kwok-Wing Leung (Grandpa Hong Fat); Sally Cahill (Maid); Roger Clown (Dr. Wagner); Jamie Jones (Pickpocket).

A Very Brady Sequel
(Paramount, 1996). Color-90 mins. PG-13-rated.

Producers, Sherwood Schwartz, Lloyd J. Schwartz, Alan Ladd, Jr.; co-producers, Michael Fottrell, Kelliann Ladd; director, Arleen Sanford; based on characters created by Sherwood Schwartz; story, Harry Elfont & Deborah Kaplan; screenplay, Elfont & Kaplan, James Berg & Stan Zimmerman; production designer, Cynthia Charette; costumes, Rosanna Norton; music, Guy Moon; supervising music producer, Steve Tyrell; camera, Mac Ahlberg; editor, Anita Brandt-Burgoyne.

Shelley Long (Carol Brady); Gary Cole (Mike Brady); Christopher Daniel Barnes (Greg Brady); Christine Taylor (Marcia Brady); Paul Sutera (Peter Brady); Jennifer Elise Cox (Jan Brady); Jesse Lee (Bobby Brady); Olivia Hack (Cindy Brady); Henriette Mantel (Alice); Tim Matheson (Roy Martin/Trevor Thomas); Whip Hubley (Explorer/Dead Husband); Whitney Rybeck (Auctioneer); Gregory White, Sue Casey (Art Patrons); RuPaul (Ms. Cummings); Diana Theodore (Ms. Cumming's Daughter); David Ramsey (Brent the Lifeguard); Phil Buckman (Jason the Lifeguard); Steven Gilborn (Mr. Phillips); Zsa Zsa Gabor (Herself); ROSIE O'DONNELL (Rich Matron with Ms. Gabor); Skip O'Brien (Construction Worker); Barbara Eden (Jeannie); Jennifer Aspen (Kathy Lawrence); Brian Van Holt (Warren Mulaney); Richard Belzer (Police Detective); Connie Ray (Flight Attendant); Anthony J. Silva, Jr. (Hotel Concierge); Don Nahaku (Car Rental Person); Michael Lundberg (George Glass); Bill Applebaum, Laura Weekes, (George Glass' Parents); John Hillerman (Dr. Whitehead).

FORTHCOMING FEATURE FILM RELEASES:

Twilight of the Golds
(Showtime Cable, 1997). Color-89 mins.

Executive producer, Garry Marshall; producers, Paul Colichman, John Davimos, Mark Harris; line producers, John Schouweiller, Lisa Levy; co-producers, Valorie Massalas, Stephen P. Jarchow; director, Mark Harris; based on the play by Jonathan Tolins; screenplay, Tolins, Seth Bass; production designer, Amy Ancona; costumes, Molly Maginnis; sound, D.J. Ritchie; camera, Tom Richmond; editor, Dana Congdon.

Jennifer Beals (Suzanne); Garry Marshall (Walter); Faye Dunaway (Phyllis); Brendan Fraser (David); Jon Tenney (Rob); ROSIE O'DONNELL (Jackie); Patrick Bristow (Brandon); John Schlesinger (Dr. Adrian Lodge); and: Jack Klugman, Sean O'Brien, Stephanie Niznik, Troy Nankin, Michelle Blakely, Lucas Richmond, Robert Barry Fleming, Kathleen Marshall, Mark Medoff, Phyllis Frelich.

Wide Awake
(Miramax, 1997). Color.

Executive producers, Bob Weinstein, Harvey Weinstein, Meryl Poster; producers, Cary Woods, Cathy Konrad; co-producer, James Bigwood; associate producer, Timothy Lonsdale; director/screenplay, M. Night Shyamalan; production designer, P. Michael Johnston; costumes, Bridget Kelly; music, Edmund Choi; sound, Brian Miksi; camera, Adam Holender; editor, Andrew Mondshein.

Joseph Cross (Joshua Beal); Timothy Reifsnyder (Dave O'Hara); Dana Delany (Mrs. Beal); Denis Leary (Mr. Beal); Robert Loggia (Grandpa Beal); ROSIE O'DONNELL (sister Terry); Camryn Manheim (Sister Sophia); Vicki Giunta (Sister Beatrice); Julia Stiles (Neena Beal); Heather Casler (Hope); Dan Lauria (Father Peters); Stefan Niemczyk (Frank Benton); Michael Pacienza (Freddie Waltman); Michael Shulman (Robert Brickman); Jaret Ross Barron (Dan); Jarrett Abello (John); Joseph Melito Jr. (Billy); Peter A. Urban Jr. (Newman); Jahmal Curtis (Student); Michael Craig Bigwood (Little Boy); Gil Robbins (Cardinal Geary); Marc H. Glick (Father Sebastian); Robert K. O'Neill (Young Priest); Deborah Stern (Mrs. Waltman); Joey Perllo (Mr. Waltman); Jerry Walsh (Football Coach); Liam Mitchell (Gym Teacher).

TELEVISION SERIES:

Gimme a Break
(NBC-TV, November 19, 1986–May 12, 1987).
Color-30 mins. [sixth and final season of the series]

Cast: Nell Carter (Nellie Ruth "Nell" Harper); Lara Jill Miller (Samantha "Sam" Kanisky); John Hoyt (Grandpa Stanley Kanisky); Joey Lawrence (Joey Donovan); Telma Hopkins (Addy Wilson); Matthew Lawrence (Matthew Donovan); Paul Sand (Marty/Esteban); Rosetta LeNoire (Maybelle Harper); ROSIE O'DONNNEL (Maggie O'Brien).

Stand by Your Man
(Fox-TV, April 5, 1992–May 17, 1992). Color-30 mins.

Cast: Melissa Gilbert-Brinkman (Rochelle Dunphy); ROSIE O'DONNELL (Lorraine Popowski); Rick Hall (Artie Popowski); Sam McMurray (Roger Dunphy); Miriam Flynn (Adrienne Stone); Don Gibb (Scab); Rusty Schwimmer (Gloria); Ellen Ratners (Sophie).

The Rosie O'Donnell Show
(Syndicated-TV, June 10, 1996–   ). Color-60 mins.

Cast: ROSIE O'DONNELL (Host); John McDaniel (Music Director/Studio Band Leader); Morris Goldberg, Rodney Jones, Ray Marchica, Tracy Wormworth (Studio Band); Gary Owens (Offcamera Voices).

BROADWAY:

Grease!
(O'Neill Theatre, New York City,
revival premiere: May 11, 1994).

Producers, Barry and Fran Weissler; a Tommy Tune production; director/choreographer, Jeff Calhoun; book, music and lyrics, Jim Jacobs & Warren Casey; scenic designer, John Arnone; costumes, Willa Kim; music director/vocal & dance music arranger, John McDaniel; orchestrator, Steve Margoshes; music coordinator, John Monaco; lighting, Howell Binkley; sound, Tom Morse.

Brian Bradley (Vince Fontaine); Marcia Lewis (Miss Lynch); Michelle Blakely (Patty Simcox); Paul Castree (Eugene Florczyk); Heather Strokes (Jan); Megan Mullally (Marty); ROSIE O'DONNELL (Betty Rizzo); Sam Harris (Doody); Hunter Foster (Roger); Jason Opsahl (Kenickie); Carlos Lopez (Sonny Latierri); Jessica Stone (Frenchy); Susan Wood (Sandy Dumbrowski); Ricky Paull Goldin (Danny Zuko); Clay Adkins, Patrick Boyd, Denis Jones (Straight A's); Patrick Boyd, Katy Grenfell (Dream Mooners); Katy Grenfell, Janice Lorraine Holt, Lorna Shane (The Heartbeats); Sandra Purpuro (Cha-Cha Degregorio); Billy Porter (Teen Angel); Clay Adkins, Melissa Bell, Patrick Boyd, Katy Grenfell, Ned Hannah, Janice Lorraine Holt, Denis Jones, Allison Metcalf, H. Hylan Scott II, Lorna Shane (*Grease* Ensemble).

Note: original cast CD album of the 1994 Broadway revival: RCA Victor 900296-62703-2.

• Sources •

Writing this book provided several intriguing research challenges. As this is the first published, full-length biography of Rosie O'Donnell, there were no "standard" earlier works to consult regarding an "official" chronology of events of Rosie's very active professional life to date. Then too, the 1990s when her show business career blossomed in many directions has been a decade of cyber space explosion. Thus, interviews, reviews, publicity releases, which in previous years would have been published in magazines, books, or circulated in hard copy industry information sheets, are now distributed primarily on the Internet. As such, this required ingenuity to track down and capture before the items vanished from retrievable online databases.

Then too, the world of stand-up comedy on the road, which was Rosie O'Donnell's training ground in the 1980s, is sadly undocumented regarding performers, individual playdates and reviews. Many of the clubs across the U.S. where O'Donnell worked, have undergone several ownership changes (with files frequently destroyed in the process) or have gone out of business altogether. Fortunately, there are several useful background books on the history of stand-up comedy, including: *Comic Lives: Inside the World of American Stand-Up Comedy* (Fireside Books, 1987) by Betsy Borms; *Revolutionary Laughter: The World of Women Comics*, edited by Roz Warren (The Crossing Press, 1995); *Standup Comedians on Television*, edited by the Museum of Television and Radio (Harry N. Abrams, Inc., 1996).

As Rosie O'Donnell's entertainment career expanded in the mid-1980s after her "Star Search" TV appearances, more and more publications began featuring this forthright comedian in their pages. Among the many magazines to print helpful, in-depth interviews of her have been: *Allure* ("Rosie Gets Real" by Tom Shales, June 1996); *Buzz* ("Red Hot Rosie" by Robert Hofler, August 1994); *Career World* ("Everything's Coming Up Rosie" by Aneeta Brown, October 1994); *Cosmopolitan* ("Wondrous Rosie O'Donnell!" by Patrick Pacheco, June 1994); *Details* ("Rosie O'Donnell" by Ryan Murphy); *Entertainment Weekly* ("Rosie the Riveting" by Julian Gary, August 7, 1992; "A

League of Her Own" by Ken Tucker, July 26, 1996); *Interview* ("Major-league Comedian" by Susan Karlin, July 1992); *Irish America* ("Rosie Revealed" by Patricia Hartley, September/October 1996); *Life* ("Love Ya [Kiss, Kiss] Don't Change" by Allison Adato, July 1996); *Mademoiselle* ("Coming Up Rosie" by Madonna, August 1993);*Mirabella* ("Rosie O'Donnell" by Trish Deitch Rohrer, June 1, 1993); *Movieline* (especially their recurring "Buzz" column); *Newsweek* ("Playing in a League of Her Own" by Jeff Giles, August 16, 1993; "Queen of Nice" by Rick Marin, July 15, 1996); *People* ("On Base with a Hit" by Marjorie Rosen, July 20, 1992; "Bringing Up Babies" by Pam Lambert, July 8, 1996); *Premiere* ("Cleanup Women" by Nancy Griffin, July 1992 and the ongoing "In the Works" column); *Theater Week* ("Rosie Does Rizzo" by Michael P. Scasserra, May 9, 1994); *TV Guide* ("In a Crowded Field of Comics, Here Are Five Fresh Faces You Won't Forget" by Jane Marion, August 3, 1991; "Rosie . . . Really" by Mary Murphy, June 15, 1996); *UpTown* ("Rosie O'Donnell, Talking the Talk" by Cindy Pearlman, July 1996; *US* ("Rosie O'Donnell" by Mark Morrison, July 1993; "Rosie O'Donnell" by Margy Rochlin, June 1996).

Equally so, many newspapers, (such as the *Chicago Tribune, The Intelligence/The Record, Long Beach Press-Telegram, Los Angeles Daily News, Los Angeles Times, New York Post, New York Times, Newsday, Toronto Sun, Washington Post, The Whoot!*), news syndicates (including the Associated Press, King Features, Knight-Ridder), trade papers (e.g., *Billboard, Daily Variety, Drama-Logue, Hollywood Reporter*) and tabloids (*Globe, National Enquirer, Star*) have documented and assessed different aspects of O'Donnell's onstage and offstage life thus far.

In the field of television, Rosie O'Donnell has been a frequent guest over recent years on such nationally seen talk shows as "The Al Roker Program" (CNBC-Cable), "CBS This Morning," "Good Morning America" (ABC-TV), "Larry King Live" (CNN-Cable); "The Late Late Show with Tom Snyder" (CBS-TV), "The Late Show with David Letterman" (CBS-TV), "NBC Today Show," "Sally Jessy Raphael" (syndicated-TV) and various entertainment news programs (including "Entertainment Tonight," "Extra," "Hard Copy" and the assorted industry update offerings on E! Entertainment TV cable network). Viewing archive copies and/or reading transcripts of such programming that featured Rosie provided a wealth of relevant information. And, not to be forgotten, is Rosie herself. Whether in her many stand-up comedy guest spots, specials and series on broadcast and cable TV or on her own "The Rosie O'Donnell Show" (syndicated-TV), the star has confirmed a great many essential facts about her life as well as revealing her evolving opinions on a wide variety of subjects.

On the Internet, particularly useful for researching this book were the official and unofficial Rosie O'Donnell web sites as well as the databases and links provided by such online sources as The All-Movie Guide, The Internet Movie Database and Mr. ShowBiz and the search engines of Alta Vista, Excite, Lycos, Search and Yahoo. In recent years, Rosie, an enthusiastic Internet user herself, has been featured on several live interviews on America Online where she has her own chat group. Not to be overlooked in exploring research options for this project were the networking capabilities provided by Internet news/user groups.

Of the many libraries and research centers utilized for this book, particularly helpful were those collections and reference shelves found at the Academy of Motion Picture Arts & Sciences, the Beverly Hills Public Library, the Hollywood Public Library, the Museum of Television and Radio and the New York Public Library at Lincoln Center (The Billy Rose Theater Collection).

Finally, of course, there are those who made time to talk with me both on and off the record about their working and/or social relationships with Rosie O'Donnell.

• About the Author •

JAMES ROBERT PARISH, a show business chronicler, is the author of over 85 published books on the performing arts. Considered an authority on the subject, he is often a guest on TV talk/news shows to discuss Hollywood—past and present.

Born in Cambridge, Massachusetts, Mr. Parish attended the U. of Pennsylvania and graduated Phi Beta Kappa with a degree in English. A graduate of the U. of Pennsylvania Law School, he is a member of the New York Bar. As president of Entertainment Copyright Research Co., Inc. he headed a major media researching facility. Later he was a reviewer-interviewer for *Variety* and *Motion Picture Daily* trade newspapers as well as an entertainment publicist.

Among his many published books are: *The Unofficial "Murder, She Wrote" Casebook, Today's Black Hollywood, Let's Talk! America's Favorite Talk Show Hosts, Hollywood Celebrity Death Book, Prostitution in Hollywood Films, Great Cop Pictures, The Slapstick Queens, The RKO Gals, Great Western Stars, The Jeanette MacDonald Story, Vincent Price Unmasked, Black Action Pictures* and *The Elvis Presley Scrapbook*. Among those he has co-written are: *Hollywood Baby Boomers, Complete Actors TV Credits, Hollywood Songsters, Great Detective Pictures, The George Raft File, The MGM Stock Company, Liza!: The Liza Minnelli Story, The Funsters, Hollywood on Hollywood,* and *Great Science Fiction Pictures*.

Besides contributing to national magazines on the subject of show business, Mr. Parish is advisor for Greenwood Press' acclaimed series, Bio-Bibliographies in the Performing Arts. He is also a consultant to publishers and data base resources on the entertainment industry.

Mr. Parish resides in Studio City, CA.

• Index •

Note: due to its extensive citation in this index, "The Rosie O'Donnell Show" has been abreviated to "Rosie" except where explicitly spelled out.